Unified Patent Court

Rules of Procedure and Other Relevant Legal Texts

Unified Patent Court

Rules of Procedure and Other Relevant Legal Texts

Editor:
W.J.G. Maas

eleven

Published, sold and distributed by Eleven
P.O. Box 85576
2508 CG The Hague
The Netherlands
Tel.: +31 70 33 070 33
Fax: +31 70 33 070 30
e-mail: sales@elevenpub.nl
www.elevenpub.com

Sold and distributed in USA and Canada
Independent Publishers Group
814 N. Franklin Street
Chicago, IL 60610, USA
Order Placement: +1 800 888 4741
Fax: +1 312 337 5985
orders@ipgbook.com
www.ipgbook.com

Eleven is an imprint of Boom uitgevers Den Haag.

ISBN 978-94-6236-350-2
ISBN 978-94-0011-231-5 (E-book)

Preface

The Unified Patent Court (UPC) is a new European court, comprising the best patent judges from all participating Member States of the European Union. Seventeen EU Member States have signed the Agreement on a Unified Patent Court of 19 February 2013 (UPCA) and this agreement will enter into force after the deposit of the ratification instrument by Germany. Three months after the German ratification of the UPCA, which is expected the end of February 2023, the court will open its doors. This means that the Unitary Patent (UP) and Unified Patent Court (UPC) will become a reality in June 2023. It will have a profound and lasting impact on the European patent landscape. Described by EPO President, António Campinos, as 'the most important change in the European patent system since the EPO took up its operations in 1977', the UPC will inevitably bring about a significant change to the patent strategies of business and patent advisors alike, as soon as it opens its doors for business.

The seventeen EU Member States which have ratified the UPCA and which will participate in the Unitary Patent system when it starts are Austria, Belgium, Bulgaria, Denmark, Estonia, Finland, France, Germany, Italy, Latvia, Lithuania, Luxembourg, Malta, the Netherlands, Portugal, Slovenia and Sweden. The seven EU Member States that have signed but not yet ratified the UPCA are Cyprus, Czech Republic, Greece, Hungary, Ireland, Romania and Slovakia. The UPC's rulings will have effect throughout the territories of those Member States that have already ratified the UPCA. As a result the UPC will cover a market of about 350 million people, which is a coverage comparable to that of the US.

The UPC will have exclusive competence for patent disputes involving UP's as well as 'classical' European patents. There are, however, some exceptions with regard to European patents, since cases may still be brought before national courts, and proprietors of European patents may 'opt out' from the UPC's exclusive competence during a transitional period of seven years, which may be prolonged with a further seven years. Despite these exceptions, it seems to be apparent that a ruling of the UPC will have a very significant economic effect and of strategic importance to (global) assertion strategies of patent owners.

This collection of laws includes i) the Rules of Procedure of the UPC and ii) the other relevant legal texts setting out the legal framework of the UP and the UPC. We hope it will facilitate your endeavours to embark on your journey to explore the 'Brave New World' of UPC patent litigation. Finally, I would like to thank Valérie ten Hoor for her assistance in compiling this publication.

Wim Maas
Partner Taylor Wessing

Table of Contents

1. Rules of Procedure of the Unified Patent Court

as adopted by decision of the Administrative Committee on 8 July 2022
entry into force: 1 September 2022

ABBREVIATIONS

Agreement: Agreement on a Unified Patent Court of 19 February 2013 (OJ C 175, 20.6.2013, p. 1) including any subsequent amendments

Directive 98/5/EC: Directive 98/5/EC of the European Parliament and of the Council of 16 February 1998 to facilitate practice of the profession of lawyer on a permanent basis in a Member State other than that in which the qualification was obtained (OJ L 77, 14.3.1998, p. 36) including any subsequent amendments

EPC: Convention on the Grant of European Patents of 5 October 1973 (European Patent Convention) including any subsequent amendments

The Hague Convention: Convention on the Service Abroad of Judicial and Extrajudicial Documents in Civil or Commercial Matters of 15 November 1965 including any subsequent amendments

Lugano Convention: Convention on Jurisdiction and the Recognition and Enforcement of Judgments in Civil and Commercial Matters of 30 October 2007 (OJ L 147, 10.6.2009, p. 5) including any subsequent amendments

Regulation (EU) 2020/1783: Regulation (EU) 2020/1783 of the European Parliament and of the Council of 25 November 2020 on cooperation between the courts of the Member States in the taking of evidence in civil or commercial matters (taking of evidence) (recast), OJ L 405, 2.12.2020, p. 1 including any subsequent amendments

Regulation (EU) No 1215/2012: Regulation (EU) No 1215/2012 of the European Parliament and of the Council of 12 December 2012 on jurisdiction and the recognition and enforcement of judgments in civil and commercial matters (OJ L 351, 20.12.2012, p. 1) including any subsequent amendments

Regulation (EU) No 1257/2012: Regulation (EU) No 1257/2012 of the European Parliament and of the Council of 17 December 2012 implementing enhanced cooperation in the area of the creation of unitary patent protection (OJ L 361, 31.12.2012, p. 1) including any subsequent amendments

Regulation (EU) No 1260/2012: Regulation (EU) No 1260/2012 of the Council of 17 December 2012 implementing enhanced cooperation in the area of the creation of unitary patent protection with regard to the applicable translation arrangements (OJ L 361, 31.12.2012, p. 89) including any subsequent amendments including any subsequent amendments

Regulation (EU) 2020/1784: Regulation (EU) 2020/1784 1783 of the European Parliament and of the Council of 25 November 2020 on the service in the Member States of judicial and extrajudicial documents in civil or commercial matters (service of documents) (recast), OJ L 405, 2.12.2020; p. 40

Statute: Statute of the Unified Patent Court (OJ C 175, 20.6.2013, p. 29) including any subsequent amendments

PREAMBLE

1. The Court shall conduct proceedings in accordance with the Agreement, the Statute and these Rules. In the event of a conflict between the provisions of the Agreement and/or the Statute on the one hand and of the Rules on the other hand, the provisions of the Agreement and/or the Statute shall prevail.
2. The Rules shall be applied and interpreted in accordance with Articles 41(3), 42 and 52(1) of the Agreement on the basis of the principles of proportionality, flexibility, fairness and equity.
3. Proportionality shall be ensured by giving due consideration to the nature and complexity of each action and its importance.
4. Flexibility shall be ensured by applying all procedural rules in a flexible and balanced manner with the required level of discretion for the judges to organise the proceedings in the most efficient and cost effective manner.
5. Fairness and equity shall be ensured by having regard to the legitimate interests of all parties.
6. In accordance with these principles, the Court shall apply and interpret the Rules in a way which shall ensure decisions of the highest quality.
7. In accordance with these principles, proceedings shall be conducted in a way which will normally allow the final oral hearing on the issues of infringement and validity at first instance to take place within one year whilst recognising that complex actions may require more time and procedural steps and simple actions less time and fewer procedural steps. Decisions on costs and/or damages may take place at the same time or as soon as practicable thereafter. Case management shall be organised in accordance with these objectives. Parties shall cooperate with the Court and set out their full case as early as possible in the proceedings.
8. The Court shall endeavour to ensure consistent application and interpretation of these Rules by all first instance divisions and the Court of Appeal. Due consideration shall also be given to this objective in any decision concerning leave to appeal against procedural orders.

APPLICATION AND INTERPRETATION OF THE RULES

Rule 1 – Application of the Rules and general principles of interpretation
1. The Court shall conduct proceedings in accordance with the Agreement, the Statute and these Rules, which include the Preamble to these Rules and the principles set out therein. In the event of a conflict between the provisions of the Agreement and/or the Statute on the one hand and of the Rules on the other hand, the provisions of the Agreement and/or the Statute shall prevail.
2. Where these Rules provide for the Court to perform any act other than an act exclusively reserved for a panel of the Court, the President of the Court of First Instance or the President of the Court of Appeal, that act may be performed by:
   (a) the presiding judge or the judge-rapporteur of the panel to which the action has been assigned;
   (b) a single legally qualified judge where the action has been assigned to a single judge;
   (c) the standing judge designated pursuant to Rule 345.5.
3. References to persons in these Rules may apply to legal persons as well as natural persons. Words importing the masculine gender shall include the feminine and vice versa. Unless the contrary intention appears, words in the singular include the plural and vice versa.

Relation with Agreement: Article 8(7)
Relation with Statute: Article 19(3) and (4)

Rule 2 – Supplementary protection certificate

1. Subject to paragraph 2, in these Rules with the exception of Rule 5 the expression 'patent' and 'proprietor' shall whenever appropriate include, respectively, a supplementary protection certificate as defined in Article 2(h) of the Agreement and granted in respect of the patent and the holder of such certificate.

2. References in these Rules to the language in which the patent was granted shall mean that language and not the language in which a supplementary protection certificate in respect of the patent was granted.

Rule 3 – Power of staff of the Registry and a sub-registry to perform functions of the Registry

Where these Rules refer to the Registry or Registrar and provide to perform any act that reference shall include – where applicable – the Deputy-Registrar and the relevant sub-registry and that act may be performed by the Registrar, the Deputy-Registrar or by a member of staff of the Registry or sub-registry of the relevant division.

Rule 4 – Lodging of documents

1. Written pleadings and other documents shall be signed and lodged at the Registry or relevant sub-registry in electronic form. Parties shall make use of the official forms available online. The receipt of documents shall be confirmed by the automatic issue of an electronic receipt, which shall indicate the date and local time of receipt.

2. Where it is not possible to lodge a document electronically for the reason that the electronic case management system of the Court has ceased to function a party may lodge a document in hard-copy form at the Registry or a sub-registry. An electronic copy of the document shall be lodged as soon as practicable thereafter.

Relation with Agreement: Article 44

Rule 5 – Lodging of an Application to opt out and withdrawal of an opt-out

1. The proprietor of a European patent (including a European patent that has expired) or the applicant for a published application for a European patent (hereinafter in this Rule 5 an 'application') who wishes to opt out that patent or application from the exclusive competence of the Court in accordance with Article 83(3) of the Agreement shall lodge an Application (hereinafter in this Rule 5 an 'Application to opt out') with the Registry.

- (a) Where the patent or application is owned by two or more proprietors or applicants, all proprietors or applicants shall lodge the Application to opt out. Where the person lodging an Application to opt out is not recorded as the proprietor or applicant in the registers referred to in Rule 8.5(a) and (b), respectively, the person shall lodge a declaration pursuant to paragraph 3(e).
- (b) The Application to opt out shall be made in respect of all of the states for which the European patent has been granted or which have been designated in the application.

2. An Application to opt out or an Application to withdraw an opt-out pursuant to paragraph 7 (hereinafter in this Rule 5 an 'Application to withdraw') shall extend to any supplementary protection certificate based on the European patent.

- (a) Where any such supplementary protection certificate has been granted at the date of lodging the Application to opt out or the Application to withdraw, the holder of the supplementary protection certificate shall, if different from the proprietor of the patent, lodge the Application to opt out or the Application to withdraw together with the proprietor.
- (b) Where any such supplementary protection certificate is granted subsequent to lodging the Application to opt out, the opt-out shall take effect automatically on grant of said supplementary protection certificate.

(c) Paragraphs 6 and 8 shall apply *mutatis mutandis*. For the purposes of paragraphs 6 and 8, reference to actions
   (i) in respect of a European patent shall apply to all supplementary protection certificates based on that European patent, and
   (ii) in respect of a supplementary protection certificate shall apply to the European patent on which such supplementary protection certificate is based and
   (iii) in respect of a supplementary protection certificate shall apply to all other supplementary protection certificates based on the same European patent.
(d) For the avoidance of doubt, it is not possible to opt out supplementary protection certificates, whether granted by the authorities of a Contracting Member State or otherwise, based on a European patent with unitary effect.

3. The Application to opt out shall contain:
   (a) the name of each proprietor or applicant for the European patent or application and of the holder of any supplementary protection certificate based on the European patent in question, and all relevant postal and, where applicable, electronic addresses;
   (b) the name and postal address and electronic address of
      (i) the representative appointed by the applicant or the proprietor in accordance with Article 48 of the Agreement or
      (ii) any other person lodging the Application to opt out on behalf of the proprietor or the applicant and the mandate for lodging the Application to opt out;
   (c) details of the patent and/or application including the EP publication number;
   (d) details of any supplementary protection certificate granted based on the patent concerned, including the number; and
   (e) for the purposes of paragraph 1(a), a declaration by or on behalf of each proprietor or applicant pursuant to Rule 8.5 that he is entitled to be registered in the national patent register.

4. Rule 8 shall not apply to Applications to opt out and to Applications to withdraw made pursuant to this Rule 5.

5. The Registrar shall as soon as practicable enter the Application to opt out in the register. Subject to paragraph 6, the opt-out which meets the requirements laid down in this Rule shall be regarded as effective from the date of entry in the register. If the requirements recorded in the register are missing or incorrect, a correction may be lodged with the Registry. The date of entry of the correction shall be noted in the register. The opt-out shall be effective from the date of correction.

6. In the event that an action has been commenced before the Court in respect of a patent and/or an application contained in an Application to opt out prior to the date of entry of the Application to opt out in the register or prior to the date of correction pursuant to paragraph 5, the Application to opt out shall be ineffective in respect of the patent and/or application in question, irrespective of whether the action is pending or has been concluded.

7. A proprietor of a patent or an application the subject of an opt-out pursuant to this Rule may lodge an Application to withdraw in respect of the patent or application, but not in respect of different states for which the European patent has been granted or which have been designated in the application. The Application to withdraw shall contain the particulars in accordance with paragraph 3. The Registrar shall as soon as practicable enter the Application to withdraw in the register and the withdrawal shall be regarded as effective from the date of entry in the register. Paragraphs 1(a) and 5 shall apply *mutatis mutandis*.

8. In the event that an action has been commenced before a court of a Contracting Member State in a matter over which the Court also has jurisdiction pursuant to Article 32 of the Agreement in respect of a patent or application contained in an Application to withdraw, prior to the entry of the Application to withdraw in the register or any time before the date pursuant to paragraph 5, the Application to

withdraw shall be ineffective in respect of the patent or application in question, irrespective of whether the action is pending or has been concluded.
9. Where an application for a European patent subject to an opt-out pursuant to this Rule proceeds to grant as a European patent with unitary effect the opt-out shall be deemed to have been withdrawn and the Registrar shall as soon as practicable enter the withdrawal in the register.
10. A patent or application the subject of an Application to withdraw which has been entered on the register may not thereafter be the subject of a further Application to opt out.
11. The Registrar shall as soon as practicable notify the European Patent Office and the national patent office of any Contracting Member States concerned of the entries in the register pursuant to paragraphs 5 and 7.
12. Applications accepted by the Registry before the entry into force of the Agreement shall be treated as entered on the register on the date of entry into force of the Agreement.

Relation with Agreement: Article 83(3) and (4)

Rule 5A – Application to remove an unauthorised application to opt out or unauthorised withdrawal of an opt-out
1. Without prejudice to the lodging of an Application to opt out or withdraw an opt-out in accordance with Rule 5, the proprietor of a European patent or the applicant for a published application for a European patent or holder of a supplementary protection certificate in relation to which an Application to opt out or withdraw the opt-out is entered in the register may lodge an Application to remove the entry of an unauthorised Application to opt out or withdrawal of the opt-out from the Registry setting out the reasons.
2. The Registrar shall mark the status of the Application to opt out or withdraw the opt-out entered in the register as subject to an Application for removal. The Registrar shall decide on the Application for removal as soon as practicable. If the final decision is to remove the Application to opt out or withdrawal of an opt-out the Registrar shall delete it in the register.
3. The decision on the Application for removal may be subject to an Application for review to the President of the Court of Appeal. The Application for review shall be lodged with the Registrar in one of the official languages of the European Patent Office, within one month of the notification of the challenged decision setting out the request, facts, evidence and arguments. If the Application for review is allowable, the President of the Court of Appeal shall order the Registrar to remove the opt-out or the withdrawal of the opt-out.

Rule 6 – Service and supply of orders, decisions, written pleadings and other documents
1. The Registry shall as soon as practicable serve, in accordance with Part 5, Chapter 2:
  (a) orders and decisions of the Court on the parties;
  (b) written pleadings and other documents of a party on the other party.
Where applicable, the Registry shall inform the parties of the opportunity to reply or to take any other appropriate step in the proceedings and of any time period for so doing.
2. The Registry shall also as soon as practicable supply to the parties copies of documents referred to in these Rules and lodged with pleadings and written evidence.
3. Where the postal or electronic address for service provided by a party pursuant to these Rules has changed that party shall give notice to the Registry and to every other party as soon as such change has taken place.

Rule 7 – Language of written pleadings and written evidence
1. Written pleadings and other documents, including written evidence, shall be lodged in the language of the proceedings unless the Court or these Rules otherwise provide.

2. Where these Rules or the Court require a pleading or other document to be translated it shall not be necessary to provide a formal certification by the translator as to the accuracy of such translation unless the accuracy is challenged by a party or such certification is ordered by the Court or required by these Rules.

Rule 8 – Party and party's representative

1. A party shall be represented in accordance with Article 48 of the Agreement unless otherwise provided by these Rules [Rules 5, 88.4 and 378.5].
2. For the purpose of all proceedings in relation to a patent, where these Rules provide that a party performs any act or that any act be performed upon a party that act shall be performed by or upon the representative for the time being of the party.
3. Except where these Rules provide otherwise, a party shall not communicate with the Court without informing the other party. Where such communication is in writing, the communication should be copied to the other party unless these Rules provide that the Court will supply a copy to the other party.
4. For the purposes of proceedings under these Rules in relation to the proprietor of a European patent with unitary effect, the person shown in the Register for unitary patent protection [Regulation (EU) No 1257/2012, Article 2(e)] as the proprietor shall be treated as such. If during proceedings before the Court a new proprietor is recorded in the Register for unitary patent protection, the former registered proprietor may apply to the Court pursuant to Rule 305.1(c) for the substitution of the new proprietor.
5. Subject to paragraph 6, for the purposes of proceedings under these Rules:
   (a) in relation to the proprietor of a European patent, the person entitled to be registered as proprietor under the law of each Contracting Member State in which such European patent has been validated shall be treated as the proprietor whether or not such person is in fact recorded in the register of patents maintained in such Contracting Member State (hereinafter 'national patent register'); and
   (b) in relation to the applicant for a European patent, the person entitled to be registered as applicant whether or not such person is in fact recorded as such in the European Patent Register kept by the European Patent Office.
   (c) For the purposes of paragraph 5, there shall be a rebuttable presumption that the person shown in each national patent register and the European Patent Register kept by the European Patent Office is the person entitled to be registered as proprietor or applicant as the case may be.
6. For the purposes of proceedings pursuant to Rules 42 and 61 in relation to a European patent, the person shown in the national patent register [Rule 8.5(a)] as the proprietor shall be treated as such for each Contracting Member State or, as far as no such person is registered in a national patent register, the last person shown recorded as proprietor in the European Patent Register kept by the European Patent Office.

Relation with Agreement: Article 48

Rule 9 – Powers of the Court

1. The Court may, at any stage of the proceedings, of its own motion or on a reasoned request by a party, make a procedural order such as to order a party to take any step, answer any question or provide any clarification or evidence, within time periods to be specified.
2. The Court may disregard any step, fact, evidence or argument which a party has not taken or submitted in accordance with a time limit set by the Court or these Rules.

3. Subject to paragraph 4, on a reasoned request by a party, the Court may:
   (a) extend, even retrospectively, a time period referred to in these Rules or imposed by the Court; and
   (b) shorten any such time period.
4. The Court shall not extend the time periods referred to in Rules 198.1, 213.1 and 224.1.

PART 1 – PROCEDURES BEFORE THE COURT OF FIRST INSTANCE

Rule 10 – Stages of the proceedings (*inter partes* proceedings)
Proceedings before the Court of First Instance shall consist of the following stages:
(a) a written procedure;
(b) an interim procedure, which may include an interim conference with the parties;
(c) an oral procedure which, subject to Rules 116.1 and 117, shall include an oral hearing of the parties unless the Court dispenses with the oral hearing with the agreement of the parties;
(d) a procedure for the award of damages, which may include a procedure to lay open books;
(e) a procedure for cost decisions.

Relation with Agreement: Articles 52, 68 and 69

Rule 11 – Settlement
1. At any stage of the proceedings, if the Court is of the opinion that the dispute is suitable for a settlement, it may propose that the parties make use of the facilities of the Patent Mediation and Arbitration Centre ('the Centre') in order to settle or to explore a settlement of the dispute. In particular, the judge-rapporteur shall during the interim procedure, especially at an interim conference in accordance with Rule 104(d), explore with the parties the possibility of a settlement, including through mediation and/or arbitration, using the facilities of the Centre. Parties who choose mediation in an attempt to settle a dispute are subsequently not prevented from initiating judicial proceedings before the Court in relation to that dispute by the expiry of limitation or prescription periods during the mediation process, which will stay the limitation or prescription periods until the end of the mediation process. If mediation proceedings are terminated without a dispute settlement agreement, the period shall continue to run from that moment.
2. Pursuant to Rule 365 the Court shall, if requested by the parties, by decision confirm the terms of any settlement or arbitral award by consent (irrespective of whether it was reached using the facilities of the Centre or otherwise), including a term which obliges the patent owner to limit, surrender or agree to the revocation of a patent or not to assert it against the other party and/or third parties. The parties may agree on costs to be awarded or may request the Court to decide on costs to be awarded in accordance with Rules 150 to 156 *mutatis mutandis*.
3. Save for the purpose of enforcing the terms of any such settlement agreement by any person no opinion expressed, suggestion made, proposal put forward, concession made or document drawn up for the purposes of settlement may be relied on as evidence by the Court or the parties in proceedings before the Court or any other court unless such matter was expressed to be made on an open basis and freely disclosable to the Court or any other court.

Relation with Agreement: Articles 35, 52(2) and 79

CHAPTER 1 – WRITTEN PROCEDURE

SECTION 1 – INFRINGEMENT ACTION

Rule 12 – Exchange of written pleadings (infringement action)

1. The written procedure shall consist of:
   (a) the lodging of a Statement of claim (by the claimant) [Rule 13];
   (b) the lodging of a Statement of defence (by the defendant) [Rules 23 and 24]; and, optionally
   (c) the lodging of a Reply to the Statement of defence (by the claimant) [Rule 29(b)]; and
   (d) the lodging of a Rejoinder to the Reply (by the defendant) [Rule 29(c)].
2. The Statement of defence may include a Counterclaim for revocation [Rule 25.1].
3. If a Counterclaim for revocation is lodged:
   (a) the claimant and any proprietor who becomes a party pursuant to Rule 25.2 (hereinafter in this Rule 12 and Rules 29 to 32, 'the proprietor') shall lodge a Defence to the Counterclaim for revocation [Rule 29(a)], which may include an Application to amend the patent by the proprietor [Rule 30];
   (b) the defendant may lodge a Reply to the Defence to the Counterclaim [Rule 29(d)]; and
   (c) the claimant and the proprietor may lodge a Rejoinder to the Reply to the Defence to the Counterclaim [Rule 29(e)].
4. If an Application to amend the patent is lodged by the proprietor, the defendant shall lodge a Defence to the Application to amend the patent in the Reply to the Defence to the Counterclaim, the proprietor may lodge a Reply to the Defence to the Application to amend and the defendant may lodge a Rejoinder to such Reply [Rule 32].
5. The judge-rapporteur may allow the exchange of further written pleadings, within time periods to be specified [Rule 36].

STATEMENT OF CLAIM

Rule 13 – Contents of the Statement of claim

1. The claimant shall lodge a Statement of claim with the division chosen by him [Article 33 of the Agreement] which shall contain:
   (a) the name of the claimant, and, where the claimant is a corporate entity, the location of its registered office, and of the claimant's representative;
   (b) the name of the party against whom the Statement is made (the defendant), and, where the defendant is a corporate entity, the location of its registered office;
   (c) postal and electronic addresses for service on the claimant and the names of the persons authorised to accept service;
   (d) postal and, where available, electronic addresses for service on the defendant and the names of the persons authorised to accept service, if known;
   (e) where the claimant is not the proprietor or not the only proprietor of the patent concerned, postal and where available, electronic addresses for service on the proprietor and the names and addresses of the persons authorised to accept service, if known;
   (f) where the claimant is not the proprietor of the patent concerned, or not the only proprietor, evidence to show the claimant is entitled to commence proceedings [Article 47(2) and (3) of the Agreement];
   (g) details of the patent concerned, including the number;
   (h) where applicable, information about any prior or pending proceedings relating to the patent concerned before the Court including any action for revocation or a declaration of non-in-

fringement pending before the central division and the date of any such action, the European Patent Office or any other court or authority;
- (i) an indication of the division which shall hear the action [Article 33(1) to (6) of the Agreement] with an explanation of why that division has competence; where the parties have agreed in accordance with Article 33(7) of the Agreement, the indication of the division which shall hear the action shall bc accompanied by evidence of the defendant's agreement;
- (j) where applicable, an indication that the action shall be heard by a single judge [Article 8(7) of the Agreement], accompanied by evidence of the defendant's agreement;
- (k) the nature of the claim, the order or the remedy sought by the claimant;
- (l) an indication of the facts relied on, in particular:
  - (i) one or more instances of alleged infringements or threatened infringements specifying the date and place of each;
  - (ii) the identification of the patent claims alleged to be infringed;
- (m) the evidence relied on [Rule 170.1], where available, and an indication of any further evidence which will be offered in support;
- (n) the reasons why the facts relied on constitute an infringement of the patent claims, including arguments of law and where appropriate an explanation of the proposed claim interpretation;
- (o) an indication of any order the claimant will seek during the interim procedure [Rule 104(e)];
- (p) where the claimant assesses that the value of the infringement action exceeds EUR500.000, an indication of the value; and
- (q) a list of the documents, including any witness statements, referred to in the Statement of claim, together with any request that all or part of any such document need not be translated and/or any request pursuant to Rule 262.2 or Rule 262A.

2. The claimant shall at the same time supply a copy of each of the documents referred to in the Statement of claim.

3. The judge-rapporteur shall decide on any request made pursuant to paragraph 1(q) as soon as practicable after his designation pursuant to Rule 18.

Rule 14 – Use of languages under Article 49(1) and (2) of the Agreement

1. Without prejudice to Articles 49(3) to (6) of the Agreement and subject to paragraph 2 and Rules 271.7, 321 to 323, proceedings shall be conducted:
- (a) in the official language or one of the official languages designated as language(s) of proceedings pursuant to Article 49(1) of the Agreement; or
- (b) in a language designated as language of proceedings by a Contracting Member State pursuant to Article 49(2) of the Agreement.

2. Where a Contracting Member State hosts a local division or participates in a regional division for which several languages have been designated pursuant to Article 49(1) and/or Article 49(2) of the Agreement:
- (a) subject to paragraphs 2(b) and (c), the claimant may choose as the language of proceedings any of the language(s) designated pursuant to Article 49(1) and/or Article 49(2) of the Agreement;
- (b) in proceedings before a local or regional division in a Contracting Member State against a defendant who has his domicile or principal place of business in that Contracting Member State where the action could not be brought pursuant to Article 33(1)(a) of the Agreement before any other local or regional division, proceedings shall be conducted in the official language of the Contracting Member State (paragraph 1(a)). Where a designation by a Contracting Member State having several official regional languages so indicates, proceedings shall be conducted in the official language of the region in which the defendant has his domicile or principal place of business. Where there are two or more such defendants whose domicile or principle place of business has different regional languages, the claimant may choose the language from the

regional languages in question. Where a designation by a Contracting Member State having several official languages so indicates, proceedings shall be conducted in the official language of the defendant. Where there are two or more such defendants with different official languages, the claimant may choose the language from the official languages in question.

(c) Where a designation of a language under Article 49(2) of the Agreement for a regional division or for one or more local division(s) hosted in a Member State so indicates, the judge-rapporteur may order in the interest of the panel to provide that judges may use in the oral proceedings the language according to paragraph 1(a) and/or to provide that the Court may make any order and deliver any decision in the language according to paragraph 1(a) together with a certified translation for the purpose of Rule 118.8 into the language according to paragraph 1(b).

3. The Registrar shall maintain a list of languages communicated by Contracting Member States pursuant to Article 49(1) and Article 49(2) of the Agreement as well as designations by Contracting Member States made pursuant to paragraph 2(b) and (c). The list shall be made publically available online.

4. The Registrar shall return any pleading lodged in a language other than the language of proceedings.

Rule 15 - Fee for the infringement action

1. The claimant shall pay the fixed fee and, where applicable, the value based fee for the infringement action in accordance with Part 6.

2. The Statement of claim shall not be deemed to have been lodged until the fixed fee and, where applicable, the value based fee for the infringement action has been paid, unless otherwise provided.

Relation with Agreement: Articles 36(3), 70 and 71

Rule 16 - Examination as to formal requirements of the Statement of claim

1. The Registry shall as soon as practicable check whether the patent concerned is the subject of an opt-out pursuant to Article 83(3) of the Agreement and Rule 5. In the event of an opt-out the Registry shall as soon as practicable inform the claimant who may withdraw or amend the Statement of claim as appropriate.

2. The Registry shall, as soon as practicable after the lodging of the Statement of claim, examine whether the requirements of Rules 13.1 (a) to (j), .2, 14 and 15.1 have been complied with.

3. If the claimant has not complied with the requirements referred to in paragraph 2, the Registry shall as soon as practicable invite the claimant to:

(a) correct the deficiencies within 14 days of service of such notification; and

(b) where applicable, pay the fee for the infringement action within said 14 days.

4. The Registry shall at the same time inform the claimant that if the claimant fails to correct the deficiencies or pay the fee within the time stated, a decision by default may be given, in accordance with Rule 355.

5. If the claimant fails to correct the deficiencies or pay the fee, the Registry shall inform a judge of the division who may reject the action as inadmissible by a decision by default. The judge may give the claimant an opportunity to be heard beforehand.

Rule 17 - Recording in the register and assignment (Court of First Instance, infringement action)

1. If the requirements referred to in Rule 16.2 or 16.3 have been complied with, the Registry shall as soon as practicable:

(a) record the date of receipt of the Statement of claim and attribute an action number to the file;

(b) record the file in the register; and

(c) inform the claimant of the action number of the file and the date of receipt.

2. The action shall be assigned to a panel of a division according to Rule 345.3. Where requested by the parties the action shall be assigned to a single judge in accordance with Rule 345.6.

3. The following shall determine the distribution of actions between the seat of the central division and its sections.

(a) Where an action involves a single patent having a single classification, the Registry shall allocate the action to the seat or the section of the central division appropriate to the classification of the patent according to Annex II of the Agreement. The Registry shall assign the action to a panel in accordance with Rule 345.3.

(b) Where an action involves more than one patent and a majority of the patents have a single classification appropriate to the seat or a single section of the central division according to Annex II of the Agreement, the Registry shall allocate the action to the seat or that section of the central division. The Registry shall assign the action to a panel in accordance with Rule 345.3.

(c) Where neither paragraph (a) nor (b) applies, especially where

(i) the action involves a single patent having more than one classification or

(ii) where the action involves more than one patent and no majority of the patents have a single classification corresponding to the seat or to one of the sections of the central division,

the Registry shall assign the action in accordance with Rule 345.3 to the panel at the seat or the section appropriate to the first classification of either the single patent or, where the action involves more than one patent, the patent first listed in the Statement of claim, according to Annex II of the Agreement. If the presiding judge of the respective panel considers that the reference of the action is appropriate, he shall accept it. If he considers otherwise, he shall instruct the Registry to refer the action in accordance with Rule 345.3 to the presiding judge of a panel of either the seat or the other section of the central division he considers appropriate, who shall likewise consider whether the re-allocation of the action is appropriate. If that presiding judge considers otherwise, he shall inform the President of the Court of First Instance, who shall allocate the action to the seat or the section of the central division he considers appropriate. The Registry shall assign the action to a panel in accordance with Rule 345.3.

4. The action shall be regarded as having commenced before the Court as from the date of receipt attributed to the Statement of claim.

Relation with Agreement: Article 7(2), Article 10

Rule 18 – Designation of the judge-rapporteur

The presiding judge of the panel to which the action has been assigned [Rule 17.2] shall designate one legally qualified judge of the panel as judge-rapporteur. The presiding judge may designate himself as judge-rapporteur. The Registry shall as soon as practicable notify the claimant and defendant of the identity of the judge-rapporteur.

PROCEDURE WHEN THE DEFENDANT RAISES A PRELIMINARY OBJECTION

Rule 19 – Preliminary objection

1. Within one month of service of the Statement of claim, the defendant may lodge a Preliminary objection concerning:

(a) the jurisdiction and competence of the Court, including any objection that an opt-out pursuant to Rule 5 applies to the patent that is the subject of the proceedings;

(b) the competence of the division indicated by the claimant [Rule 13.1(i)];

(c) the language of the Statement of claim [Rule 14].

2. A Preliminary objection shall contain:

(a) particulars in accordance with Rule 24(a) to (c);

(b) the decision or order sought by the defendant;

(c) the grounds upon which the Preliminary objection is based; and

(d) where appropriate the facts and evidence relied on.

3. The Preliminary objection shall be drawn up in the language pursuant to Rule 14.
4. If the action has been commenced before a regional division the defendant may by a Preliminary objection request a transfer of the action to the central division pursuant to Article 33(2) of the Agreement. The Preliminary objection shall in such a case contain all facts and evidence supporting the existence of the same infringement in the territories of three or more regional divisions.
5. The Registry shall as soon as practicable invite the claimant to comment on the Preliminary objection. Where applicable, the claimant may of his own motion correct any deficiency [paragraph 1(b) or (c)], within 14 days of service of notification of the Preliminary objection. Alternatively the claimant may submit written comments within the same period. The judge-rapporteur shall be informed of any correction made or written comments submitted by the claimant. If the deficiency referred to in paragraph 1(b) is corrected and the claimant has indicated another division, which is competent, the judge-rapporteur shall refer the action to the division indicated by the claimant.
6. The period for lodging the Statement of defence [Rule 23] shall not be affected by the lodging of a Preliminary objection, unless the judge-rapporteur decides otherwise.
7. The defendant's failure to lodge a Preliminary objection within the time period referred to in paragraph 1 shall be treated as a submission to the jurisdiction and competence of the Court and the competence of the division chosen by the claimant.

Rule 20 – Decision or order on a Preliminary objection
1. As soon as practicable after the expiry of the period referred to in Rule 19.5, the judge-rapporteur shall decide the Preliminary objection. The judge-rapporteur shall give the parties an opportunity to be heard. The decision shall include instructions to the parties and to the Registry concerning the next step in the proceedings.
2. Where the Preliminary objection is to be dealt with in the main proceedings, the judge-rapporteur shall inform the parties.

Rule 21 – Appeal against decision or order on a Preliminary objection
1. A decision of the judge-rapporteur allowing the Preliminary objection may be appealed pursuant to Rule 220.1(a). An order of the judge-rapporteur rejecting the Preliminary objection may only be appealed pursuant to Rule 220.2.
2. If an appeal is lodged, proceedings at first instance may be stayed by the judge-rapporteur or the Court of Appeal on a reasoned request by a party.

VALUE-BASED FEE FOR THE INFRINGEMENT ACTION

Rule 22 – Determination of value-based fee for the infringement action
1. The value of the infringement action shall be determined by the judge-rapporteur under Rule 370.6, taking into account the value as assessed by the parties, by way of an order during the interim procedure.
2. Where the value of the infringement action exceeds EUR 500.000, the claimant shall pay a value-based fee for the infringement action, in accordance with Part 6. Rule 16.3 to .5 shall apply *mutatis mutandis.*

STATEMENT OF DEFENCE

Rule 23 – Lodging of the Statement of defence
The defendant shall lodge a Statement of defence within three months of service of the Statement of claim.

Rule 24 - Contents of the Statement of defence
The Statement of defence shall contain:
(a) the names of the defendant and of the defendant's representative;
(b) postal and electronic addresses for service on the defendant and the names and addresses of the persons authorised to accept service;
(c) the action number of the file;
(d) an indication whether the defendant has lodged a Preliminary objection [Rule 19];
(e) an indication of the facts relied on, including any challenge to the facts relied on by the claimant;
(f) the evidence relied on [Rule 170.1], where available, and an indication of any further evidence which will be offered in support;
(g) the reasons why the action shall fail, arguments of law and any argument arising from the provisions of Article 28 of the Agreement and where appropriate any challenge to the claimant's proposed claim interpretation;
(h) an indication of any order the defendant will seek in respect of the infringement action during the interim procedure [Rule 104(e)];
(i) a statement whether the defendant disputes the claimant's assessment of the value of the infringement action and the grounds for such dispute; and
(j) a list of the documents, including any witness statements, referred to in the Statement of defence together with any request that all or part of any such document need not be translated and/or any request pursuant to Rule 262.2 or Rule 262A. Rule 13.2 and .3 shall apply *mutatis mutandis.*

Rule 25 - Counterclaim for revocation
1. If the Statement of defence includes an assertion that the patent alleged to be infringed is invalid the Statement of defence shall include a Counterclaim against the proprietor of the patent for revocation of said patent in accordance with Rule 42. The Counterclaim for revocation shall contain:
(a) an indication of the extent to which revocation of the patent is requested;
(b) one or more grounds for revocation, which shall as far as possible be supported by arguments of law, and where appropriate an explanation of the defendant's proposed claim construction;
(c) an indication of the facts relied on;
(d) the evidence relied on, where available, and an indication of any further evidence which will be offered in support;
(e) an indication of any order the defendant will seek during the interim procedure [Rule 104(e)];
(f) a statement of his position, if any, on the options provided for in Article 33(3) of the Agreement and Rule 37.4;
(g) a list of the documents, including any witness statements, referred to in the Counterclaim for revocation together with any request that all or part of any such documents need not be translated and/or any request pursuant to Rule 262.2 or Rule 262A. Rule 13.2 and .3 shall apply *mutatis mutandis*; and
(h) insofar as the proprietor of the patent is not claimant in the infringement proceedings, the information required by Rule 13.1(b) and (d) in respect of said proprietor.

2. Where the claimant is not the proprietor or not the only proprietor of the patent concerned, the Registry shall as soon as practicable serve a copy of the Counterclaim for revocation on the relevant proprietor in accordance with Rule 13.1(e) and shall supply a copy of each document referred to in paragraph 1(h). Rule 271 shall apply *mutatis mutandis*. The proprietor in question shall become a party to the revocation proceedings and shall be treated as defendant in all subsequent proceedings. The proprietor shall provide details pursuant to Rule 13.1(e) if not already provided by the claimant.

Rule 26 – Fee for the Counterclaim for revocation
The defendant shall pay the fee for the Counterclaim for revocation in accordance with Part 6. Rule 15.2 shall apply *mutatis mutandis.*

Rule 27 – Examination as to formal requirements of the Statement of defence and Counterclaim for revocation
1. The Registry shall, as soon as practicable after the lodging of the Statement of defence:
   (a) examine whether the requirements of Rule 24(a) to (d) have been complied with; and
   (b) if the Statement of defence includes a Counterclaim for revocation, examine whether the requirements of Rule 25.1(g) and (h), and the obligation to pay the fee pursuant to Rule 26 has been complied with.
2. If the Registry considers that the Statement of defence or the Counterclaim for revocation does not comply with any of the requirements referred to in paragraph 1, it shall as soon as practicable invite the defendant to:
   (a) correct the deficiencies noted, within 14 days of service of such notification; and
   (b) where applicable, pay the fee for the Counterclaim for revocation, within said 14 days.
3. The Registry shall at the same time inform the defendant that if the defendant fails to correct the deficiencies or pay the fee within the time stated, a decision by default may be given, in accordance with Rule 355.
4. If the defendant fails to correct the deficiencies or to pay the fee for the Counterclaim for revocation, as appropriate, within said 14 days, the Registry shall inform the judge-rapporteur who may give a decision by default. He may give the defendant an opportunity to be heard beforehand.

Rule 28 – Further schedule
As soon as practicable after service of the Statement of defence, the judge-rapporteur shall, after consulting the parties, set a date and time for an interim conference (where necessary [Rule 101.1]) and set a date for the oral hearing. The judge-rapporteur may set one alternative date.

DEFENCE TO THE COUNTERCLAIM FOR REVOCATION, REPLY TO THE STATEMENT OF THE DEFENCE AND APPLICATION TO AMEND THE PATENT AND REJOINDER TO THE REPLY

Rule 29 – Lodging of Defence to the Counterclaim for revocation, Reply to the Statement of defence and Rejoinder to the Reply
(a) Within two months of service of a Statement of defence which includes a Counterclaim for revocation, the claimant shall lodge a Defence to the Counterclaim for revocation together with any Reply to the Statement of defence and any Application to amend the patent pursuant to Rule 30, if applicable.
(b) Within two months of service of a Statement of defence which does not include a Counterclaim for revocation, the claimant may lodge a Reply to the Statement of defence.
(c) Within one month of service of a Reply to the Statement of defence which does not include a Counterclaim for revocation the defendant may lodge a Rejoinder to the Reply to the Statement of defence. The Rejoinder to the Reply to the Statement of defence shall be limited to a response to the matters raised in the Reply to the Statement of defence.
(d) Within two months of service of the Defence to Counterclaim the defendant may lodge a Reply to the Defence to the Counterclaim together with any Rejoinder to the Reply to the Statement of defence and any Defence to an Application to amend the patent pursuant to Rule 32, if applicable.
(e) Within one month of the service of the Reply to the Defence to the Counterclaim, the claimant may lodge a Rejoinder to the Reply together with any Reply to the Defence to an Application to amend

the patent pursuant to Rule 32, if applicable. The Rejoinder to the Reply to the Statement of defence shall be limited to a response to the matters raised in the Reply to the Statement of defence.

(f) Where the claimant is not the proprietor of the patent, all references to the claimant in this Rule 29 regarding an Application to amend the patent shall be read as including the proprietor.

Rule 29A – Contents of the Defence to the Counterclaim

The Defence to the Counterclaim for revocation shall contain:

(a) an indication of the facts relied on, including any challenge to the facts relied on by the defendant;
(b) the evidence relied on [Rule 170.1], where available, and an indication of any further evidence which will be offered in support;
(c) the reasons why the Counterclaim for revocation shall fail, including arguments of law and any argument as to why any dependent claim of the patent is independently valid;
(d) an indication of any order the claimant and the proprietor will seek in respect of the revocation action at the interim conference [Rule 104(e)];
(e) the claimant's and the proprietor's response to the defendant's choice of option, if any, provided for in Article 33(3) of the Agreement and Rule 37.4; and
(f) a list of the documents, including any witness statements, referred to in the Defence to the Counterclaim together with any request that all or part of any such document shall not be translated and/or any request pursuant to Rule 262.2 or Rule 262A. Rule 13.2 and .3 shall apply *mutatis mutandis*.

Rule 30 – Application to amend the patent

1. The Defence to the Counterclaim for revocation may include an Application by the proprietor of the patent to amend the patent which shall contain:

   (a) the proposed amendments of the claims of the patent concerned and/or specification, including where applicable and appropriate one or more alternative sets of claims (auxiliary requests), in the language in which the patent was granted; where the language of the proceedings [Rule 14.3] is not the language in which the patent was granted, the proprietor shall lodge a translation of the proposed amendments in the language of the proceedings, and where the patent is a European patent with unitary effect in the language of the defendant's domicile in a Member State of the EU or of the place of the alleged infringement or threatened infringement in a Contracting Member State if so requested by the defendant;
   (b) an explanation as to why the amendments satisfy the requirements of Articles 84 and 123(2), (3) EPC and why the proposed amended claims are valid and, if applicable, why they are infringed; and
   (c) an indication whether the proposals are conditional or unconditional; the proposed amendments, if conditional, must be reasonable in number in the circumstances of the case.

2. Any subsequent request to amend the patent may only be admitted into the proceedings with the permission of the Court.

3. Where other proceedings involving the patent subject to an Application to amend the patent are pending, the claimant shall notify the Court or the authority in question that such an Application has been made and provide the information required in paragraph 1(a).

DEFENCE TO THE APPLICATION TO AMEND THE PATENT

Rule 32 – Lodging of the Defence to the Application to amend the patent, the Reply to the Defence and the Rejoinder to the Reply

1. Within two months of service of an Application to amend the patent, the defendant shall lodge a Defence to the Application to amend the patent setting out whether he opposes the Application to amend the patent and, if so, why:
   (a) the proposed amendments are not allowable; and
   (b) the patent cannot be maintained as requested.
2. Where appropriate in view of the proposed amendments, the Defence to the Application to amend the patent may contain submissions in accordance with Rule 44(d) to (h) and alternative non-infringement submissions.
3. The proprietor may lodge a Reply to the Defence to the Application to amend the patent within one month of service of the Defence and the defendant may within one month of the service of the Reply lodge a Rejoinder to the Reply. The Rejoinder shall be limited to the matters raised in the Reply.

APPLICATION FOR ALLOCATING A TECHNICALLY QUALIFIED JUDGE TO THE PANEL

Rule 33 – Application by a party for allocating a technically qualified judge

1. Any party to the proceedings may lodge an Application for allocating a technically qualified judge to the panel which shall contain an indication of the relevant field of technology.
2. The Application shall be lodged as early as possible in the written procedure. An Application lodged after the closure of the written procedure [Rule 35] shall only be granted if justified in view of changed circumstances, such as new submissions presented by the other party, and allowed by the Court.
3. If the requirements of paragraphs 1 and 2 have been complied with, the President of the Court of First Instance shall allocate a technically qualified judge to the panel, after consulting the judge-rapporteur.

Rule 34 – Request by the judge-rapporteur for allocating a technically qualified judge

1. The judge-rapporteur may at any time during the written procedure, after consulting the presiding judge and the parties, request the President of the Court of First Instance to allocate a technically qualified judge to the panel.
2. Where a technically qualified judge is allocated to the panel, the judge-rapporteur may at any time consult the technically qualified judge.

LAST STEPS IN THE WRITTEN PROCEDURE

Rule 35 – Closure of the written procedure

Following the exchange of written pleadings in accordance with Rule 12.1 and, where applicable, in accordance with Rule 12.2 to .4, the judge-rapporteur shall:

(a) inform the parties of the date on which he intends to close the written procedure, without prejudice to Rule 36; and
(b) where an interim conference is necessary [Rules 28 and 101.1], confirm the date and the time set for the interim conference [Rule 28] or inform the parties that an interim conference will not be held.

Rule 36 – Further exchanges of written pleadings

Without prejudice to the powers of the judge-rapporteur pursuant to Rule 110.1, on a reasoned request by a party lodged before the date on which the judge-rapporteur intends to close the written procedure [Rule 35(a)], the judge-rapporteur may allow the exchange of further written pleadings, within a period to be specified. Where the exchange of further written pleadings is allowed, the written procedure shall be deemed closed upon expiry of the specified period.

Rule 37 – Application of Article 33(3) of the Agreement

1. As soon as practicable after the closure of the written procedure the panel shall decide by way of order how to proceed with respect to the application of Article 33(3) of the Agreement. The parties shall be given an opportunity to be heard [Rule 264]. The panel shall set out in its order brief reasons for its decision.
2. The Panel may by order take an earlier decision if appropriate having considered the parties' pleadings and having given the parties an opportunity to be heard [Rule 264].
3. Where the panel decides to proceed in accordance with Article 33(3)(a) of the Agreement, the judge-rapporteur shall request the President of the Court of First Instance to allocate to the panel a technically qualified judge if not already allocated pursuant to Rules 33 and 34.
4. Where the panel decides to proceed in accordance with Article 33(3)(b) of the Agreement, the panel may stay the infringement proceedings pending a final decision in the revocation proceedings and shall stay the infringement proceedings where there is a high likelihood that the relevant claims of the patent will be held to be invalid on any ground by the final decision in the revocation proceedings.
5. Where the panel decides to proceed in accordance with Article 33(3)(b) of the Agreement and not to stay the proceedings, the judge-rapporteur of the regional or local division shall communicate to the central division the dates set for the interim conference and for the oral hearing according to Rule 28.

COUNTERCLAIM FOR REVOCATION REFERRED TO THE CENTRAL DIVISION UNDER ARTICLE 33(3)(B) OF THE AGREEMENT

Rule 38 – Written procedure when the central division deals with a Counterclaim for revocation under Article 33(3)(b) of the Agreement

When a Counterclaim for revocation is referred to the central division, it shall be dealt with as follows:

(a) Rule 17.2 and .3 shall apply *mutatis mutandis*;
(b) Rule 18 shall apply *mutatis mutandis*: the presiding judge of the panel to which the Counterclaim for revocation has been assigned shall designate one legally qualified judge of the panel as judge-rapporteur;
(c) The judge-rapporteur shall give any further directions necessary for the future conduct of the written procedure before the central division;
(d) Rule 28 shall apply *mutatis mutandis*: the judge-rapporteur shall after consulting the parties set a date and a time for the interim conference (where necessary [Rules 28 and 101]) and set a date, and one alternative date, for the oral hearing.

Rule 39 – Language of the proceedings before the central division

1. Where the language of the proceedings before the local division or the regional division which referred the Counterclaim for revocation to the central division is not the language in which the patent was granted, the judge-rapporteur may order that the parties lodge, within a period of one month, a translation in the language in which the patent was granted of any written pleadings and such other documents lodged during the written procedure as the judge-rapporteur may direct.
2. Where appropriate, the judge-rapporteur may specify in his order that only excerpts of parties' written pleadings and other documents shall be translated.
3. Where the language of the proceedings before the local division or the regional division is the language in which the patent was granted the pleadings served in accordance with Rules 24, 25, 29, 29a, 30 and 32 shall stand.

Rule 40 – Accelerated proceedings before the central division

The judge-rapporteur shall accelerate proceedings before the central division where
(a) an Application for provisional measures has been lodged [Rule 206]; or
(b) the regional or local division has referred the Counterclaim for revocation to the central division and where the infringement action has not been stayed.

In the latter case, the judge-rapporteur of the panel of the central division shall endeavour to set a date for the oral hearing on the revocation action prior to the date of the oral hearing of the infringement action.

ACTION REFERRED TO THE CENTRAL DIVISION UNDER ARTICLE 33(3)(C) OF THE AGREEMENT

Rule 41 – Written procedure when the central division deals with the action under Article 33(3)(c) of the Agreement

When an action is referred to the central division under Article 33(3)(c) of the Agreement, it shall be dealt with as follows:
(a) Rule 17.2 and .3 shall apply *mutatis mutandis*. The parties may request that the action be heard by a single judge;
(b) Rule 18 shall apply *mutatis mutandis*: the presiding judge of the panel to which the action has been assigned shall designate one judge of the panel as judge-rapporteur;
(c) dates already set under Rule 28 shall be confirmed wherever possible;
(d) Rule 39 shall apply *mutatis mutandis*: the judge-rapporteur may order that the parties lodge a translation in the language in which the patent was granted of any written pleadings lodged during the written procedure; where appropriate, the judge-rapporteur may specify in his order that only excerpts of parties' written pleadings and other documents shall be translated. Otherwise the pleadings lodged during the written procedure shall stand;
(e) The judge-rapporteur shall give any further directions necessary for the future conduct of the written procedure before the central division.

SECTION 2 – REVOCATION ACTION

Rule 42 – Action to be directed against the patent proprietor

1. Any action for the revocation of a patent shall be directed against the proprietor of the patent.
2. If the action for revocation is directed against the proprietor in accordance with Rule 8.6 ('the registered proprietor') but the registered proprietor is not a proprietor within the meaning of Rule 8.5(a) or (b) ('the Rule 8.5 proprietor') each such registered proprietor shall as soon as practicable after service of the Statement for revocation apply to the Court pursuant to Rule 305.1(c) for the substitution of the registered proprietor by the Rule 8.5 proprietor.

Relation with Agreement: Articles 47(5) and 65(1)

Rule 43 – Exchange of written pleadings (revocation action)

1. The written procedure shall consist of:
   (a) the lodging of a Statement for revocation (by the claimant) [Rule 44]; and
   (b) the lodging of a Defence to revocation (by the defendant) [Rule 49]; and optionally
   (c) the lodging of a Reply to the Defence to revocation (by the claimant) [Rule 51];
   (d) the lodging of a Rejoinder to the Reply (by the defendant) [Rule 52].
2. The Defence to revocation may include:
   (a) an Application to amend the patent; and

(b) a Counterclaim for infringement by the proprietor of the patent.
3. If an Application to amend the patent is lodged, the claimant shall lodge a Defence to the Application to amend the patent. The defendant may lodge a Reply to the Defence to the Application. The claimant may lodge a Rejoinder to the Reply. The Rejoinder shall be limited to a response to the matters raised in the Reply.
4. If a Counterclaim for infringement is lodged, the claimant shall lodge a Defence to the Counterclaim for infringement [Rule 56], the defendant may lodge a Reply to the Defence to the Counterclaim [Rule 56.3] and the claimant may lodge a Rejoinder to the Reply [Rule 56.4].
5. Rule 12.5 shall apply.

STATEMENT FOR REVOCATION

Rule 44 – Contents of the Statement for revocation

The claimant shall, subject to point (b), lodge a Statement for revocation at the Registry in accordance with Article 7(2) of the Agreement and Annex II thereto. The Statement for revocation shall contain:
(a) particulars in accordance with Rule 13.1(a) to (d) and (g), (h);
(b) where the parties have agreed to bring the action before a local division or a regional division in accordance with Article 33(7) of the Agreement, an indication of the division which shall hear the action, accompanied by evidence of the defendant's agreement;
(c) where applicable, an indication that the action shall be heard by a single judge [Article 8(7) of the Agreement], accompanied by evidence of the defendant's agreement;
(d) an indication of the extent to which revocation of the patent is requested;
(e) one or more grounds for revocation, which shall as far as possible be supported by arguments of law, and where appropriate an explanation of the claimant's proposed claim construction;
(f) an indication of the facts relied on;
(g) the evidence relied on, where available, and an indication of any further evidence which will be offered in support;
(h) an indication of any order the claimant will seek during the interim procedure [Rule 104(e)]; and
(i) a list of the documents, including any witness statements, referred to in the Statement for revocation together with any request that all or part of any such document need not be translated and/or any request pursuant to Rule 262.2 and Rule 262A. Rule 13.2 and .3 shall apply *mutatis mutandis.*

Rule 45 – Language of the Statement for revocation

1. Subject to paragraph 2, the Statement for revocation shall be drawn up in the language in which the patent was granted.
2. Where the parties have agreed to bring the action before a local or a regional division in accordance with Article 33(7) of the Agreement, the Statement for revocation shall be drawn up in one of the languages referred to in Rule 14.1(a) and (b).

Relation with Agreement: Article 49

Rule 46 – Fee for the revocation action

The claimant shall pay the fee for the revocation action in accordance with Part 6. Rule 15.2 shall apply *mutatis mutandis.*

Relation with Agreement: Articles 70 and 71

Rule 47 – Examination as to formal requirements, recording in the register, assignment (Court of First Instance, revocation action) and designation of the judge-rapporteur
1. Rules 16 to 18 shall apply *mutatis mutandis.*
2. The Registrar shall notify the European Patent Office that the patent in question is subject to an action for revocation.

Relation with Agreement: Articles 10 and 33

Rule 48 – Preliminary objection
Rule 19.1 to .3 and .5 to .7 as well as Rules 20 and 21 shall apply *mutatis mutandis.*

DEFENCE TO REVOCATION

Rule 49 – Lodging of the Defence to revocation
1. The defendant shall lodge a Defence to revocation within two months of service of the Statement for revocation.
2. The Defence to revocation may include:
  (a) an Application to amend the patent;
  (b) a Counterclaim for infringement.

Rule 50 – Contents of the Defence to revocation and Counterclaim for infringement
1. The Defence to revocation shall contain the matters referred to in Rule 24(a) to (c).
Rule 29A(a) to (d) and (f) shall apply *mutatis mutandis.*
2. Any Application to amend the patent shall contain the matters referred to in Rule 30.1(a), (c) and an explanation as to why the amendments satisfy the requirements of Articles 84 and 123(2), (3) EPC and why the proposed amended claims are valid. Rule 30.2 shall apply.
3. Any Counterclaim for infringement shall contain the matters referred to in Rule 13.1(k) to (q). Rule 13.2 and .3 shall apply.

Rule 51 – Reply to Defence to revocation
Within two months of service of the Defence to revocation the claimant may lodge a Reply to the Defence to revocation together with any Defence to an Application to amend the patent pursuant to Rule 43.3 and 55 as well as any Defence to the Counterclaim for infringement pursuant to Rule 56.1, if applicable.

Rule 52 – Rejoinder to the Reply
Within one month of the service of the Reply the defendant may lodge a Rejoinder to the Reply to the Defence to revocation together with any Reply to the Defence to an Application to amend the patent pursuant to Rule 43.3 and 55 as well as any Reply to the Defence to the Counterclaim for infringement pursuant to Rule 56.3, if applicable. The Rejoinder shall be limited to a response to the matters raised in the Reply.

Rule 53 – Fee for the Counterclaim for infringement
The defendant shall pay the fixed fee and, where applicable, the value based fee for the Counterclaim for infringement in accordance with Part 6. Rule 15 and Rule 16.3 to 5 shall apply *mutatis mutandis.*

Rule 54 – Examination as to formal requirements and further schedule
Rules 27 and 28 shall apply *mutatis mutandis.*

DEFENCE TO THE APPLICATION TO AMEND THE PATENT AND DEFENCE TO THE COUNTERCLAIM FOR INFRINGEMENT

Rule 55 – Lodging of the Defence to the Application to amend the patent, the Reply to the Defence and the Rejoinder to the Reply
Rule 32 shall apply *mutatis mutandis.*

Rule 56 – Lodging of the Defence to the Counterclaim for infringement
1. Within two months of service of a Counterclaim for infringement, the claimant shall lodge a Defence to the Counterclaim for infringement.
2. The Defence to the Counterclaim for infringement shall contain the matters referred to in Rule 24.1(e) to (h) and (j) and a statement whether the claimant disputes the defendant's assessment of the value of the Counterclaim pursuant to Rule 50.3 and the reasons for such dispute.
3. The defendant may lodge a Reply to the Defence to the Counterclaim for infringement within one month.
4. Within one month of the service of the Reply to the Defence to the Counterclaim for infringement the claimant may lodge a Rejoinder to the Reply together with any Rejoinder to the Reply to the Defence to the Application to amend the patent pursuant to Rule 43.3 and 55. The Rejoinder shall be limited to matters raised in the Reply.

Rule 57 – Request for allocating a technically qualified judge
Rules 33 and 34 shall apply *mutatis mutandis.*

Rule 58 – Closure of the written procedure subject to the possible exchange of further pleadings
Rules 35 and 36 shall apply *mutatis mutandis.*

Rule 60 – Determination of the value-based fee for the Counterclaim for infringement
1. The value of the Counterclaim for infringement shall be determined by the judge-rapporteur under Rule 370.6, taking into account the value as assessed by the parties, by way of an order during the interim procedure.
2. Where the value of the Counterclaim for infringement exceeds EUR 500.000, the defendant shall pay a value-based fee in accordance with Part 6. Rule 16.3 to .5 shall apply *mutatis mutandis.*

SECTION 3 – ACTION FOR DECLARATION OF NON-INFRINGEMENT

Rule 61 – Declaration of non-infringement
1. A declaration that the performance of a specific act does not, or a proposed act would not, constitute an infringement of a patent may be made by the Court in proceedings between the person doing or proposing to do the act and the patent proprietor or licensee entitled to commence infringement proceedings pursuant to Article 47 of the Agreement, if the patent proprietor or such licensee has asserted that the act is an infringement, or, if no such assertion has been made by the patent proprietor or licensee, if:

(a) that person has applied in writing to the proprietor or licensee for a written acknowledgment to the effect of the declaration claimed, and has provided him with full particulars in writing of the act in question; and
(b) the proprietor or licensee has refused or failed to give any such acknowledgment within one month.

2. The action for a declaration shall be directed against the proprietor of the patent or the licensee who has asserted an infringement or refused or failed to give an acknowledgement pursuant to paragraph 1(b).
3. If the action for a declaration of non-infringement is directed against the proprietor of the patent in accordance with Rule 8.6 ('the registered proprietor') but the registered proprietor is not a proprietor within the meaning of Rule 8.5(a) or (b) ('the Rule 8.5 proprietor') each such registered proprietor shall as soon as possible after service of the Statement for a declaration of non-infringement apply to the Court pursuant to Rule 305.1(c) for the substitution of the registered proprietor by the Rule 8.5 proprietor.

Rule 62 – Exchange of written pleadings (action for declaration of non-infringement)
1. The written procedure shall consist of:
   (a) the lodging of a Statement for a declaration of non-infringement (by the claimant) [Rule 63];
   (b) the lodging of a Defence to the Statement for a declaration of non-infringement (by the defendant) [Rules 67 and 68]; and, optionally
   (c) the lodging of a Reply to the Defence to the Statement for a declaration of non-infringement [Rule 69];
   (d) the lodging of a Rejoinder to the Reply [Rule 69].
2. Rule 12.5 shall apply.

Rule 63 – Contents of the Statement for a declaration of non-infringement
The claimant shall, subject to point (b), lodge at the Registry in accordance with Article 33(4), Article 7(2) of the Agreement and Annex II thereto, a Statement for a declaration of non-infringement which shall contain:
(a) particulars in accordance with Rule 13.1(a) to (h) and particulars confirming that the requirements of Rule 61 are met;
(b) where the parties have agreed to bring the action before a local division or a regional division in accordance with Article 33(7) of the Agreement, an indication of the division which shall hear the action, accompanied by evidence of the defendant's agreement;
(c) where applicable, an indication that the action shall be heard by a single judge [Article 8(7) of the Agreement], accompanied by evidence of the defendant's agreement;
(d) the declaration sought by the claimant;
(e) the reasons why the performance of a specific act does not, or a proposed act would not, constitute an infringement of the patent concerned, including arguments of law and where appropriate an explanation of the claimant's proposed claim construction;
(f) an indication of the facts relied on;
(g) the evidence relied on, where available, and an indication of any further evidence which will be offered in support;
(h) an indication of any order the claimant will seek at the interim conference [Rule 104(e)];
(i) where the claimant assesses that the value of the declaratory action exceeds EUR 500.000, an indication of the value; and
(j) a list of the documents, including any witness statements, referred to in the Statement for a declaration together with any request that all or part of any such document need not be translated and/or any request pursuant to Rule 262.2 or Rule 262A. Rule 13.2 and .3 shall apply *mutatis mutandis.*

Rule 64 – Language of the Statement for a declaration of non-infringement
Rule 45 shall apply *mutatis mutandis.*

Rule 65 – Examination as to formal requirements, recording in the register, assignment and designation of the judge-rapporteur
Rules 16 to 18 shall apply *mutatis mutandis.*

Rule 66 – Preliminary objection
Rule 19.1 to .3 and .5 to .7 as well as Rules 20 and 21 shall apply *mutatis mutandis.*

Rule 67 – Lodging of the Defence to the Statement for a declaration of non-infringement
The defendant shall lodge a Defence to the Statement for a declaration of non-infringement within two months of service of the Statement for a declaration of non-infringement.

Rule 68 – Contents of the Defence to the Statement for a declaration of non-infringement
The Defence to the Statement for a declaration of non-infringement shall contain the matters referred to in Rule 24(a) to (j). Rule 13.2 and .3 shall apply *mutatis mutandis.*

Rule 69 – Reply to Defence to the Statement for a declaration of non-infringement and Rejoinder to the Reply
1. The claimant may lodge a Reply to the Defence to the Statement for a declaration of non-infringement within one month.
2. The defendant may lodge a Rejoinder to the Reply within one month of service of the Reply. The Rejoinder shall be limited to the matters raised in the Reply.

Rule 70 – Fee for the action for a declaration of non-infringement
The claimant shall pay the fixed fee and, where applicable, the value based fee for the action for a declaration of non-infringement in accordance with Part 6. Rule 15.2 and Rule 16.3 to .5 shall apply *mutatis mutandis.*

Rule 71 – Examination as to formal requirements and further schedule
Rules 27 and 28 shall apply *mutatis mutandis.*

Rule 72 – Request for allocating a technically qualified judge
Rules 33 and 34 shall apply *mutatis mutandis.*

Rule 73 – Closure of the written procedure subject to the possible exchange of further pleadings
Rules 35 and 36 shall apply *mutatis mutandis.*

Rule 74 – Value-based fee for the action for a declaration of non-infringement
1. The value of the action for a declaration of non-infringement shall be determined by the judge-rapporteur under Rule 370.6, taking into account the value as assessed by the parties, by way of an order during the interim procedure.
2. Where the value exceeds EUR500.000 the claimant shall pay a value-based fee for the action for a declaration of non-infringement in accordance with Part 6. Rule 16.3 to .5 shall apply *mutatis mutandis.*

SECTION 4 – ACTIONS WITHIN ARTICLE 33(5) AND (6) OF THE AGREEMENT

Rule 75 – Revocation action and subsequent infringement action in a local or regional division (Article 33(5) of the Agreement)

1. Where a claimant has lodged a Statement for revocation [Rule 44] before the central division and the defendant or a licensee entitled to commence proceedings pursuant to Article 47 of the Agreement subsequently initiates an infringement action in a local or regional division against the claimant in respect of the same patent the following procedures shall apply.
2. The Registry at the local or regional division shall proceed in accordance with Rules 16 and 17. The Registry shall as soon as practicable notify the President of the Court of First Instance of the revocation action in the central division, the infringement action in the local or regional division and any Counterclaim for revocation in the infringement action. The presiding judges of the panels seized shall be informed likewise about actions in the other divisions.
3. Where a Counterclaim for revocation is brought in the infringement action and there is identity of parties as between the two actions, unless otherwise agreed by the parties, the panel appointed in the central division to hear the revocation action shall stay all further proceedings in the revocation action pending a decision of the panel hearing the action for infringement pursuant to Article 33(3) of the Agreement and Rule 37.
4. The panel hearing the action for infringement shall when exercising its discretion under Article 33(3) of the Agreement take into consideration how far the revocation action in the central division was advanced prior to the stay referred to in paragraph 3.
5. Where the panel hearing the action for infringement decides to proceed in accordance with Article 33(3)(a) of the Agreement, Rules 33 and 34 shall apply *mutatis mutandis* to the action for infringement.
6. Where the panel hearing the action for infringement decides to proceed in accordance with Article 33(3)(b) or (c) of the Agreement, Rules 37.4 and 39 to 41 shall apply *mutatis mutandis.*

Rule 76 – Actions for declaration of non-infringement within Article 33(6) of the Agreement

1. Where a claimant has lodged an action for declaration of non-infringement (Rule 61) before the central division against the patent proprietor or a licensee entitled to commence infringement proceedings pursuant to Article 47 of the Agreement and the defendant proprietor or licensee subsequently initiates an action for infringement in a local or regional division against the claimant in respect of the same patent and with respect to the same alleged infringement the following procedure shall apply.
2. The Registry shall proceed in accordance with Rule 16 and 17. The Registry shall as soon as practicable notify the President of the Court of First Instance of the co-pending actions and the dates attributed to them. The presiding judges of the panels seized shall be informed likewise about the action in the other division.
3. If the date attributed by the Registry to the action for infringement pursuant to Rule 17.1(a) is within three months of the date attributed to the action for declaration of non-infringement the panel of the central division shall stay all further proceedings in the action for a declaration. If the date attributed to the action for infringement is outside the said three month period there shall be no stay but the presiding judges of the central division and the local or regional division concerned shall consult to agree on the future progress of proceedings including the possibility of a stay of one action pursuant to Rule 295(f).

Rule 77 – Action for declaration of non-infringement and action for revocation

An action for declaration of non-infringement may be lodged together with an action for revocation of the patent in question. Fees shall be paid in accordance with both Rules 46 and Rules 70 and 74.

SECTION 5 – ACTION FOR COMPENSATION FOR LICENCES ON THE BASIS OF ARTICLE 8 OF REGULATION (EU) NO 1257/2012

Rule 80 – Compensation for a licence of right

1. The Application for appropriate compensation [Article 32(1)(h) of the Agreement] shall contain:
   (a) particulars in accordance with Rule 13.1(a) to (d);
   (b) information on the filing of the statement as referred to in Article 8(1) of Regulation (EU) No 1257/2012;
   (c) the licence agreement referred to in Article 8(2) of Regulation (EU) No 1257/2012.
2. Rules 132, 133, 134, 135 and 137 to 140 apply *mutatis mutandis* to the procedure for appropriate compensation.

Relation with Agreement: Article 32(1)(h)

SECTION 6 – ACTION AGAINST DECISIONS OF THE EUROPEAN PATENT OFFICE IN CARRYING OUT THE TASKS REFERRED TO IN ARTICLE 9 OF REGULATION (EU) NO 1257/2012

Relation with Agreement: Articles 32(1)(i), 47(7) and 66

Rule 85 – Stages of the proceedings (*ex parte* proceedings)

1. Subject to paragraph 2, where an action is brought against a decision of the European Patent Office in carrying out the tasks referred to in Article 9 of Regulation (EU) No 1257/2012 (hereinafter 'decision of the Office'), proceedings before the Court of First Instance shall consist of:
   (a) a written procedure, which shall include a possibility for interlocutory review by the European Patent Office;
   (b) an interim procedure, which may include an interim conference; and
   (c) an oral procedure which, at the request of the claimant or at the instance of the Court, may include an oral hearing.
2. This Rule and Rules 88 (save as expressly provided for in Rule 97.2), 89 and 91 to 96 shall not apply to an expedited action against a decision of the Office pursuant to Rule 97.

Rule 86 – Suspensive effect

An action against a decision of the Office shall have suspensive effect.

Rule 87 – Grounds for annulling or altering a decision of the Office

An action against a decision of the Office may be brought on grounds of:
(a) infringement of Regulation (EU) No 1257/2012 or of Regulation (EU) No 1260/2012 or of any rule of law relating to their application;
(b) infringement of any of the implementing rules of the European Patent Office for carrying out the tasks referred to in Article 9(1) of Regulation (EU) No 1257/2012;
(c) infringement of an essential procedural requirement;
(d) misuse of power.

Rule 88 – Application to annul or alter a decision of the Office

1. The claimant shall lodge an Application at the Registry, in accordance with Article 7(2) of the Agreement and Annex II thereto, to annul or alter a decision of the Office in the language in which the patent was granted, within two months of service of the decision of the Office.
2. The Application to annul or alter a decision of the Office shall contain:

(a) the names of the claimant and, where applicable, of the claimant's representative;
(b) where the claimant is not the proprietor of or applicant for the European patent with unitary effect, an explanation and evidence that he is adversely affected by the decision of the Office and entitled to start proceedings [Article 47(7) of the Agreement];
(c) postal and electronic addresses for service on the claimant and the names and addresses of the persons authorised to accept service;
(d) a reference to the contested decision of the Office;
(e) where applicable, information about any prior or pending proceedings relating to the patent concerned before the Court, the European Patent Office or any other court or authority;
(f) an indication whether the action shall be heard by a single judge;
(g) the order or the remedy sought by the claimant;
(h) one or more grounds for annulling or altering the contested decision, in accordance with Rule 87;
(i) the facts, evidence and arguments relied on; and
(j) a list of the documents, including any witness statements, referred to in the Application together with any request that all or part of any such document need not be translated and/or any request pursuant to Rule 262.2 or Rule 262A. Rule 13.2 and 3 shall apply *mutatis mutandis.*

3. The claimant shall pay the fee for the action against a decision of the Office, in accordance with Part 6. Rule 15.2 shall apply *mutatis mutandis.*
4. Rule 8 shall not apply.

Relation with Agreement: Articles 32(1)(i), 33(9), 47(7), 48(7) and 49(6)

Rule 89 – Examination as to formal requirements (*ex parte* proceedings)
1. The Registry shall, as soon as practicable after an Application to annul or alter a decision of the Office has been lodged, examine whether the requirements of Articles 47(7) and 49(6) of the Agreement and Rule 88.1, .2(a) to (d) and .3 have been complied with.
2. If the Registry considers that any of the requirements referred to in paragraph 1 has not been complied with, it shall invite the claimant to:
(a) correct the deficiencies noted, within 14 days from the date of service of such notification; and
(b) where applicable, pay the fee for the action against a decision of the Office, within said 14 days.

3. The Registry shall at the same time inform the claimant that if the claimant fails to correct the deficiencies or pay the fee within the time stated, a decision by default may be given in accordance with Rule 355.
4. If the claimant fails to correct the deficiencies noted or to pay the fee for the action against a decision of the Office, the Registry shall inform the President of the Court of First Instance who may reject the action as inadmissible by a decision by default. He may give the claimant an opportunity to be heard beforehand.

Rule 90 – Recording in the register (*ex parte* proceedings)
If the requirements referred to in Rule 89.1 have been complied with, the Registry shall as soon as practicable:
(a) record the date of receipt of the Application to annul or alter a decision of the Office and attribute an action number to the file;
(b) record the file in the register;
(c) inform the claimant of the action number of the file and the date of receipt; and
(d) forward the Application to the European Patent Office, with an indication that the Application is admissible.

Rule 91 – Interlocutory revision by the European Patent Office

1. If the European Patent Office considers that the Application to annul or alter a decision of the Office is well founded, it shall within two months of the date of receipt of the Application:

(a) rectify the contested decision in accordance with the order or remedy sought by the claimant [Rule 88.2(g)]; and

(b) inform the Court that the decision has been rectified.

2. Where the Court is informed by the European Patent Office that the contested decision has been rectified, it shall inform the claimant that the action is closed. It may order full or partial reimbursement of the fee for the action against a decision of the Office, in accordance with Part 6.

Rule 92 – Assignment to panel or to single judge, designation of judge-rapporteur

Where the action is not closed in accordance with Rule 91.2, the action shall, as soon as practicable after the expiry of the period referred to in Rule 91.1, be assigned to a panel of the central division or to a single judge if requested by the claimant [Rule 88.2(f)] in accordance with Rule 345.3. Rule 18 shall apply.

Rule 93 – Examination of the Application to annul or alter a decision of the Office

1. In the examination of the Application to annul or alter a decision of the Office, the judge-rapporteur may invite the claimant to lodge further written pleadings, within a time period to be specified.

2. Where appropriate, the judge-rapporteur may, after consulting the claimant, set a date and time for an interim conference.

3. Rule 35 shall apply *mutatis mutandis*.

Rule 94 – Invitation to the President of the European Patent Office to comment

The judge-rapporteur may, on his own initiative or on request by the President of the European Patent Office, invite the President of the European Patent Office to comment in writing on any question arising in the course of proceedings under this Section including any appeal by the claimant pursuant to Rule 220. The claimant shall be entitled to submit his observations on the President's comments.

Rule 95 – *Lex specialis* for the interim procedure (*ex parte* procedure)

During the interim procedure, the judge-rapporteur shall invite the claimant to indicate whether he wishes that an oral hearing be convened. The judge-rapporteur may convene an oral hearing at his own instance.

Rule 96 – *Lex specialis* for the oral procedure (*ex parte* procedure)

1. Rules 110.3, 111, 115 and 118.6 shall apply to the oral hearing and to the decision of the Court.

2. If an oral hearing is not convened, the panel shall decide in accordance with Rule 117.

Rule 97 – Application to annul a decision of the Office to reject a request for unitary effect

1. The proprietor of a patent whose request for unitary effect has been rejected by the Office shall lodge an Application at the Registry in accordance with Article 7(2) of the Agreement and Annex II thereto, to reverse the decision of the Office, in the language in which the patent was granted, within three weeks of service of the decision of the European Patent Office.

2. The Application shall contain particulars in accordance with Rule 88.2(a), (c), (d) and (g) to (j) and the proprietor shall pay the fee for the action against the decision of the Office in accordance with Part 6. Rule 15.2 and Rule 89 shall apply *mutatis mutandis*.

3. If the requirements referred to in paragraph 2 have been complied with, Rule 90 shall apply *mutatis mutandis*.

4. The Registry shall as soon as practicable forward the Application to the standing judge who may invite the President of the European Patent Office to comment on the Application, but shall in any event decide the Application within three weeks of the date of receipt of the Application.
5. A Statement of appeal by the proprietor of the patent or the President of the European Patent Office against the decisions of the standing judge pursuant to paragraph 4 may be lodged within three weeks of service of the said decision. The Statement of appeal shall contain the particulars previously lodged pursuant to paragraph 2 and also the reasons for setting aside the contested decision. The appellant shall pay the fee for the appeal in accordance with Part 6. Rule 15.2 shall apply *mutatis mutandis*. If the requirements of this paragraph 5 have been complied with, the Registry shall record the appeal in accordance with Rule 230.1 and shall as soon as practicable assign the appeal to the standing judge of the Court of Appeal [Rule 345.5 and 345.8] who may invite the other party to comment on the appeal but shall in any event decide the appeal within three weeks of receipt by the Registry of the Statement of appeal.
6. The Registry shall as soon as practicable notify the Office of the decision on the Application or on the appeal as the case may be.

Rule 98 - Costs
The parties shall bear their own costs in any action pursuant to Rule 85 or 97.

CHAPTER 2 – INTERIM PROCEDURE

Rule 101 - Role of the judge-rapporteur (Case management)
1. During the interim procedure, the judge-rapporteur shall make all necessary preparations for the oral hearing. He may in particular, where appropriate, and subject to the mandate of the panel, hold an interim conference with the parties which may be held on more than one occasion and may exercise the powers provided for in Rule 334.
2. The judge-rapporteur shall have the obligation to ensure a fair, orderly and efficient interim procedure.
3. Without prejudice to the principle of proportionality, the judge-rapporteur shall complete the interim procedure within three months of the closure of the written procedure.

Relation with Agreement: Articles 43 and 52(2)

Rule 102 - Referral to the panel
1. The judge-rapporteur may refer any matter to the panel for decision and the panel may of its own motion review any decision or order of the judge-rapporteur or the conduct of the interim procedure.
2. Any party may request that a decision or order of the judge-rapporteur be referred to the panel for a review pursuant to Rule 333. Pending review, the decision or order of the judge-rapporteur shall be effective.

Rule 103 - Preparation for the interim conference
1. Whether or not the judge-rapporteur decides to hold an interim conference, he may order the parties, within time periods to be specified, in particular to:
   (a) provide further clarification on specific points;
   (b) answer specific questions;
   (c) produce evidence;
   (d) lodge specific documents including each party's summary of the orders to be sought at the interim conference.

The judge-rapporteur shall at the same time inform the party concerned that if the party fails to comply with the order within the time period specified, a decision by default may be given in accordance with Rule 355.
2. If a party fails to comply with an order of the judge-rapporteur within the time period specified, the judge-rapporteur may give a decision by default pursuant to Rule 355.

INTERIM CONFERENCE

Rule 104 – Aim of the interim conference
The interim conference shall enable the judge-rapporteur to:
(a) identify main issues and determine which relevant facts are in dispute;
(b) where appropriate, clarify the position of the parties as regards those issues and facts;
(c) establish a schedule for the further progress of the proceedings;
(d) explore with the parties the possibilities to settle the dispute or to make use of the facilities of the Centre;
(e) where appropriate, issue orders regarding production of further pleadings, documents, experts (including court experts), experiments, inspections, further written evidence, the matters to be the subject of oral evidence and the scope of questions to be put to the witnesses;
(f) where appropriate, but only in the presence of the parties, hold preparatory discussions with witnesses and experts with a view to properly preparing for the oral hearing;
(g) make any other decision or order as he deems necessary for the preparation of the oral hearing including, after consultation with the presiding judge, an order for a separate hearing of witnesses and experts before the panel;
(h) set a date for any separate hearing pursuant to point (g) of this Rule, confirm the date for the oral hearing and order, where appropriate, after consultation with the presiding judge and the parties that the oral hearing or a separate hearing of witnesses and experts be wholly or partly by video conference in accordance with Rule 112.3;
(i) decide the value of the action in accordance with Rule 370.6.;
(j) decide the value of the proceeding for the purpose of applying the scale of ceilings for recoverable costs (Rule 152.3);
(k) order the parties to submit, in advance of the decision at the oral hearing, a preliminary estimate of the legal costs that they will seek to recover.

Relation with Agreement: Article 52(2)

Rule 105 – Holding the interim conference
1. The interim conference should, where practicable, be held by telephone conference or by video conference.
2. On request by a party, subject to paragraph 1 and the approval of the judge-rapporteur, the interim conference may be held in Court. If the interim conference is held in Court, it shall be open to the public unless the Court decides to make it, to the extent necessary, confidential in the interests of one or both parties or third parties or in the general interests of justice or public order.
3. The judge-rapporteur may hold the interim conference in any language agreed by the parties' representatives.
4. Rule 103 shall apply *mutatis mutandis*.
5. Following the interim conference, the judge-rapporteur shall issue an order setting out the decisions taken.

Rule 106 – Recording of the interim conference
The interim conference shall be audio recorded. The recording shall be made available at the premises of the Court to the parties or their representatives after the hearing.

Relation with Agreement: Articles 44 and 45

PREPARATION FOR THE ORAL HEARING

Rule 108 – Summons to the oral hearing
The judge-rapporteur shall summon the parties to the oral hearing which shall take place before the panel on the date(s) set under Rules 28 and/or 41(c) and 104(h). If no date(s) have been set the judge-rapporteur shall set a date for the oral hearing. At least two months' notice shall be given, unless the parties agree to a shorter time period.

Rule 109 – Simultaneous interpretation during oral hearings
1. At the latest one month before the oral hearing including any separate hearing of witnesses and experts a party may lodge a Request for simultaneous interpretation which shall contain:
  (a) an indication of the language to or from which the party requests simultaneous interpretation during the oral hearing;
  (b) the reasons for the Request;
  (c) the field of technology concerned;
  (d) any other information of relevance for the Request.
2. The judge-rapporteur shall decide whether and to what extent simultaneous interpretation is appropriate and shall instruct the Registry to make all necessary arrangements for simultaneous interpretation. In the event that the judge-rapporteur refuses to order simultaneous interpretation the parties may request arrangements to be made, so far as practically possible, for simultaneous interpretation at their cost.
3. The judge-rapporteur may decide of his own motion to order simultaneous interpretation and shall instruct the Registry and inform the parties accordingly.
4. A party wishing to engage an interpreter at its own expense shall inform the Registry at the latest two weeks before the oral hearing.
5. Costs for simultaneous interpretation are costs of the proceedings to be decided upon under Rule 150 except where a party engages an interpreter at its own expense under paragraph 4; these costs are borne solely by that party.

Relation with Agreement: Article 51(2)

Rule 110 – Closure of the interim procedure
1. As soon as the judge-rapporteur considers that the state of preparation of the file is adequate, he shall inform the presiding judge and the parties that the interim procedure is closed in view of the oral hearing.
2. Where final dates have been set pursuant to Rules 103 and 104 the interim procedure shall be deemed closed on the last date set.
3. The oral procedure shall start immediately after the interim procedure is closed. The presiding judge shall, in consultation with the judge-rapporteur, take over the management of the action.

CHAPTER 3 – ORAL PROCEDURE

Rule 111 – Role of the presiding judge (Case management)

The presiding judge shall:
(a) have all authority to ensure a fair, orderly and efficient oral procedure; and
(b) ensure that the action is ready for decision on the merits at the end of the oral hearing.

Rule 112 – Conduct of the oral hearing

1. The oral hearing shall be held before the panel and shall be under the control of the presiding judge.
2. The oral hearing shall consist of:
   (a) the hearing of the parties' oral submissions;
   (b) the hearing of witnesses and experts under the control of the presiding judge.
3. The Court may decide to:
   (a) allow a party, representative or accompanying person, to attend the oral hearing by videoconference,
   (b) hear a party, witnesses or expert through electronic means, such as video conference or
   (c) hold the oral hearing by videoconference if all parties agree or the Court considers it appropriate to do so due to exceptional circumstances.

In all cases, the oral hearing shall be transmitted simultaneously in picture and sound to the court room.
4. The presiding judge and the judges of the panel may provide a preliminary introduction to the action and put questions to the parties, to the parties' representatives and to any witness or expert.
5. Under the control of the presiding judge, the parties may put questions to the witness or expert. The presiding judge may prohibit any question which is not designed to adduce admissible evidence.
6. With the consent of the Court a witness may give evidence in a language other than the language of proceedings.

Relation with Agreement: Articles 52(3) and 53(1)

Rule 113 – Duration of the oral hearing

1. Without prejudice to the application of the principle of proportionality, the presiding judge shall endeavour to complete the oral hearing within one day. The presiding judge may set time limits for parties' oral submissions in advance of the oral hearing.
2. Oral testimony at the oral hearing or at any separate hearing shall be limited to issues identified by the judge-rapporteur or the presiding judge as having to be decided on the basis of oral evidence.
3. The presiding judge may, after consulting the panel, limit a party's oral submissions if the panel is sufficiently informed.

Rule 114 – Adjournment where the Court considers that further evidence is required

In exceptional cases, the Court may, after hearing the parties' oral submissions, decide to adjourn proceedings and call for further evidence.

Rule 115 – The oral hearing

The oral hearing and any separate hearing of witnesses shall be open to the public unless the Court decides to make a hearing, to the extent necessary, confidential in the interests of one or both parties or third parties or in the general interests of justice or public order. The hearing shall be audio recorded. The recording shall be made available to the parties or their representatives at the premises of the Court after the hearing. Rule 103 shall apply *mutatis mutandis*.

Relation with Agreement: Article 45

Rule 116 – Absence of a party from the oral hearing
1. A party which does not wish to be represented at the oral hearing shall inform the Registry in good time. Where both parties have informed the Registry that they do not wish to be represented at the oral hearing, the Court may decide the action in accordance with Rule 117.
2. The Court shall not be obliged to delay any step in the procedure, including the decision on the merits, by reason only of the absence of a party from the oral hearing.
3. A party that is not represented at the oral hearing shall be treated as relying only on its written case.
4. If due to an exceptional occurrence a party is prevented from being represented at the oral hearing, the Court shall on a reasoned request of that party, adjourn the oral hearing.
5. The provisions of this Rule are without prejudice to the power of the Court to give a decision by default pursuant to Rule 355.

Rule 117 – Absence of both parties from the oral hearing
Where both parties have informed the Registry that they do not wish to be represented at the oral hearing the Court shall take a decision on the merits on the basis of the pleadings and evidence submitted by the parties and the court expert, if applicable, and otherwise in accordance with Rules 118 and 350 to 354.

Rule 118 – Decision on the merits
1. In addition to the orders and measures and without prejudice to the discretion of the Court referred to in Articles 63, 64, 67 and 80 of the Agreement the Court may, if requested, order the payment of damages or compensation according to Articles 68 and 32(1)(f) of the Agreement. The amount of the damages or the compensation may be stated in the order or determined in separate proceedings [Rules 125-144].
2. If, while there are infringement proceedings before a local or regional division, a revocation action is pending between the same parties before the central division or an opposition is pending before the European Patent Office, the local or regional division:
   (a) may render its decision on the merits of the infringement claim, including its orders, under the condition subsequent pursuant to Article 56(1) of the Agreement that the patent is not held to be wholly or partially invalid by the final decision in the revocation proceedings or a final decision of the European Patent Office or under any other term or condition; or
   (b) may stay the infringement proceedings pending a decision in the revocation procedure or a decision of the European Patent Office and shall stay the infringement proceedings if it is of the view that there is a high likelihood that the relevant claims of the patent will be held to be invalid on any ground by the final decision in the revocation proceedings or of the European Patent Office where such decision of the European Patent Office may be expected to be given rapidly.
3. Where, in the decision on the merits of a revocation action, the patent is found to be entirely or partially invalid, the Court shall revoke the patent entirely or partially according to Article 65 of the Agreement.
4. Where the Court has made orders in accordance with paragraph 2(a) any party may apply to the local or regional division within two months following a final decision of the central division or the Court of Appeal or the European Patent Office as the case may be on the validity of the patent for orders consequential on such final decision [Rule 354.2].
5. The Court shall decide in principle on the obligation to bear legal costs in accordance with Article 69 of the Agreement. The Court may order in advance of the decision that the parties submit a preliminary estimate of the legal costs that they will seek to recover.

6. The Court shall give the decision on the merits as soon as possible after the closure of the oral hearing. The Court shall endeavour to issue the decision on the merits in writing within six weeks of the oral hearing. The Court shall give reasons for its decision.
7. The Court may give its decision immediately after the closure of the oral hearing and provide its reasons on a subsequent date.
8. The orders of the Court referred to in paragraphs 1 and 2(a) shall be enforceable on the defendant only after the claimant has notified the Court which part of the orders he intends to enforce, a certified translation of the orders in accordance with Rule 7.2, where applicable, into the official language of a Contracting Member State in which the enforcement shall take place has been provided by the claimant and the said notice and, where applicable, a certified translation of the orders have been served on the defendant by the Registry. The Court may subject any order or measure to a security to be given by the successful party to the unsuccessful party as determined by the Court in accordance with Rule 352.

Relation with Agreement: Article 77

Rule 119 – Interim award of damages
The Court may order an interim award of damages to the successful party in the decision on the merits, subject to any conditions that the Court may order. Such award shall at least cover the expected costs of the procedure for the award of damages and compensation on the part of the successful party.

CHAPTER 4 – PROCEDURE FOR THE DETERMINATION OF DAMAGES AND COMPENSATION

Rule 125 – Separate proceedings for determining the amount of damages ordered
The determination of the amount of damages ordered for the successful party may be the subject of separate proceedings. The determination shall include the determination of the amount of compensation, if any, to be awarded as a result of the provisional protection conferred by a published European patent application [Article 32(1)(f) of the Agreement, Article 67 EPC] and compensation to be paid pursuant to Rules 118.1, 198.2, 213.2 and 354.2. The expression 'damages' used in Chapter 4 shall be deemed to include such compensation and interest at the rate and for the period that the Court shall decide.

Rule 126 – Start of proceedings for the determination of damages
Where the successful party wishes to have the amount of damages determined, it shall no later than one year from service of the final decision on the merits (including any final decision on appeal) on both infringement and validity (or in the case of an award under Rules 118.1, 198.2, 213.2 or 354.2 from the date of the order for such award) lodge an Application for the determination of damages, which may include a request for an order to lay open books.

Relation with Agreement: Article 68

SECTION 1 – APPLICATION FOR THE DETERMINATION OF DAMAGES

Rule 131 – Contents of the Application for the determination of damages
1. The Application for the determination of damages shall contain:
   (a) particulars in accordance with Rule 13.1(a) to (d);
   (b) the date of the decision on the merits and the action number of the file;
   (c) if required a request for an order to lay open books (Rules 141 to 144) in which case the applicant shall provide the matters set out in Rule 141(b) to (e).

2. After any procedure for the laying open of books is complete, or, if that has not been requested in the Application referred to in paragraph 1 the applicant shall indicate:

(a) the redress (damages, licence fees, profits) and the interest thereon requested by him;
(b) an indication of the facts relied on, in particular calculations concerning lost profits or profits made by the unsuccessful party;
(c) the evidence relied on;
(d) a statement as to whether the decision on the merits is the subject of an appeal;
(e) his assessment of the amount of damages due to him.

Rule 132 – Fee for the Application for the determination of damages
The applicant shall pay the fixed fee and, where applicable, the value based fee for the determination of damages in accordance with Part 6. Rule 15.2 shall apply *mutatis mutandis.*

Rule 133 – Determination of the value-based fee for the determination of damages
Where the value of the action exceeds EUR500.000 the applicant shall pay a value based fee for the determination of damages in accordance with Part 6.

Rule 134 – Examination as to formal requirements of the Application for the determination of damages
1. The Registry shall, as soon as practicable after the lodging of the Application for the determination of damages, examine whether the requirements of Rules 126, 131.1 and .2(d) and (e) and 132 have been complied with.
2. If the Application for the determination of damages does not comply with the requirements referred to in paragraph 1, the Registry shall invite the applicant to correct the deficiencies noted within a time period to be specified.
3. Rule 16.4 to .5 shall apply *mutatis mutandis.*

Rule 135 – Recording in the register (Application for the determination of damages) and service
1. If the requirements referred to in Rule 131.1 and .2(d) and (e) have been complied with, the Registry shall as soon as practicable:

(a) record the date of receipt of the Application for the determination of damages;
(b) record the Application in the register;
(c) inform the applicant of the date of receipt;
(d) inform the panel which has given the decision on the merits on infringement that an Application for the determination of damages has been lodged;
(e) serve the Application upon the unsuccessful party.

2. The panel which has given the decision on the merits on infringement shall be the panel for the determination of damages unless for any reason this is not possible or practical in which case the presiding judge of the division concerned shall appoint a fresh panel. Rules 17.2 and 18 shall apply *mutatis mutandis.*

Rule 136 – Stay of the Application for a determination of damages
The Court may stay the Application for a determination of damages pending any appeal on the merits pursuant to Rule 295(h) on a reasoned request by the unsuccessful party. The applicant shall be given the opportunity to be heard. If the Court continues the proceedings on the Application, it may order the applicant to render a security according to Rule 352.

Rule 137 – Reply of the unsuccessful party

1. If the unsuccessful party accepts the claim made in the Application for the determination of damages, it shall within two months inform the Registry. The judge-rapporteur shall make the order for the determination of damages in accordance with the Application for the determination of damages.
2. If the unsuccessful party contests the claim made in the Application for the determination of damages, it shall within two months of service of the Application for the determination of damages or, where there was a procedure for the laying open of books, within two months of service of the indication pursuant to Rule 131.2, lodge a Defence to the Application for the determination of damages.

Rule 138 – Contents of the Defence to the Application for the determination of damages

The Defence to the Application for the determination of damages shall contain:

(a) the names of the unsuccessful party and of that party's representative;
(b) postal and electronic addresses for service on the unsuccessful party and the names and addresses of the persons authorised to accept service;
(c) the action number attributed to the file;
(d) the reasons why the Application for the award of damages is contested;
(e) an indication of the facts relied on; and
(f) the evidence relied on.

Rule 139 – Reply to the Defence to the Application for the determination of damages and Rejoinder to the Reply

The applicant may within one month lodge a Reply to the Defence to the Application for the determination of damages, limited to the matters raised in the Defence. The unsuccessful party may lodge a Rejoinder to the Reply within one month of service of the Reply, limited to the matters raised in the Reply.

Rule 140 – Further procedure (Application for the determination of damages)

1. The judge-rapporteur may order further exchange of written pleadings, within time periods to be specified.
2. The provisions of Part 1, Chapters 2 (Interim procedure) and 3 (Oral procedure) shall apply *mutatis mutandis* but with such reduced timetable as the judge-rapporteur may order. He shall decide on the obligation to bear the legal costs of the proceedings for the determination of damages in accordance with Article 69 of the Agreement.

SECTION 2 – REQUEST TO LAY OPEN BOOKS

Rule 141 – Contents of the Request to lay open books

If the applicant has made a request pursuant to Rule 131.1(c), Rules 134 to 136 shall apply *mutatis mutandis*. The Request shall contain:

(a) particulars in accordance with Rule 131.1(a) and (b);
(b) details of any information ordered by the Court and given by the other party pursuant to Rule 191;
(c) a description of the information held by the unsuccessful party to which the applicant requests access, in particular documents relating to turnover and profits generated by the infringing products or regarding the extent of use of the infringing process as well as accounts and bank documents, and any related document concerning the infringement;
(d) the reasons why the applicant needs access to this information;
(e) the facts relied on; and
(f) the evidence offered in support.

Rule 142 - Defence of the unsuccessful party, Reply to the Defence and Rejoinder to the Reply
1. If the unsuccessful party accepts the Request to lay open books, it shall within two months of service of the Request to lay open books inform the Registry. The judge-rapporteur shall make the order to lay open books in accordance with the Request to lay open books.
2. If the unsuccessful party contests the Request to lay open books, it shall within two months of service of the Request to lay open books lodge a Defence to the Request to lay open books.
3. The applicant may within 14 days of service of the Defence to the Request lodge a Reply to the Defence to the Request to lay open books, limited to the matters raised in the Defence. The unsuccessful party may within 14 days of service of the Reply lodge a Rejoinder, limited to the matters raised in the Reply.

Rule 143 - Further procedure
Rule 140 shall apply *mutatis mutandis.*

Rule 144 - Decision on the Request to lay open books
1. The Court may:
(a) order the unsuccessful party to open its books to the applicant within a time period to be specified and subject to such terms as the Court may deem appropriate having regard *inter alia* to Article 58 of the Agreement and Rule 190.1 and .4;
(b) inform the applicant and specify a time period within which the procedure for the award of damages shall be continued.
2. Where the Request to lay open books is not allowable, the Court shall inform the applicant and specify a time period within which the procedure for the award of damages shall be continued [Rule 131.2].

CHAPTER 5 – PROCEDURE FOR COST DECISION

Rule 150 - Separate proceedings for cost decision
1. A cost decision may be the subject of separate proceedings following a decision on the merits and, if applicable, a decision for the determination of damages. The cost decision shall cover costs incurred in the proceedings by the Court such as costs for simultaneous interpretation and costs incurred pursuant to Rules 173, 180.1, 185.7, 188 and 201 and, subject to the Rules 152 to 156, the costs of the successful party including Court fees paid by that party [Rule 151(d)]. Costs for interpretation and translation which is necessary for the judges of the Court in order to conduct the case in the language of proceedings are borne solely by the Court.
2. The Court may order an interim award of costs to the successful party in the decision on the merits [Rule 119] or in a decision for the determination of damages, subject to any conditions that the Court may decide.

Rule 151 - Start of proceedings for cost decision
Where the successful party (hereinafter 'the applicant') wishes to seek a cost decision, it shall within one month of service of the decision lodge an Application for a cost decision which shall contain:
(a) particulars in accordance with Rule 13.1(a) to (d);
(b) the date of the decision and the action number of the file;
(c) a statement as to whether the decision on the merits is the subject of an appeal, if known at the date of the Application;
(d) an indication of the costs for which compensation is requested, which may include recovery of court fees and costs of representation, of witnesses, of experts, and other expenses; and
(e) the preliminary estimate of the legal costs that the party submitted pursuant to Rule 118.5.

Rule 152 - Compensation for representation costs
1. The applicant shall be entitled to recover reasonable and proportionate costs for representation.
2. The Administrative Committee shall adopt a scale of ceilings for recoverable costs by reference to the value of the proceedings. The scale may be adjusted from time to time.
3. Where a claim, counterclaim, application, request or appeal subject to only a fixed fee is made, the party concerned shall, in the first submission, assess its respective value for the purpose of calculating the applicable ceiling. The other party shall be heard. Rule 370.6 shall apply *mutatis mutandis.*

Rule 153 - Compensation for costs of experts
The compensation for costs of experts of the parties [Rule 181] exceeding the expenses referred to in Rule 180.1 shall be based on the rates that are customary in the respective sector, with due regard to the required expertise, the complexity of the issue and the time spent by the expert for the services rendered.

Rule 154 - Compensation for costs of witnesses
Where the Court has ordered the deposit of a sum sufficient to cover the expenses of a witness in accordance with Rule 180.2 or of a party's expert in accordance with Rule 181, compensation may be requested for payments made by the Registry towards the expenses incurred by a witness or an expert.

Rule 155 - Compensation for costs of interpreters and translators
1. The compensation for costs of interpreters shall be the rates that are customary in the country of the division in question, depending on the interpreter's training and professional experience.
2. The compensation for costs of translators shall be the rates that are customary in the country of the division in question, depending on the translator's training and professional experience.

Rule 156 - Further procedure
1. The judge-rapporteur may request the applicant to provide written evidence of all costs requested in Rule 151(d). The judge-rapporteur shall allow the unsuccessful party an opportunity to comment in writing on the costs requested including any item of costs that should be apportioned or borne by each party in accordance with Article 69(1) to (3) of the Agreement.
2. The judge-rapporteur shall decide in writing on the costs to be awarded or apportioned in accordance with Article 69(1) to (3) of the Agreement.
3. The costs shall be paid within the period ordered by the judge-rapporteur.

Rule 157 - Appeal against the cost decision
The decision of the judge-rapporteur as to costs only may be appealed to the Court of Appeal in accordance with Rule 221.

Relation with Agreement: Article 69

CHAPTER 6 – SECURITY FOR COSTS

Rule 158 - Security for costs of a party
1. At any time during proceedings, following a reasoned request by one party, the Court may order the other party to provide, within a specified time period, adequate security for the legal costs and other expenses incurred and/or to be incurred by the requesting party, which the other party may be liable to bear. Where the Court decides to order such security, it shall decide whether it is appropriate to order the security by deposit or bank guarantee.

2. The Court shall give the parties an opportunity to be heard before making an order for security. Rule 354 shall apply to the enforcement of the order.
3. The order for security shall indicate that an appeal may be lodged in accordance with Article 73 of the Agreement and Rule 220.2.
4. The Court shall, when specifying the time period in paragraph 1, inform the party concerned that if the party fails to provide adequate security within the time stated, a decision by default may be given, in accordance with Rule 355.
5. If a party fails to provide adequate security within the time stated, the Court may give a decision by default pursuant to Rule 355.

Relation with the Agreement: Article 69(4)

Rule 159 – Security for costs of the Court
Except where deposits are rendered pursuant to Rule 180.2, the Court may order that either or both parties provide adequate security (either by deposit or bank guarantee) to cover costs incurred and/or to be incurred in the proceedings by the Court, pending a cost decision pursuant to Rule 150.1. Rule 158.2 and .3 shall apply.

PART 2 – EVIDENCE

Rule 170 – Means of evidence and means of obtaining evidence
1. In proceedings before the Court, the means of evidence shall include in particular the following:
- (a) written evidence, whether printed, hand-written or drawn, in particular documents, written witness statements, plans, drawings, photographs;
- (b) expert reports and reports on experiments carried out for the purpose of the proceedings;
- (c) physical objects, in particular devices, products, embodiments, exhibits, models;
- (d) electronic files and audio/video recordings.

2. Means of obtaining evidence shall include in particular the following:
- (a) hearing of the parties;
- (b) requests for information;
- (c) production of documents;
- (d) summoning, hearing and questioning of witnesses;
- (e) appointing, receiving opinions from, summoning and hearing and questioning of experts;
- (f) ordering inspection of a place or a physical object;
- (g) conducting comparative tests and experiments;
- (h) sworn statements in writing (written witness statements).

3. Means of obtaining evidence shall further include [Article 59 and 60 of the Agreement]:
- (a) ordering a party or a third party to produce evidence;
- (b) ordering measures to preserve evidence.

Rule 171 – Offering of evidence
1. A party making a statement of fact that is contested or likely to be contested by the other party shall indicate the means of evidence to prove it. In case of failure to indicate the means of evidence regarding a contested fact, the Court shall take such failure into account when deciding the issue in question.
2. A statement of fact that is not specifically contested by any party shall be held to be true as between the parties.

Rule 172 – Duty to produce evidence

1. Evidence available to a party regarding a statement of fact that is contested or likely to be contested by the other party must be produced by the party making that statement of fact.
2. The Court may at any time during the proceedings order a party making a statement of fact to produce evidence that lies in the control of that party. If the party fails to produce the evidence, the Court shall take such failure into account when deciding on the issue in question.

Relation with Agreement: Article 53

Rule 173 – Judicial Cooperation in the taking of evidence

For the judicial cooperation in the taking of evidence, the Court shall apply any method provided by:
1. The Regulation (EU) No 2020/1783, where it applies;
2. The Hague Convention of 18 March 1970 on the Taking of Evidence Abroad in Civil or Commercial Matters, where it applies, or any other applicable convention or agreement; or
3. to the extent that there is no such convention or agreement in force, national law on the procedures to be followed for the judicial cooperation in the taking of evidence.

CHAPTER 1 – WITNESSES AND EXPERTS OF THE PARTIES

Rule 175 – Written witness statement

1. A party seeking to offer witness evidence shall lodge a written witness statement or a written summary of the evidence to be given.
2. A written witness statement shall be signed by the witness and shall include a statement of the witness that he is aware of his obligation to tell the truth and of his liability under applicable national law in the event of any breach of this obligation. The statement shall set out the language in which the witness shall give oral evidence, if necessary.
3. The written witness statement or written summary of the evidence to be given shall set out:
   (a) any current or past relationship between the witness and the party offering the evidence; and
   (b) any actual or potential conflict of interest that may affect the impartiality of the witness.

Rule 176 – Application for the hearing of a witness in person

Subject to the orders of the Court referred to in Rules 104(e) and 112.2(b) a party seeking to offer oral witness evidence shall make an Application for the hearing of a witness in person which shall set out:
(a) the reasons why the witness should be heard in person;
(b) the facts which the party expects the witness to confirm; and
(c) the language in which the witness shall give evidence.

Rule 177 – Summoning of witnesses to the oral hearing

1. The Court may order that a witness be heard in person:
   (a) of its own motion;
   (b) where a written witness statement is challenged by the other party; or
   (c) on an Application for the hearing of a witness in person [Rule 176].
2. An order of the Court summoning a witness to the oral hearing shall in particular indicate:
   (a) the name, address and description of the witness;
   (b) the date and place of the oral hearing;
   (c) an indication of the facts of the action about which the witness is to be examined;
   (d) information about the reimbursement of expenses incurred by the witness;
   (e) a statement that the witness will be questioned by the Court and the parties; and

(f) the language of the proceedings and the possibility of arranging simultaneous interpretation between that language and the language of the witness, if necessary [Rule 109].

3. In its order summoning the witness, the Court shall also inform the witness of his duties and rights as a witness under Rules 178 and 179, including the sanctions which may be imposed on a defaulting witness.

Rule 178 – Hearing of witnesses

1. After the identity of the witness has been established and before hearing his evidence, the presiding judge shall ask the witness to make the following declaration:

'I solemnly, sincerely and truly declare and affirm that the evidence I shall give shall be the truth, the whole truth and nothing but the truth.'

2. The witness shall give his evidence to the Court.

3. The hearing of a witness who has signed a written witness statement shall begin with the confirmation of the evidence given therein. The witness may elaborate on the evidence contained in his written witness statement.

4. The presiding judge and the judges of the panel may put questions to the witness.

5. Under the control of the presiding judge, the parties may put questions to the witness. The presiding judge may prohibit any question which is not designed to adduce admissible evidence.

6. With the consent of the Court a witness may give evidence in a language other than the language of proceedings.

Rule 179 – Duties of witnesses

1. Witnesses who have been duly summoned shall obey the summons and attend the oral hearing.

2. Without prejudice to paragraph 3, if a witness who has been duly summoned fails to appear before the Court or refuses to give evidence or to make the declaration referred to in Rule 178.1, the Court may impose upon him a pecuniary sanction not exceeding EUR50.000 and may order that a further summons be served at the witness's own expense.

3. Nobody shall be obliged to sign a written witness statement or to give evidence at an oral hearing if he is a spouse, partner equal to a spouse under applicable national law, descendant, sibling or parent of a party. A witness may also refuse to answer questions if answering them would violate a professional privilege or other duty of confidentiality imposed by the national law applicable to the witness or expose him or his spouse, partner equal to a spouse under applicable national law, descendant, sibling or parent to criminal prosecution under applicable national law.

4. The Court may decide to report to the competent authorities of the Contracting Member States whose courts have criminal jurisdiction in case of the giving of false evidence on the part of a witness.

Rule 180 – Reimbursement of expenses of witnesses

1. A witness shall be entitled to reimbursement of:

(a) expenses for travelling and stay; and

(b) loss of income caused by his hearing in person.

After the witness has carried out his duties and upon his request, the Registry shall make a payment to the witness towards the expenses incurred.

2. The Court shall make the summoning of a witness conditional upon the deposit by the party relying on the witness of a sum sufficient to cover the expenses referred to in paragraph 1.

Rule 181 – Experts of the parties

1. Subject to the orders of the Court referred to in Rules 104(e) and 112.2(b) a party may provide any expert evidence that it considers necessary. Rules 175 to 180 shall apply *mutatis mutandis* to experts of the parties.

2. An order of the Court under Rule 177 summoning the expert shall additionally set out that:
   - (a) an expert has a duty to assist the Court impartially on matters relevant to his area of expertise which overrides any duty to the party retaining him; and
   - (b) an expert is to be independent and objective, and shall not act as an advocate for any party to the proceedings.

CHAPTER 2 – COURT EXPERTS

Rule 185 – Appointment of a court expert

1. Where the Court must resolve a specific technical or other question in relation to the action, it may of its own motion, and after hearing the parties, appoint a court expert.
2. The parties may make suggestions regarding the identity of the court expert, his technical or other relevant background and the questions to be put to him.
3. The court expert shall be responsible to the Court and shall possess the expertise, independence and impartiality required for being appointed as court expert. The parties shall be entitled to be heard on the expertise, independence and impartiality of the court expert.
4. The Court shall appoint a court expert by way of order which shall in particular specify:
   - (a) the name and address of the expert appointed;
   - (b) a short description of the facts of the action;
   - (c) the evidence submitted by the parties in respect of the technical or other question;
   - (d) the questions put to the expert, with the appropriate level of detail, including where appropriate suggestions relating to any experiments to be carried out;
   - (e) when and under what conditions the expert may receive other relevant information;
   - (f) the time period for the presentation of the expert report;
   - (g) information about the reimbursement of expenses incurred by the expert;
   - (h) information about the sanctions which may be imposed on a defaulting expert; and
   - (i) his duties under Rule 186.
5. The expert shall receive a copy of the order, together with the documents and other evidence that the Court considers to be necessary for carrying out his task.
6. The expert shall be required upon receipt of the order to confirm in writing that he will present the expert report within the time period specified by the Court.
7. The Court shall agree with the expert on a fee covering his written expert report and his participation in the oral hearing. The Court may reduce this fee by an equitable amount if the expert does not deliver his report within the time period specified by the Court or if the report did not have the quality to be expected of the expert.
8. If an appointed court expert does not present his report within the time period specified or, if extended at the expert's request, the extended period, the Court may appoint another expert in his place. The Court may hold the expert liable for all or part of the costs of appointing and reimbursing another expert.
9. The Registry shall maintain an indicative list of technical experts.

Rule 186 – Duties of a court expert

1. The court expert shall present an expert report in writing within the time period specified by the Court [Rule 185.4(f)].
2. The court expert shall be under the supervision of the Court and shall inform the Court of his progress in carrying out his task.
3. The court expert shall give expert advice only on questions which have been put to him.

4. The court expert shall not communicate with one party without the other party being present or without the consent of the other party. He shall document all communications with the parties in his report.
5. The court expert shall not communicate the contents of his report to third parties.
6. The court expert shall attend the oral hearing if requested to do so by the Court and shall answer questions from the Court and the parties.
7. The court expert has an overriding duty to assist the Court impartially on matters relevant to his area of expertise. He is to be independent and objective, and shall not act as an advocate for any party to the proceedings.

Rule 187 – Expert report
Once the report of the court expert has been presented to the Court, the Court shall invite the parties to comment on it either in writing or during the oral hearing.
Rule 188 – Hearing of a court expert
Rules 178 to 180 shall apply *mutatis mutandis* to a court expert.

Relation with Agreement: Article 57

CHAPTER 3 – ORDER TO PRODUCE EVIDENCE AND TO COMMUNICATE INFORMATION

ORDER TO PRODUCE EVIDENCE

Rule 190 – Order to produce evidence
1. Where a party has presented reasonably available and plausible evidence in support of its claims and has, in substantiating those claims, specified evidence which lies in the control of the other party or a third party, the Court may on a reasoned request by the party specifying such evidence, order that other party or third party to produce such evidence. For the protection of confidential information the Court may order that the evidence be disclosed to certain named persons only and be subject to appropriate terms of non-disclosure.
2. During the written and interim procedures, a party may request such an order to produce evidence.
3. The judge-rapporteur may make such order in the written procedure or in the interim procedure having given the other/third party an opportunity to be heard.
4. An order to produce evidence shall in particular specify:
   (a) under which conditions, in what form and within what time period the evidence shall be produced;
   (b) any sanction which may be imposed if the evidence is not produced according to the order.
5. Where the Court orders a third party to produce evidence, the interests of that third party shall be duly taken into account.
6. An order to produce evidence shall be subject to the provisions of Rules 179.3, 287 and 288. The order shall indicate that an appeal may be brought in accordance with Article 73 of the Agreement and Rule 220.1.
7. If a party fails to comply with an order to produce evidence, the Court shall take such failure into account when deciding on the issue in question.

Relation with Agreement: Article 59

ORDER TO COMMUNICATE INFORMATION

Rule 191 – Application for order to communicate information
The Court may in response to a reasoned request by a party order the other party or any third party to communicate such information in the control of that other party or third party as is specified in Article 67 of the Agreement or such other information as is reasonably necessary for the purpose of advancing that party's case. Rule 190.1 second sentence, .5 and .6 shall apply *mutatis mutandis*.

Relation with the Agreement: Article 67

CHAPTER 4 – ORDER TO PRESERVE EVIDENCE (*SAISIE*) AND ORDER FOR INSPECTION

ORDER TO PRESERVE EVIDENCE (*SAISIE*)

Rule 192 – Application for preserving evidence
1. An Application for preserving evidence may be lodged by a party (within the meaning of Article 47 of the Agreement) (hereinafter 'the applicant') at the division where the applicant has commenced infringement proceedings on the merits. If the application is lodged before proceedings on the merits have been started it shall be lodged at the division where the applicant intends to start proceedings on the merits.
2. The Application for preserving evidence shall contain:
   (a) particulars in accordance with Rule 13.1(a) to (i);
   (b) a clear indication of the measures requested [Rule 196.1], including the exact location of the evidence to be preserved where it is known or suspected with good reason;
   (c) the reasons why the proposed measures are needed to preserve relevant evidence; and
   (d) the facts and evidence relied on in support of the Application.

Where main proceedings on the merits of the case have not yet been started before the Court, the Application shall in addition contain a concise description of the action which will be started before the Court, including an indication of the facts and evidence which may be relied on in support.
3. Where the applicant requests that measures to preserve evidence be ordered without hearing the other party (hereinafter 'the defendant'), the Application for preserving evidence shall in addition set out the reasons for not hearing the defendant having regard in particular to Rule 197. The applicant shall be under a duty to disclose any material fact known to it which might influence the Court in deciding whether to make an order without hearing the defendant. The application shall not be entered on the register until notice has been given to the defendant pursuant to Rule 197.2.
4. Where the Application for preserving evidence is lodged after main proceedings on the merits of the case have been started before the Court, the Application shall be drawn up in the language of the proceedings. Where the Application is lodged before main proceedings on the merits of the case have been started before the Court, Rule 14 shall apply *mutatis mutandis*.
5. The applicant shall pay the fee for the Application for preserving evidence, in accordance with Part 6. Rule 15.2 shall apply *mutatis mutandis*.

Relation with Agreement: Article 60

Rule 193 – Examination as to formal requirements, recording in the register, assignment to panel, designation of judge-rapporteur, single judge
1. Where main proceedings on the merits of the case have not yet been started before the Court, the Application for preserving evidence shall be dealt with in accordance with Rule 16 (formalities exam-

ination by Registry), Rule 17.1(a) to (c) and .2 (date of receipt, recording in the register, action number, assignment to panel) and Rule 18 (designation only of judge-rapporteur by presiding judge).
2. Where main proceedings on the merits of the case have already been started before the Court, an Application for preserving evidence shall immediately be examined by the Registry in accordance with Rule 16 and forwarded to the panel to which the action has been assigned or to the judge to whom the action has been assigned [Rules 17.2, 194.3 and .4].
3. The judge deciding on an Application for preserving evidence shall have all necessary powers of the Court.

Rule 194 - Examination of the Application for preserving evidence
1. The Court shall have the discretion - including where the Application is made pursuant to Rule 192.3 - to:
  (a) inform the defendant about the Application and invite him to lodge, within a time period to be specified, an Objection to the Application for preserving evidence which shall contain:
    (i) the reasons why the Application shall fail;
    (ii) the facts and evidence relied on, in particular any challenge to the facts and evidence relied on by the applicant;
    (iii) where main proceedings on the merits of the case have not yet been started before the Court, the reasons why the action which will be started before the Court shall fail and an indication of the facts and evidence relied on in support;
  (b) summon the parties to an oral hearing;
  (c) summon the applicant to an oral hearing without the presence of the defendant;
  (d) decide the Application without having heard the defendant.
2. In exercising its discretion, the Court shall take into account:
  (a) the urgency of the action;
  (b) whether the reasons for not hearing the defendant [Rules 192.3 and 197] appear well-founded;
  (c) the probability that evidence may be destroyed or otherwise cease to be available [Rule 197].
3. The presiding judge may decide that he or the judge-rapporteur or other single judge or the standing judge may decide on the Application.
4. In cases of extreme urgency the standing judge appointed in accordance with Rule 345.5 may decide immediately on an Application to preserve evidence and the procedure to be followed on the Application.
5. If the Court decides to inform the defendant about the Application the Court will first give the applicant the possibility to withdraw the Application. In the event of such withdrawal the applicant may request that the Court shall order that the Application and its contents shall remain confidential.
6. If the patent the subject of the Application is also the subject of a Protective letter pursuant to Rule 207 the applicant may withdraw the Application pursuant to paragraph 5.

Rule 195 - Oral hearing
1. Where the Court decides to summon the parties to an oral hearing, the date for the oral hearing shall be set as soon as possible after the date of receipt of the Application for preserving evidence.
2. Rules 111 to 116 shall apply *mutatis mutandis*. Where the applicant is absent from the oral hearing without a reasonable excuse, the Court shall reject the Application for preserving evidence.
3. The decision of the Court on the Application for preserving evidence shall be given in writing as soon as possible after the closure of the oral hearing. If the Court deems appropriate, the decision may be given orally to the parties at the end of the oral hearing but shall as soon as practicable thereafter be given in writing.

Relation with Agreement: Article 60

Rule 196 – Order on the Application for preserving evidence

1. The Court may order, in particular, the following:
   (a) preserving evidence by detailed description, with or without the taking of samples;
   (b) physical seizure of allegedly infringing goods;
   (c) physical seizure of the materials and implements used in the production and/or distribution of these goods and any related document;
   (d) the preservation and disclosure of digital media and data and the disclosure of any passwords necessary to access them.

For the protection of confidential information the Court may order that any of the above be disclosed only to certain named persons and subject to appropriate terms of non-disclosure.

2. An order to preserve evidence shall specify that, unless otherwise ordered by the Court, the outcome of the measures to preserve evidence may only be used in the proceedings on the merits of the case.

3. The order to preserve evidence shall be enforceable immediately, unless the Court decides otherwise. The Court may set conditions to the enforceability of the order, specifying in particular:
   (a) who may represent the applicant when the measures to preserve evidence are being carried out and under what conditions;
   (b) any security which shall be provided by the applicant.

If necessary, the Court may set penalties applicable to the applicant if these conditions are not observed.

4. The order to preserve evidence shall specify a person who shall carry out the measures referred to in paragraph 1 and present a written Report on the measures to preserve evidence, all in accordance with the national law of the place where the measures are executed, to the Court within a time period to be specified.

5. The person referred to in paragraph 4 shall be a professional person or expert, who guarantees expertise, independence and impartiality. Where appropriate and allowed under applicable national law, the person may be a bailiff or assisted by a bailiff. In no circumstances may an employee or director of the applicant be present at the execution of the measures.

6. The Court may order the applicant to provide adequate security for the legal costs and other expenses and compensation for any injury incurred or likely to be incurred by the defendant which the applicant may be liable to bear. The Court shall do so where the order to preserve evidence was made without the defendant having been heard, unless there are special circumstances not to do so. The Court shall decide whether it is appropriate to order the security by deposit or bank guarantee.

7. The order to preserve evidence shall indicate that an appeal may be lodged in accordance with Article 73 of the Agreement and Rule 220.1.

Relation with Agreement: Article 60(1)-(4)

Rule 197 – Order to preserve evidence without hearing the defendant

1. The Court may order measures to preserve evidence [Rule 196.1] without the defendant having been heard, in particular where any delay is likely to cause irreparable harm to the applicant or where there is a demonstrable risk of evidence being destroyed or otherwise ceasing to be available.

2. Where measures to preserve evidence are ordered without the defendant having been heard, Rule 195 shall apply *mutatis mutandis* to the oral hearing without the presence of the defendant. In such cases, the defendant shall be given notice, immediately at the time of the execution of the measures.

3. Within 30 days after the execution of the measures, the defendant may request a review of the order to preserve evidence. The Request for review shall set out:
   (a) the reasons why the order to preserve evidence shall be revoked or modified; and
   (b) the facts and evidence relied on.

4. The Court shall order an oral hearing to review the order without delay. Rule 195 shall apply. The Court may modify, revoke or confirm the order. In case the order is modified or revoked the Court

shall oblige the persons to whom confidential information has been disclosed to keep this information confidential [Rule 196.1].

Relation with Agreement: Article 60(6)

Rule 198 – Revocation of an order to preserve evidence
1. The Court shall ensure that an order to preserve evidence is revoked or otherwise cease to have effect, upon request of the defendant, without prejudice to the damages which may be claimed, if, within a time period not exceeding 31 calendar days or 20 working days, whichever is the longer, from the date specified in the Court's order with due account to the date where the Report referred to in Rule 196.4 shall be presented, the applicant does not start proceedings on the merits of the case before the Court.
2. Where the measures to preserve evidence are revoked, or where they lapse due to any act or omission by the applicant, or where it is subsequently found that there has been no infringement or threat of infringement of the patent, the Court may order the applicant, upon request of the defendant, to provide the defendant appropriate compensation for any injury caused by those measures [Rule 354.2].

Relation with Agreement: Article 60(8) and (9)

ORDER FOR INSPECTION

Rule 199 – Order for inspection
1. The Court may, on a reasoned request by a party, order an inspection of products, devices, methods, premises or local situations in situ. For the protection of confidential information the Court may order that any of the above be disclosed only to certain named persons and subject to appropriate terms of non-disclosure in accordance with Article 58 of the Agreement.
2. Rules 192 to 198 shall apply *mutatis mutandis.*

Relation with Agreement: Article 60

CHAPTER 5 – OTHER EVIDENCE

Rule 200 – Order to freeze assets
1. Where a party has presented reasonably available and plausible evidence in support of its claim that a patent has been or is about to be infringed the Court may, whether before or after proceedings have been commenced, order a party not to remove from its jurisdiction any assets or particular assets located therein nor to deal in any assets, whether located within its jurisdiction or not.
2. Rules 192 to 198 shall apply *mutatis mutandis.*

Relation with Agreement: Article 61

Rule 201 – Experiments ordered by the Court
1. Without prejudice to the possibility for parties or parties' experts to carry out experiments, the Court may, on a reasoned request by a party, order an experiment to prove a statement of fact for the purpose of proceedings before the Court.
2. A party requesting to be allowed to prove a statement of fact by means of experiments shall lodge a request as soon as practicable in the written procedure or the interim procedure to carry out experiments which shall:
  (a) identify the facts intended to be established by the experiments, describe the proposed experiments in detail and the reasons for carrying out the proposed experiments;

(b) propose an expert to carry out such experiments; and
(c) disclose any previous attempts to carry out similar experiments.

3. Other parties to the proceedings shall be invited to state whether they dispute the facts intended to be established by the experiments. They shall also be invited to comment on the request, including the identity of the expert proposed and the description of the experiments.

4. Unless otherwise ordered by the Court the party requesting experiments shall initially bear the costs of the experiment.

5. The order of the Court allowing the experiments shall specify the detailed experiments and:
(a) the name and address of the expert who is to carry out the experiments as Court's expert and draw up the report on the experiments;
(b) the time period for carrying out the experiments and, where appropriate, the exact time and place where they are to be carried out;
(c) if necessary, other conditions for carrying out the experiments; and
(d) the time period for presenting the report on the experiments and, where appropriate, directions relating to the contents of the report.

6. Where appropriate, the Court may order that the experiments be carried out in the presence of the parties and their experts.

7. Once the report on the experiments is presented to the Court, it shall invite the parties to comment on it either in writing or during the oral hearing. The expert may be summoned to the oral hearing.

PART 3 – PROVISIONAL MEASURES

Rule 205 – Stages of the proceedings (summary proceedings)

Provisional measures are treated by way of summary proceedings which shall consist of the following stages:
(a) a written procedure; and
(b) an oral procedure, which may include an oral hearing of the parties or of one of the parties.

Rule 206 – Application for provisional measures

1. An Application for provisional measures may be lodged by a party (hereinafter 'the applicant') before or after main proceedings on the merits of the case have been started before the Court.

2. An Application for provisional measures shall contain:
(a) particulars in accordance with Rule 13.1(a) to (i);
(b) a indication of the provisional measures which are being requested [Rule 211.1];
(c) the reasons why provisional measures are necessary to prevent a threatened infringement, to forbid the continuation of an alleged infringement or to make such continuation subject to the lodging of guarantees;
(d) the facts and evidence relied on in support of the Application, including evidence to support the claim that provisional measures are necessary including the matters referred to in Rule 211.2 and .3; and
(e) a concise description of the action which will be started before the Court, including an indication of the facts and evidence which will be relied on in support of the main proceedings on the merits of the case.

3. Where the applicant requests that provisional measures be ordered without hearing the other party (hereinafter 'the defendant'), the Application for provisional measures shall in addition contain:
(a) the reasons for not hearing the defendant having regard in particular to Rule 197; and
(b) information about any prior correspondence between the parties concerning the alleged infringement.

4. The applicant shall be under a duty to disclose any material fact known to it which might influence the Court in deciding whether to make an order without hearing the defendant including any pending proceedings and/or any unsuccessful attempt in the past to obtain provisional measures in respect of the patent.
5. Rule 14 shall apply *mutatis mutandis*. The applicant shall pay the fee for the Application for provisional measures, in accordance with Part 6. Rule 15.2 shall apply *mutatis mutandis*.

Relation with Agreement: Articles 32(1)(c) and 62

Rule 207 - Protective letter
1. If a person entitled to start proceedings under Article 47 of the Agreement considers it likely that an Application for provisional measures against him as a defendant may be lodged before the Court in the near future, he may file a Protective letter.
2. The Protective letter shall be filed with the Registry in the language of the patent and shall contain:
- (a) the name of the defendant or defendants filing the Protective letter and of the defendant's representative;
- (b) the name of the presumed applicant for provisional measures;
- (c) postal and electronic addresses for service on the defendant filing the Protective letter and the names of the persons authorised to accept service;
- (d) postal and, where available, electronic addresses for service on the presumed applicant for provisional measures and the names of the persons authorised to accept service if known;
- (e) where available, the number of the patent concerned and, where applicable, information about any prior or pending proceedings referred to in Rule 13.1(h); and
- (f) the statement that the letter is a Protective letter.

3. The Protective letter may contain:
- (a) an indication of the facts relied on, which may include a challenge to the facts expected to be relied on by the presumed applicant and/or, where applicable, any assertion that the patent is invalid and the grounds for such assertion;
- (b) any available written evidence relied on;
- (c) the arguments of law, including the reasons why any Application for provisional measures should be rejected.

4. The defendant or defendants filing the Protective letter shall pay the fee for filing a Protective letter, in accordance with Part 6. Rule 15.2 shall apply *mutatis mutandis*.
5. The Registry shall as soon as practicable examine whether the requirements of paragraphs 2(a) to (f) and 4 have been complied with. If these requirements have been complied with, the Registry shall as soon as practicable:
- (a) record the date of receipt and assign a number to the Protective letter;
- (b) subject to paragraph 7, record the Protective letter in the register;
- (c) provide details of the Protective letter to all divisions; and
- (d) where an Application for provisional measures has already been lodged, inform the panel or the single judge dealing with the Application about the filing of the Protective letter.

6. If the defendant has not complied with the requirements of paragraph 2 the Registry shall as soon as practicable invite the defendant to:
- (a) correct the deficiencies within 14 days of service of such notification; and
- (b) where applicable, pay the fee referred to in paragraph 4.

7. The protective letter shall not be publicly available on the register until it has been forwarded to the applicant pursuant to paragraph 8.

8. Where an Application for provisional measures is subsequently lodged the Registrar shall forward a copy of the protective letter to the panel or judge appointed under Rule 208 together with the Application for provisional measures and shall forward a copy to the applicant as soon as practicable.
9. If no Application for provisional measures has been lodged within six months from the date of receipt of the Protective letter, the Protective letter shall be removed from the register unless the person who has lodged the Protective letter has prior to the expiry of such period applied for an extension of six months and paid a fee for the extension in accordance with Part 6. Further extensions may be obtained on further payments of the fee.
10. Rule 15.2 shall apply *mutatis mutandis.*

Rule 208 – Examination as to formal requirements, recording in the register, assignment to panel, designation of judge-rapporteur, single judge
1. The Application for provisional measures shall be examined by the Registry in accordance with Rule 16. The Registry shall in addition examine whether any Protective letter relevant for the Application is recorded in the register.
2. Where main proceedings on the merits of the case have not yet been started before the Court, Rule 17 (date of receipt, recording in the register, action number, assignment to panel) and Rule 18 (designation of judge-rapporteur by presiding judge) shall apply *mutatis mutandis.* In urgent cases, the presiding judge may decide that he or an experienced judge of the panel, acting as single judge, may decide on the Application in accordance with Rules 209 to 213 with a reduced time-table.
3. Where main proceedings on the merits of the case have already been started before the Court, the Application for provisional measures shall immediately be forwarded to the panel to which the action has been assigned or to the single judge. In urgent cases (where the action has not been assigned to a single judge), the presiding judge may decide that he or the judge-rapporteur, acting as single judge, may decide on the Application in accordance with Rules 209 to 213 with a reduced time-table.
4. The single judge deciding on the Application for provisional measures shall have all necessary powers of the Court.

Relation with Statute: Article 19

Rule 209 – Examination of the Application for provisional measures
1. Without prejudice to the Court's decision on the Application for provisional measures, the Court shall have the discretion – including where the Application is made pursuant to Rule 206.3 – to:
- (a) inform the defendant about the Application and invite him to lodge, within a time period to be specified, an Objection to the Application for provisional measures which shall contain:
  - (i) the reasons why the Application shall fail;
  - (ii) the facts and evidence relied on, in particular any challenge to the facts and evidence relied on by the applicant; and
  - (iii) where main proceedings on the merits of the case have not yet been started before the Court, the reasons why the action which will be started before the Court shall fail and the facts and evidence relied on in support;
- (b) summon the parties to an oral hearing;
- (c) summon the applicant to an oral hearing without the presence of the defendant.

2. In exercising its discretion pursuant to paragraph 1, the Court shall in particular take into account:
- (a) whether the patent has been upheld in an opposition procedure before the European Patent Office or has been the subject of proceedings in any other court;
- (b) the urgency of the action;
- (c) whether the applicant has requested provisional measures without hearing the defendant and whether the reasons for not hearing the defendant appear well-founded; and

(d) any Protective letter filed by the defendant; the Court shall in particular consider summoning parties to an oral hearing if a relevant Protective letter has been filed by the defendant.

3. In cases of extreme urgency the standing judge appointed in accordance with Rule 345.5 may decide immediately on the Application for provisional measures and the procedure to be followed on the Application.

4. If the applicant has applied for provisional measures without hearing the defendant and the Court decides not to grant provisional measures without hearing the defendant the applicant may withdraw the Application and may request that the Court order that the Application and the contents of the Application remain confidential.

5. If the patent the subject of the Application is also the subject of a protective letter pursuant to Rule 207 the applicant may withdraw the Application pursuant to paragraph 4.

Rule 210 - Oral hearing

1. Where the Court decides to summon the parties to an oral hearing, the date for the oral hearing shall be set as soon as possible after the date of receipt of the Application for provisional measures.

2. The Court may order the parties to provide further information, documents and other evidence before or during the oral hearing, including evidence to enable the Court to make its decision in accordance with Rule 211. Part 2 of these Rules on Evidence shall be applicable only to the extent determined by the Court.

3. Rules 111 to 116 shall apply *mutatis mutandis*. Where the applicant is absent from the oral hearing without a reasonable excuse, the Court shall reject the Application for provisional measures.

4. The decision of the Court on the Application for provisional measures shall be given in writing as soon as possible after the closure of the oral hearing. If the Court deems appropriate, its decision may be given orally to the parties at the end of the oral hearing, prior to providing its decision in writing.

Rule 211 - Order on the Application for provisional measures

1. The Court may in particular order the following provisional measures:

(a) injunctions against a defendant;

(b) the seizure or delivery up of the goods suspected of infringing a patent right so as to prevent their entry into or movement within the channels of commerce;

(c) if an applicant demonstrates circumstances likely to endanger the recovery of damages, a precautionary seizure of the movable and immovable property of the defendant, including the blocking of his bank accounts and other assets;

(d) an interim award of costs.

2. In taking its decision the Court may require the applicant to provide reasonable evidence to satisfy the Court with a sufficient degree of certainty that the applicant is entitled to commence proceedings pursuant to Article 47, that the patent in question is valid and that his right is being infringed, or that such infringement is imminent.

3. In taking its decision the Court shall in the exercise of its discretion weigh up the interests of the parties and, in particular, take into account the potential harm for either of the parties resulting from the granting or the refusal of the injunction.

4. The Court shall have regard to any unreasonable delay in seeking provisional measures.

5. The Court may order the applicant to provide adequate security for appropriate compensation for any injury likely to be caused to the defendant which the applicant may be liable to bear in the event that the Court revokes the order for provisional measures. The Court shall do so where interim measures are ordered without the defendant having been heard unless there are special circumstances not to do so. The Court shall decide whether it is appropriate to order the security by deposit or bank guarantee. The order shall be effective only after the security has been given to the defendant in accordance with the Court's decision.

6. The order on provisional measures shall indicate that an appeal may be brought in accordance with Article 73 of the Agreement and Rule 220.1.

Relation with Agreement: Article 62(2) and (4)

Rule 212 - Order on provisional measures without hearing the defendant
1. The Court may order provisional measures without the defendant having been heard, in particular where any delay is likely to cause irreparable harm to the applicant or where there is a demonstrable risk of evidence being destroyed. Rule 197 shall apply *mutatis mutandis.*
2. Where provisional measures are ordered without the defendant having been heard, Rule 210 shall apply *mutatis mutandis* to the oral hearing without the presence of the defendant. In such cases, the defendant shall be given notice of the provisional measures without delay and at the latest immediately at the time of execution of the measures.
3. The defendant may request a review. Rule 197.3 and .4 shall apply *mutatis mutandis.*

Relation with Agreement: Article 60(5) and (6)

Rule 213 - Revocation of provisional measures
1. The Court shall ensure that provisional measures are revoked or otherwise cease to have effect, upon request of the defendant, without prejudice to the damages which may be claimed, if, within a time period not exceeding 31 calendar days or 20 working days, whichever is the longer, from the date specified in the Court's order, the applicant does not start proceedings on the merits of the case before the Court. When specifying the date, the Court shall take due account, where applicable, of the date on which the Report referred to in Rule 196.4 shall be presented.
2. Where provisional measures are revoked, or where they lapse due to any act or omission by the applicant, or where it is subsequently found that there has been no infringement or threat of infringement of the patent, the Court may order the applicant, upon request of the defendant, to provide the defendant with appropriate compensation for any injury caused by those measures [Rule 354.2].

Relation with Agreement: Article 60(9).

PART 4 - PROCEDURES BEFORE THE COURT OF APPEAL

Rule 220 - Appealable decisions
1. An appeal by a party adversely affected may be brought against:
   (a) final decisions of the Court of First Instance;
   (b) decisions terminating proceedings as regards one of the parties;
   (c) orders referred to in Articles 49(5), 59, 60, 61, 62 or 67 of the Agreement.
2. Orders other than those referred to in paragraph 1 and Rule 97.5, may be either the subject of an appeal together with the appeal against the decision or may be appealed with the leave of the Court of First Instance within 15 days of service of the Court's decision to that effect.
3. In the event of a refusal of the Court of First Instance to grant leave within 15 days of the order of one of its panels a request for a discretionary review to the Court of Appeal may be made within 15 calendar days from the end of that period. Rule 333.3 shall apply *mutatis mutandis*. The request shall set out the matters referred to in Rule 221.2.
4. The Registrar shall assign the request for a discretionary review to the standing judge (Rule 345.5 and .8). The standing judge may deny the request without giving reasons. If the standing judge allows the request after having heard the other party, he shall order what further steps, if any, the parties shall take and within what time limits and the President of the Court of Appeal shall assign the review to

a panel of the Court of Appeal for a decision. The Court of Appeal may consult the presiding judge or the judge-rapporteur of the panel of the Court of First Instance which has refused the leave order.
5. The Court of Appeal may hear appeals against separate decisions on the merits in infringement proceedings and in validity proceedings together.

Relation with Agreement: Article 73

Rule 221 - Application for leave to appeal against cost decisions
1. A party adversely affected by a decision referred to in Rule 157 may lodge an Application for leave to appeal to the Court of Appeal within 15 days of service of the decision of the Court.
2. The Application for leave to appeal shall set out:
   (a) the reasons why the appeal should be heard;
   (b) where necessary, the facts, evidence and arguments relied on.
3. The Application for leave to appeal shall be assigned to the standing judge (Rule 345.5 and .8) who shall decide on granting leave to appeal.
4. If leave to appeal a cost decision is granted the standing judge shall decide the appeal.

Rule 222 - Subject-matter of the proceedings before the Court of Appeal
1. Requests, facts, evidence and arguments submitted by the parties under Rules 221, 225, 226, 236 and 238 shall, subject to paragraph 2, constitute the subject-matter of the proceedings before the Court of Appeal. The Court of Appeal shall consult the file of the proceedings before the Court of First Instance.
2. Requests, facts and evidence which have not been submitted by a party during proceedings before the Court of First Instance may be disregarded by the Court of Appeal. When exercising discretion, the Court shall in particular take into account:
   (a) whether a party seeking to lodge new submissions is able to justify that the new submissions could not reasonably have been made during proceedings before the Court of First Instance;
   (b) the relevance of the new submissions for the decision on the appeal;
   (c) the position of the other party regarding the lodging of the new submissions.

Relation with Agreement: Article 73(4)

Rule 223 - Application for suspensive effect
1. A party may lodge an Application for suspensive effect, in accordance with Article 74 of the Agreement.
2. The Application for suspensive effect shall set out:
   (a) the reasons why the lodging of the appeal shall have suspensive effect;
   (b) the facts, evidence and arguments relied on.
3. The Court of Appeal shall decide the Application without delay.
4. In cases of extreme urgency the applicant may apply at any time without formality for an order for suspensive effect to the standing judge [Rule 345.5 and .8]. The standing judge shall have all the powers of the Court of Appeal and shall decide the procedure to be followed on the application, which may include a subsequent written Application.
5. There shall be no suspensive effect for an appeal of an order pursuant to Rule 220.2, Rule 220.3 or 221.3.

Relation with Agreement: Article 74

CHAPTER 1 – WRITTEN PROCEDURE

SECTION 1 – STATEMENT OF APPEAL, STATEMENT OF GROUNDS OF APPEAL

Rule 224 – Time periods for lodging the Statement of appeal and the Statement of grounds of appeal

1. A Statement of appeal shall be lodged by the appellant:
   (a) within two months of service of a decision referred to in Rule 220.1(a) and (b); or
   (b) within 15 days of service of an order referred to in Rule 220.1(c) or a decision referred to in Rule 220.2 or 221.3.
2. The Statement of grounds of appeal shall be lodged by the appellant:
   (a) within four months of service of a decision referred to in Rule 220.1(a) and (b); or
   (b) within 15 days of service of an order referred to in Rule 220.1(c) or a decision referred to in Rule 220.2 or 221.3.

Relation with Agreement: Article 73(1) and (2)

Rule 225 – Contents of the Statement of appeal

The Statement of appeal shall contain:
(a) the names of the appellant and of the appellant's representative;
(b) the names of the respondent and of the respondent's representative;
(c) postal and electronic addresses for service on the appellant and on the respondent, as well as the names of the persons authorised to accept service;
(d) the date of the decision or order appealed against and the action number attributed to the file in proceedings before the Court of First Instance; and
(e) the order or remedy sought by the appellant, including any order for expedition of the appeal pursuant to Rule 9.3(b) and the reasons justifying such order for expedition.

Rule 226 – Contents of the Statement of grounds of appeal

The Statement of grounds of appeal shall contain:
(a) an indication of which parts of the decision or order are contested;
(b) the reasons for setting aside the contested decision or order; and
(c) an indication of the facts and evidence on which the appeal is based in accordance with Rule 222.1 and .2.

Rule 227 – Language of the Statement of appeal and of the Statement of grounds of appeal

The Statement of appeal and the Statement of grounds of appeal shall be drawn up:
(a) without prejudice to Article 50(3) of the Agreement, in the language of the proceedings before the Court of First Instance; or
(b) where the parties have agreed in accordance with Article 50(2) of the Agreement, in the language in which the patent was granted. Where the parties have agreed in accordance with Article 50(2) of the Agreement, evidence of the respondent's agreement shall be lodged by the appellant together with the Statement of appeal.

Relationship with Agreement: Article 50

Rule 228 – Fee for the appeal

The appellant shall pay the fixed fee and, where applicable, the value based fee for the appeal, in accordance with Part 6. Rule 15.2 shall apply *mutatis mutandis*.

Rule 229 – Examination as to formal requirements of the Statement of appeal
1. The Registry shall, as soon as practicable after the lodging of the Statement of appeal, examine whether the requirements of Rules 224.1, 225, 227 and 228 have been complied with.
2. If the appellant has not complied with the requirements referred to in Rules 225, 227 or 228, the Registry shall invite the appellant to:
   (a) correct the deficiencies within 14 days of service of such notification; and
   (b) where applicable, pay the fee for the appeal within said 14 days.
3. The Registry shall at the same time inform the appellant that if the appellant fails to correct the deficiencies or to pay the fee within the time stated, a decision by default may be given in accordance with Rule 357.
4. If the appellant has not met the requirements of Rules 225, 227 and 228 and fails to correct the deficiencies or pay the fee the Registry shall inform the President of the Court of Appeal who shall reject the appeal as inadmissible by a decision by default. He may give the appellant an opportunity to be heard beforehand.
5. If the appellant has not met the requirements of Rule 224.1, the Registry shall inform the President of the Court of Appeal who shall reject the appeal as inadmissible. He may give the appellant an opportunity to be heard beforehand.

Rule 230 – Recording in the register (Court of Appeal)
1. If the Statement of appeal complies with the requirements referred to in Rule 229.1, the Registry shall:
   (a) record the date of receipt to the Statement of appeal and an action number to the appeal file;
   (b) record the appeal file in the register;
   (c) inform the appellant of the action number and the date of receipt; and
   (d) serve the Statement of appeal on all parties to the proceedings at first instance.
2. The action shall be assigned to a panel according to Rule 345.3 and .8.
3. The panel shall as soon as practicable decide whether to grant any order for expedition pursuant to Rule 225(e) having given the parties an opportunity to be heard.

Rule 231 – Designation of the judge-rapporteur
The presiding judge of the panel to which the action has been assigned shall designate one legally qualified judge of the panel as judge-rapporteur. The presiding judge may designate himself as the judge-rapporteur. The Registry shall as soon as practicable notify the appellant and respondent of the identity of the judge-rapporteur.

Rule 232 – Translation of file
1. If the language of the proceedings before the Court of Appeal is not the language of the proceedings before the Court of First Instance, the judge-rapporteur may order the appellant to lodge, within a time period to be specified, translations into the language of the proceedings before the Court of Appeal of:
   (a) written pleadings and other documents lodged by the parties before the Court of First Instance, as specified by the judge-rapporteur;
   (b) decisions or orders of the Court of First Instance.

The judge-rapporteur shall at the same time inform the appellant that if the appellant fails to lodge the translations within the time period specified, a decision by default may be given in accordance with Rule 357.
2. If the appellant fails to lodge the translations under paragraph 1 within the time period specified, the judge-rapporteur shall reject the appeal by a decision by default in accordance with Rule 357. He may give the appellant an opportunity to be heard beforehand.

3. The appellant may request that documented costs of translations be taken into account when the Court fixes the amount of costs in accordance with Part 1, Chapter 5.

Relation with Agreement: Article 50(2) and (3)

Rule 233 - Preliminary examination of the Statement of grounds of appeal
1. The judge-rapporteur shall examine whether the Statement of grounds of appeal satisfies the requirements of Rule 226.
2. If the Statement of grounds of appeal does not comply with the requirements of Rule 226, the judge-rapporteur shall give the appellant leave to amend the Statement of grounds of appeal within such period as he may decide. If the appellant fails to amend the Statement within such period the judge-rapporteur may reject the appeal as inadmissible. He shall give the appellant an opportunity to be heard beforehand.
3. Grounds of appeal which are not raised within the period specified for the Statement of grounds of appeal in Rule 224.2 shall not be admissible.

Rule 234 - Challenge to the decision to reject an appeal as inadmissible
1. The appellant may challenge a decision to reject the appeal as inadmissible under Rules 224.1 or 233.2 within one month of service of the decision, without providing new grounds of appeal.
2. The action shall be assigned to a panel according to Rule 345.3 and .8.
3. If a decision to reject an appeal as inadmissible is set aside, the appeal shall take its normal course.

SECTION 2 – STATEMENT OF RESPONSE

Rule 235 - Statement of response
1. Within three months of service of the Statement of grounds of appeal pursuant to Rule 224.2(a), any other party to proceedings before the Court of First Instance (hereinafter 'respondent') may lodge a Statement of response, which shall be served on the appellant.
2. Within 15 days of service of grounds of appeal pursuant to Rule 224.2(b), any other party to proceedings before the Court of First Instance (hereinafter 'respondent') may lodge a Statement of response, which shall be served on the appellant.
3. If the respondent fails to lodge a Statement of response, the Court of Appeal may give a reasoned decision.

Rule 236 - Contents of the Statement of response
1. The Statement of response shall contain:
   (a) the names of the respondent and the respondent's representative;
   (b) postal and electronic addresses for service on the respondent and the names and addresses of the persons authorised to accept service;
   (c) the action number of the appeal file; and
   (d) a response to the grounds of appeal.
2. The respondent may support the decision of the Court of First Instance on grounds other than those given in the decision.

Rule 237 - Statement of cross-appeal
1. A party who has not lodged a Statement of appeal within the period referred to in Rule 224.1 may still bring an appeal by way of cross-appeal within the period referred to in Rule 235 if one of the other parties has lodged a Statement of appeal.

2. A Statement of cross-appeal shall be included in the Statement of response. It shall comply with the requirements of Rules 225 and 226. Rules 229, 233 and 234 shall apply *mutatis mutandis* to the Statement of cross-appeal.
3. A Statement of cross-appeal shall not be admissible in any other way or at any other time.
4. A cross-appeal shall be treated as an appeal as far as the fee for the appeal is concerned. Rule 228 shall apply *mutatis mutandis.*
5. If the Statement of appeal is withdrawn, any Statement of cross-appeal shall be deemed to be withdrawn.

SECTION 3 – REPLY TO A STATEMENT OF CROSS-APPEAL

Rule 238 - Reply to a Statement of cross-appeal and further schedule
1. The appellant may, within two months of service of any Statement of cross-appeal under Rules 237, 235.1, lodge a Reply to the Statement of cross-appeal which shall contain a response to the grounds of appeal raised in the Statement of cross-appeal.
2. The appellant may, within 15 days of service of the Statement of cross-appeal under Rules 237 and 235.2, lodge a Reply to the Statement of cross-appeal which shall contain a response to the grounds of appeal raised in the Statement of cross-appeal.
3. Rule 28 shall apply *mutatis mutandis.*

SECTION 4 – REFERRAL TO THE FULL COURT

Rule 238A - Decision to refer
1. The panel to which the action has been assigned may refer it to the full Court of Appeal if the panel considers, on a proposal from the presiding judge, the case to be of exceptional importance and, in particular, where the decision in the action may affect the consistency and unity of the case law of the Court.
2. The presiding judge of the panel shall request the President of the Court of Appeal and the two judges of the Court of Appeal who are members of the Presidium to appoint the judges of the Court of Appeal to the full Court. The appointees shall be the President of the Court of Appeal and not less than ten (legally and technically qualified) judges of the Court of Appeal to represent the initial two panels of the Court of Appeal. In the event that the Court of Appeal shall have more than two panels the appointees to the full Court shall increase by five judges, (legally and technically qualified), for each additional panel.
3. Decisions of the full Court shall be by no less than a three-quarters majority of the judges of the full Court.

CHAPTER 2 – INTERIM PROCEDURE

Rule 239 - Role of the judge-rapporteur
1. Upon the expiry of the periods specified in Rules 224 to 238 the judge-rapporteur shall make all necessary preparations for the oral hearing. Subject always to the provisions of Rule 222, the judge-rapporteur shall, to the extent appropriate, have the powers and exercise the duties set out in Rules 101 to 110 *mutatis mutandis.*
2. As soon as the judge-rapporteur considers that the appeal is ready for oral hearing he shall summon the parties to the oral hearing. Except for appeals against the orders referred to in Rule 220.1(c) and 220.2, and subject to any order for expedition pursuant to Rule 230.3, at least two months' notice shall be given unless the parties agree to a shorter time period. The interim procedure shall be deemed

closed and oral procedure shall start immediately on the giving of such summons. The presiding judge shall, in consultation with the judge-rapporteur take over the management of the action.

CHAPTER 3 – ORAL PROCEDURE

Rule 240 – Conduct of the oral hearing
Subject to Rule 241 the oral hearing shall be held before the panel and shall be directed by the presiding judge. Subject always to Rule 222, Rules 111, 112, 115, 116 and 117 shall apply *mutatis mutandis*.

Rule 241 – Conduct of the oral hearing for an appeal of a cost decision
The oral hearing for an appeal of a cost decision pursuant to Rule 157 shall be heard by the standing judge [Rule 345.5 and .8] who shall have all the powers of the Court of Appeal.

CHAPTER 4 – DECISIONS AND EFFECT OF DECISIONS

Rule 242 – Decision of the Court of Appeal
1. The Court of Appeal shall either reject the appeal or set the decision or order aside totally or in part substituting its own decision or order, including an order for costs both in respect of the proceedings at first instance and on appeal.
2. The Court of Appeal may:
   (a) exercise any power within the competence of the Court of First Instance;
   (b) in exceptional circumstances refer the action back to the Court of First Instance for decision or for retrial [Rule 243]. It shall not normally be an exceptional circumstance justifying a referral back that the Court of First Instance failed to decide an issue which it is necessary for the Court of Appeal to decide on appeal.

Relation with Agreement: Article 75

Rule 243 – Referral back
1. The decision referring an action back to the Court of First Instance shall specify whether the same panel whose earlier decision or order is revoked shall deal further with the action or whether another panel shall be appointed by the presiding judge of the division concerned.
2. Where an action is referred back to the Court of First Instance, the Court shall be bound by the decision of the Court of Appeal and its ratio decidendi.

Relation with Agreement: Article 75

CHAPTER 5 – PROCEDURE FOR APPLICATION FOR REHEARING

Rule 245 – Lodging of an Application for rehearing
1. An Application for rehearing may be lodged by any party adversely affected by a final decision (hereinafter 'the final decision') of the Court of First Instance for which the time for lodging an appeal has expired or of the Court of Appeal (hereinafter 'the petitioner').
2. The Application for rehearing shall be lodged at the Court of Appeal within the following periods:
   (a) where the Application for rehearing is based on the ground of a fundamental procedural defect, within two months of the discovery of the fundamental defect or of service of the final decision, whichever is the later;

(b) where the Application for rehearing is based on an act which has been held, by a final court decision, to constitute a criminal offence, within two months of the date on which the criminal offence has been so held or service of the final decision, whichever is the later;
(c) but in any event no later than ten years of service of the final decision.

Relation with Agreement: Article 81

Rule 246 – Contents of the Application for rehearing
1. The Application for rehearing shall contain:
(a) the names of the petitioner and of the petitioner's representative;
(b) postal and electronic addresses for service on the petitioner and the names and addresses of the persons authorised to accept service; and
(c) an indication of the decision to be reviewed.
2. The Application for rehearing shall indicate the reasons for setting aside the final decision, as well as the facts and evidence on which the Application is based.

Rule 247 – Fundamental procedural defects
A fundamental procedural defect under Article 81(1) of the Agreement may have occurred, for example, where:
(a) a judge of the Court took part in the decision in breach of Article 17 of the Agreement or Article 7 of the Statute;
(b) a person not appointed as a judge of the Court sat on the panel which took the final decision;
(c) a fundamental violation of Article 76 of the Agreement occurred in the proceedings which have led to the final decision;
(d) the decision was made without deciding on a request relevant to that decision; or
(e) a breach of Article 6 of the Convention for the Protection of Human Rights and Fundamental Freedoms has occurred.

Rule 248 – Obligation to raise objections
1. An Application for rehearing based on the ground of a fundamental procedural defect is only admissible where an objection in respect of the procedural defect was raised during the proceedings before the Court of First Instance or the Court of Appeal and dismissed by the Court, except where such objection could not have been raised during the proceedings before the Court of First Instance or the Court of Appeal.
2. An application for rehearing based upon the ground of a fundamental procedural defect is not admissible where the party could have brought an appeal in respect of the defect but failed to do so.

Rule 249 – Definition of criminal offence
A criminal offence shall only be considered to have occurred if it is finally held to be such an offence by a competent court or authority. A conviction is not necessary.

Rule 250 – Fee for the rehearing
The petitioner shall pay the fee for the rehearing, in accordance with Part 6. Rule 15.2 shall apply *mutatis mutandis*. The Court may waive payment of the fee in the circumstances contemplated by Rule 245.2(a) or (b).

Rule 251 – Recording in the register
Rule 230.1 shall apply *mutatis mutandis*.

Rule 252 – Suspensive effect
The lodging of an Application for rehearing shall not have suspensive effect unless the Court of Appeal decides otherwise.

Relation with Agreement: Article 81(2)

Rule 253 – Examination as to formal requirements of the Application for rehearing
1. The Registry shall, as soon as practicable after the lodging of the Application for rehearing, examine whether the requirements of Rules 245, 246 and 250 have been complied with.
2. If the petitioner has not complied with the requirements referred to in paragraph 1, the Registry shall invite the petitioner to:
   (a) correct the deficiencies within 14 days; and
   (b) where applicable, pay the fee for the rehearing within 14 days.
If the petitioner fails to correct the deficiencies or pay the fee the case shall be assigned to the standing judge by the Registrar (Rule 345.5 and .8) who may reject the Application for rehearing as inadmissible. He shall give the petitioner an opportunity to be heard beforehand.

Rule 254 – Assignment of Application for rehearing to a panel
1. Immediately after the Application for rehearing has been recorded in the register, the Registry shall serve a copy of the Application for rehearing on all other parties and shall inform the President of the Court of Appeal that a Request for rehearing has been lodged.
2. The action shall be assigned to a panel consisting of three legally qualified judges. The President of the Court of Appeal may order that judges of the Court who participated in taking the decision to be reviewed shall not sit on the panel.

Rule 255 – Examination of the Application for rehearing
After hearing the parties the panel may make:
(a) a decision to reject the Application for rehearing as not allowable; such a decision shall be by a majority vote of the judges on the panel.
(b) a decision to allow the Application for rehearing; such a decision shall set aside or suspend the decision under review, in whole or in part, and re-open the proceedings for a new hearing and decisions. Where proceedings are re-opened, the panel shall give directions for the future proceedings.

Relation with Agreement: Article 81(3)

PART 5 – GENERAL PROVISIONS

CHAPTER 1 – GENERAL PROCEDURAL PROVISIONS

Rule 260 – Examination by the Registry of its own motion
1. In any proceedings before the Court, the Registry shall, as soon as practicable in the proceedings, of its own motion, examine whether an opt-out has effect for the patent concerned.
2. Where the Registry notes that two or more actions concerning the same patent are initiated before several divisions (whether or not between the same parties), it shall as soon as practicable inform the divisions concerned.

Relation with Agreement: Article 83(3) and (4)
Relation with Statute: Articles 23 and 24

Rule 261 - Date of pleadings
All pleadings and documents lodged with pleadings shall bear a time and a date which shall be the time and date of receipt of pleadings at the Registry. The time shall be the local time of the Registry. The Registrar shall be responsible for time and date marking.

Rule 262 - Public access to the register
1. Without prejudice to Articles 58 and 60(1) of the Agreement and subject to Rules 190.1, 194.5, 196.1, 197.4, 199.1, 207.7, 209.4, 315.2 and 365.2, and following, where applicable, redaction of personal data within the meaning of Regulation (EU) 2016/679 and confidential information according to paragraph 2

(a) decisions and orders made by the Court shall be published,

(b) written pleadings and evidence, lodged at the Court and recorded by the Registry shall be available to the public upon reasoned request to the Registry; the decision is taken by the judge-rapporteur after consulting the parties.

2. A party may request that certain information of written pleadings or evidence be kept confidential and provide specific reasons for such confidentiality. To this end content of the register is made publicly available according to paragraph 1 (b) only 14 days after it has been available to all recipients. The Registrar shall ensure that beyond this time period information subject of a request for confidentiality shall not be made available pending an Application pursuant to paragraph 3 or an appeal pursuant to Rule 220.2. When a party lodges a request that parts of written pleadings or evidence shall be kept confidential, he shall also provide copies of the said documents with the relevant parts redacted when making the request.
3. A member of the public may lodge an Application with the Court for an order that any information excluded from public access pursuant to paragraph 2 may be made available to the applicant.
4. The Application shall contain:

(a) details of the information alleged to be confidential, so far as possible;

(b) the grounds upon which the applicant believes the reasons for confidentiality should not be accepted; and

(c) the purpose for which the information is needed.

5. The Court shall invite written comments from the parties prior to making any order.
6. The Court shall allow the Application unless legitimate reasons given by the party concerned for the confidentiality of the information outweigh the interest of the applicant to access such information.
7. The Registrar shall as soon as practicable take all such steps with regard to access to the register as may be necessary to give effect to an order of the Court under this Rule.

Relation with Agreement: Articles 10, 45, 58 and 60(1)
Relation with Statute: Article 24(2)

Rule 262A - Protection of Confidential Information
1. Without prejudice to Article 60(1) of the Agreement and Rules 190.1, 194.5, 196.1, 197.4, 199.1, 207.7, 209.4, 315.2 and 365.2 a party may make an Application to the Court for an order that certain information contained in its pleadings or the collection and use of evidence in proceedings may be restricted or prohibited or that access to such information or evidence be restricted to specific persons.
2. The Application shall contain the grounds upon which the applicant believes the information or evidence in question should be restricted in accordance with Article 58 of the Agreement.
3. The Application shall be made at the same time as lodging a document containing the information or evidence and shall provide a copy of the unredacted relevant document and, if applicable, a copy of the redacted document.

4. The Court shall invite written comments from the representatives of the other parties prior to making any order.
5. The Court may allow the Application considering in particular whether the grounds relied upon by the applicant for the order significantly outweigh the interest of the other party to have full access to the information and evidence in question.
6. The number of persons referred to in paragraph 1 shall be no greater than necessary in order to ensure compliance with the right of the parties to the legal proceedings to an effective remedy and to a fair trial, and shall include, at least, one natural person from each party and the respective lawyers or other representatives of those parties to the legal proceedings.
7. The Registrar shall as soon as practicable take all such steps with regard to access to the evidence as may be necessary to give effect to the order of the Court under this Rule.

Relation with Agreement: Article 58

Rule 263 – Leave to change claim or amend case
1. A party may at any stage of the proceedings apply to the Court for leave to change its claim or to amend its case, including adding a counterclaim. Any such application shall explain why such change or amendment was not included in the original pleading.
2. Subject to paragraph 3, leave shall not be granted if, all circumstances considered, the party seeking the amendment cannot satisfy the Court that:
  (a) the amendment in question could not have been made with reasonable diligence at an earlier stage; and
  (b) the amendment will not unreasonably hinder the other party in the conduct of its action.
3. Leave to limit a claim in an action unconditionally shall always be granted.
4. The Court may re-consider fees already paid in the light of an amendment.

Rule 264 – An opportunity to be heard
Where these Rules provide that a party shall or may be given an opportunity to be heard before the Court makes an order or takes some action, the Court shall or may (as the case may be) request the parties to provide written submissions within a specified period and/or shall or may invite the parties to an oral hearing on a fixed date by the Court. The Court may also order that a hearing takes place by telephone or video conference. Rules 105 and 106 shall apply *mutatis mutandis*.

Rule 265 – Withdrawal
1. As long as there is no final decision in an action, a claimant may apply to withdraw his action. The Court shall decide the application after hearing the other party. The application to withdraw shall not be permitted if the other party has a legitimate interest in the action being decided by the Court.
2. If withdrawal is permitted, the Court shall:
  (a) give a decision declaring the proceedings closed;
  (b) order the decision to be entered on the register; and
  (c) issue a cost decision in accordance with Part 1, Chapter 5.
The withdrawal of an action by the claimant shall have no effect on any counterclaim in the action. The Court may however refer any counterclaim for revocation to the Central Division.

Rule 266 – Preliminary references to the Court of Justice of the European Union
1. At any stage of the proceedings where a question is raised before the Court and the Court considers that a decision on the question by the Court of Justice of the European Union ('CJEU') is necessary before the Court can give judgment, the Court of First Instance may and the Court of Appeal shall request the CJEU to give a ruling thereon.

2. The Court shall in requesting a ruling follow the procedure set out in the Rules of the CJEU.
3. If the Court requests the CJEU to apply its expedited procedure the request shall in addition set out:
   (a) the matters of fact and law which establish its urgency; and
   (b) the reasons why an expedited ruling is appropriate.
4. The Registrar shall as soon as practicable forward the request and any request to apply the expedited procedure to the Registrar of the CJEU.
5. The Court may stay the proceedings. Where it does not stay proceedings, it shall not give judgement until the CJEU has given a ruling on the question.

Rule 267 - Actions pursuant to Article 22 of the Agreement
Where an action for damages has been brought against a Contracting Member State pursuant to Article 22 of the Agreement, the President of the Court of Appeal shall, as soon as practicable following a request from the competent authority in the Contracting Member State, provide the competent authority with copies of all pleadings, evidence, decisions and orders available to the Court in its proceedings that are relevant to the action for damages. The President of the Court of Appeal shall have an opportunity to comment.

CHAPTER 2 – SERVICE

SECTION 1 – SERVICE WITHIN THE CONTRACTING MEMBER STATES

Rule 270 - Scope of this Section
1. For service of the Statement of claim within the Contracting Member States the law of the European Union on the service of documents in civil and commercial matters [Regulation (EU) 2020/1784] and the rules set out in this Section, in particular Rule 271.2 shall apply.
2. For the purpose of Rules 270 to 275 the term Statement of claim shall, where appropriate, mean all originating pleadings in actions referred to in Article 32(1) of the Agreement.

Rule 271 - Service of the Statement of claim
1. The Registry shall serve the Statement of claim by electronic means if the conditions referred to in Article 19 of the Regulation (EU) 2020/1784 are met
   (a) on the defendant at an electronic address which the defendant has provided for the purpose of service in the proceedings; or
   (b) on a representative of the defendant if the defendant has provided the electronic address of a representative pursuant to Rule 8.1 as an address at which the defendant may be served with the Statement of claim; or
   (c) on a representative of the defendant pursuant to Rule 8.1 if the representative has notified the Registry or the claimant that he accepts service of the Statement of claim on behalf of the defendant at an electronic address.
2. Where a representative pursuant to Rule 8.1 accepts service on behalf of a party service may be effected within the closed electronic system of the UPC Case Management System (CMS).
3. For the purpose of serving a Statement for revocation [Rule 44] or of serving a Statement for declaration of non-infringement [Rule 63], reference to representative under paragraph 2(b) or (c) shall additionally include professional representatives and legal practitioners as defined in Article 134 EPC who are recorded as the appointed representative for the patent, the subject of the proceedings, in the Register for unitary patent protection [Regulation (EU) No 1257/2012, Article 2(e)] or in the national patent register [Rule 8.5(a)].
4. Where service by electronic means cannot be effected, the Registry shall serve the Statement of claim on the defendant by:

(a) any other method foreseen by the law of the European Union on the service of documents in civil and commercial matters [Regulation (EU) 2020/1784], in particular by registered letter with acknowledgement of receipt or equivalent [Article 18 Regulation (EU) 2020/1784]; or
(b) where service in accordance with paragraph 4(a) could not be effected any method permitted by the law of the Member State of the European Union where service is to be effected or authorised by the Court under Rule 275.

5. Service under this Section shall be effected at the following place:
(a) where the defendant is a company or other legal person, at its statutory seat, central administration or principal place of business within the Contracting Member States or at any place within the Contracting Member States where the company or other legal person has a permanent or temporary place of business;
(b) where the defendant is an individual, at his usual or last known residence within the Contracting Member States; or
(c) for the purpose of serving a Statement for revocation [Rule 44] or of serving a Statement for a declaration of non-infringement [Rule 63], at the place of business of a professional representative or legal practitioner as defined in Article 134 EPC who is recorded as the appointed representative for the patent, the subject of the proceedings, in the Register for unitary patent protection [Regulation (EU) No 1257/2012, Article 2(e)] or of the patent office of a Contracting Member State.

6. Subject to Rule 272.2 and .3, a Statement of claim served in accordance with paragraphs 1 to 5 is deemed to be served on the defendant:
(a) where service takes place by means of electronic communication, on the day when the relevant electronic message was sent (GMT+1);
(b) where service takes place by registered letter with acknowledgement of receipt or equivalent such letter shall be deemed to be served on the addressee on the tenth day following posting unless it has failed to reach the addressee, has in fact reached him on a later date or the acknowledgement of receipt or equivalent has not been returned. Such service shall, except where paragraph 8 applies, be deemed effective even if acceptance of the letter has been refused.

7. The Registry shall advise the defendant that he may refuse to accept a Statement of Claim if it is not written or not accompanied by a translation into a language that he understands or that is an official language of the place where service is to be effected, by enclosing with the document to be served form L in Annex I of Regulation (EU) 2020/1784.

8. Where the defendant is entitled to refuse service and where he has notified the refusal to the Registry within two weeks of the attempted service together with an indication of the language(s) he understands, the Registry shall inform the claimant. The claimant shall provide to the Registry translations of at least the Statement of claim and the information required in Rule 13.1(a) to (p) in a language provided for by paragraph 7.

Rule 272 – Notice of service and non-service of the Statement of claim

1. The Registry shall inform the claimant of the date on which the Statement of claim is deemed served under Rule 271.6.

2. Where the Registry has served the Statement of claim by registered letter with acknowledgement of receipt or equivalent and the Statement of claim is returned to the Registry for any reason, the Registry shall inform the claimant.

3. Paragraph 2 shall apply *mutatis mutandis* where the Registry has served the Statement of claim by means of electronic communication and the relevant electronic message appears not to have been received.

SECTION 2 – SERVICE OUTSIDE THE CONTRACTING MEMBER STATES

Rule 273 - Scope of this Section
This Section applies to service of a Statement of claim outside the Contracting Member States.

Rule 274 - Service outside the Contracting Member States
1. Where a Statement of claim is to be served outside the Contracting Member States, it shall be so served by the Registry
   (a) by any method provided by:
      (i) The law of the European Union on the service of documents in civil and commercial matters [Regulation (EU) 2020/1784] where it applies;
      (ii) The Hague Service Convention or any other applicable convention or agreement where it applies; or
      (iii) to the extent that there is no such convention or agreement in force, either by service through diplomatic or consular channels from the Contracting Member State in which the sub-registry of the relevant division is established;
   (b) where service in accordance with paragraph 1(a) could not be effected by any method permitted by the law of the state where service is to be effected or as authorised by the Court under Rule 275.
2. No Statement of claim may be served under this Rule 274 in a manner which is contrary to the law of the state where service is effected.
3. The Registry shall inform the claimant of the date on which the Statement of claim is deemed served under paragraph 1.
4. The Registry shall inform the claimant if for any reason service pursuant to paragraph 1 cannot be effected.

SECTION 3 – SERVICE BY AN ALTERNATIVE METHOD

Rule 275 - Service of the Statement of claim by an alternative method or at an alternative place
1. Where service in accordance with Section 1 or 2 could not be effected the Court on an application by the claimant that there is a good reason to authorise service by a method or at a place not otherwise permitted by this Chapter, the Court may by way of order permit service by an alternative method or at an alternative place.
2. On a reasoned request by the claimant, the Court may order that steps already taken to bring the Statement of claim to the attention of the defendant by an alternative method or at an alternative place is good service.
3. An order under this rule shall specify:
   (a) the method or place of service;
   (b) the date on which the Statement of claim is deemed served; and
   (c) the period for filing the Statement of defence.
4. No order for alternative service under this Rule shall be made permitting service in a manner that is contrary to the law of the state where service is to be effected.

SECTION 4 – SERVICE OF ORDERS, DECISIONS AND WRITTEN PLEADINGS

Rule 276 - Service of orders and decisions
1. Any order or decision of the Court shall be served on each of the parties in accordance with the provisions of Sections 1, 2 or 3 of this Chapter 2, as the case may be.

2. Decisions by default pursuant to Rule 355 resulting from failure of the defendant to lodge a Defence to revocation [Rule 50] or failure to lodge a Defence to the Statement for a declaration of non-infringement [Rule 67] within the time limit set by these Rules or by the Court, may be served on the defendant at the place of business of a professional representative or legal practitioner as defined in Article 134 EPC who is recorded as the appointed representative for the subject European patent with unitary effect, the subject of the proceedings, in the Register for unitary patent protection [Regulation (EU) No 1257/2012, Article 2(e)] or in the national patent register [Rule 8.5(a)].

Rule 277 – Decisions by default under Part 5, Chapter 11
No decision by default shall be entered under Part 5, Chapter 11 unless the Court is satisfied that either:
(a) the Statement of claim was served by a method prescribed by the internal law of the state addressed for the service of documents in domestic actions upon persons who are within its territory; or
(b) the Statement of claim was actually served on the defendant under this Chapter 2.

Rule 278 – Service of written pleadings and other documents
1. As soon as practicable after written pleadings have been received at the Registry, the Registry shall serve the pleadings and any other document lodged with the pleadings on the other party by means of electronic communication except if the pleading contains a request for an ex parte proceeding.
2. Where service by means of electronic communication cannot be effected, the Registry shall serve the written pleadings on the party by:
  (a) registered letter with acknowledgement of receipt or equivalent; or
  (b) any method authorised by the Court under Rule 275.
3. Service under paragraph 2(a) shall be effected at the following place:
  (a) where the party is a company or other legal person: at its statutory seat, central administration, principal place of business or at any place within the Contracting Member States where the company or other legal person has a place of business;
  (b) where the party is an individual: at his usual or last known residence within the Contracting Member States.
4. Rule 271.6 and 272 shall apply *mutatis mutandis.*
5. Where a party is represented pursuant to Rule 8.1, the pleadings and other documents referred to in paragraph 1 shall be served on that representative. Paragraph 2 shall apply *mutatis mutandis.*

Rule 279 – Change of electronic address for service
Where the electronic address for service of a party changes, that party must give notice in writing of the change as soon as it has taken place to the Registry and every other party [Rule 6.3].

CHAPTER 3 – RIGHTS AND OBLIGATIONS OF REPRESENTATIVES

Rule 284 – Duty of representatives not to misrepresent facts or cases
A representative of a party shall not misrepresent cases or facts before the Court either knowingly or with good reasons to know.

Relation to Agreement: Article 48(6)

Rule 285 – Powers of attorney
1. A representative who claims to be representing a party shall be accepted as such provided however the Court may order a representative to produce a written authority if his representative powers are challenged.

2. In the event of a successful challenge to a representative's authority pursuant to paragraph 1 the Court may make an order pursuant to Rule 291.

Rule 286 – Certificate that a representative is authorised to practice before the Court
1. A representative pursuant to Article 48(1) of the Agreement shall lodge at the Registry a certificate that he is a lawyer authorised to practise before a court of a Member State of the European Union. A lawyer within the meaning of Article 48(1) of the Agreement is a person who is authorised to pursue professional activities under a title referred to in Article 1 of Directive 98/5/EC and by way of exception a person with equivalent legal professional qualifications who, owing to national rules, is permitted to practice in patent infringement and invalidity litigation but not under such title. In subsequent actions the representative may refer to the certificate previously lodged.
2. A representative pursuant to Article 48(2) of the Agreement shall lodge at the Registry the European Patent Litigation Certificate as defined by the Administrative Committee or otherwise justify that he has appropriate qualifications to represent a party before the Court. In subsequent actions such representative may refer to the certificate or other evidence of appropriate qualification previously lodged.

Rule 287 – Attorney-client privilege
1. Where a client seeks advice from a lawyer or a patent attorney he has instructed in a professional capacity, whether in connection with proceedings before the Court or otherwise, then any confidential communication (whether written or oral) between them relating to the seeking or the provision of that advice is privileged from disclosure, whilst it remains confidential, in any proceedings before the Court or in arbitration or mediation proceedings before the Centre.
2. This privilege applies also to communications between a client and a lawyer or patent attorney employed by the client and instructed to act in a professional capacity, whether in connection with proceedings before the Court or otherwise.
3. This privilege extends to the work product of the lawyer or patent attorney (including communications between lawyers and/or patent attorneys employed in the same firm or entity or between lawyers and/or patent attorneys employed by the same client) and to any record of a privileged communication.
4. This privilege prevents the lawyer or patent attorney and his client from being questioned or examined about the contents or nature of their communications.
5. This privilege may be expressly waived by the client.
6. For the purpose of Rules 287 and 288:
   (a) the expression 'lawyer' shall mean a person as defined in Rule 286.1 and any other person who is qualified to practise as a lawyer and to give legal advice under the law of the state where he practises and who is professionally instructed to give such advice.
   (b) the expression 'patent attorney' shall include a person who is recognised as eligible to give advice under the law of the state where he practises in relation to the protection of any invention or to the prosecution or litigation of any patent or patent application and is professionally consulted to give such advice.
7. The expression 'patent attorney' shall also include a professional representative before the European Patent Office pursuant to Article 134 (1) EPC.

Relation to Agreement: Article 48(4)

Rule 288 – Litigation privilege
Where a client, or a lawyer or patent attorney as specified in Rule 287.1, .2, .6 and .7 instructed by a client in a professional capacity, communicates confidentially with a third party for the purposes of obtaining information or evidence of any nature for the purpose of or for use in any proceedings,

including proceedings before the European Patent Office, such communications shall be privileged from disclosure in the same way and to the same extent as provided for in Rule 287.

Relation to Agreement: Article 48(5)

Rule 289 – Privileges, immunities and facilities

1. Representatives appearing before the Court shall enjoy immunity in respect of words spoken or written by them concerning the action or the parties.
2. Representatives shall enjoy the following further privileges and facilities:
   (a) papers and documents relating to the proceedings shall be exempt from both search and seizure;
   (b) any allegedly infringing product or device relating to the proceedings shall be exempt from both search and seizure when brought to the Court for the purposes of the proceedings.

In the event of a dispute, customs officials or police may seal those papers, documents or allegedly infringing products or devices. They shall then be immediately forwarded to the Court for inspection in the presence of the Registrar and of the person concerned.

3. Representatives shall be entitled to travel in the course of duty without hindrance.
4. The privileges, immunities and facilities specified in paragraphs 1 to 3 are granted exclusively in the interests of the proper conduct of proceedings.
5. The Court may waive the immunity where it considers that a representative is guilty of conduct which is contrary to the proper conduct of proceedings.

Relation with Agreement: Article 48

Rule 290 – Powers of the Court as regards representatives

1. As regards representatives who appear before it, the Court shall have the powers normally accorded to courts of law, under the conditions laid down in Rule 291.
2. Representatives who appear before the Court shall strictly comply with any code of conduct adopted for such representatives by the Administrative Committee.

Rule 291 – Exclusion from the proceedings

1. If the Court considers that the conduct of a party's representative towards the Court, towards any judge of the Court or towards any member of the staff of the Registry is incompatible with the dignity of the Court or with the requirements of the proper administration of justice, or that such representative uses his rights for purposes other than those for which they were granted, or that such representative is otherwise in breach of any code of conduct adopted pursuant to Rule 290.2 it shall so inform the person concerned. On the same grounds, the Court may at any time, after having given the person concerned an opportunity to be heard, exclude that person from the proceedings by way of order. That order shall have immediate effect.
2. Where a party's representative is excluded from the proceedings, the proceedings shall be stayed for a period fixed by the presiding judge in order to enable the party concerned to appoint another representative.

Rule 292 – Patent attorneys' right of audience

1. For the purposes of Article 48(4) of the Agreement, the term 'patent attorneys' assisting a representative referred to in Article 48(1) and/or (2) of the Agreement shall mean persons meeting the requirements of Rule 287.6(b) or .7 and practising in a Contracting Member State.
2. Such patent attorneys shall be allowed to speak at hearings of the Court at the discretion of the Court and subject to the representative's responsibility to coordinate the presentation of a party's case.

3. Rules 285 and 287 to 291 shall apply *mutatis mutandis.*

Relation with Agreement: Article 48(4)

Rule 293 - Change of a representative
Any change of representative shall take effect from the receipt by the Registry of notification that a new representative shall in future be representing the party concerned. Until the moment where such statement is received, the former representative remains responsible for the conduct of the proceedings and for communications between the Court and the party concerned.

Rule 294 - Removal from the register of representatives
An Application to remove a representative's name, being a representative qualified pursuant to Article 48(1) of the Agreement, from the register of representatives may be made:
(a) by the representative himself in the event he retires or for any other reason ceases to satisfy the requirements of Rule 286;
(b) by a representative on behalf of a listed representative who has died.

CHAPTER 4 – STAY OF PROCEEDINGS

Rule 295 - Stay of proceedings
The Court may stay proceedings:
(a) where it is seized of an action relating to a patent which is also the subject of opposition proceedings or limitation proceedings (including subsequent appeal proceedings) before the European Patent Office or a national authority where a decision in such proceedings may be expected to be given rapidly;
(b) where it is seized of an action relating to a supplementary protection certificate which is also the subject of proceedings before a national court or authority;
(c) where an appeal is brought before the Court of Appeal against a decision or order of the Court of First Instance:
 (i) disposing of the substantive issues in part only;
 (ii) disposing of an admissibility issue or a Preliminary objection;
(d) at the joint request of the parties;
(e) pursuant to Rule 37;
(f) pursuant to Rules 75 and 76;
(g) pursuant to Rule 118;
(h) pursuant to Rule 136;
(i) pursuant to Rule 266;
(j) pursuant to Rules 310 and 311;
(k) pursuant to Rule 346;
(l) to give effect to Union law, in particular the provisions of Regulation (EU) No 1215/2012 and the Lugano Convention;
(m) in any other case where the proper administration of justice so requires.

Rule 296 - Duration and effects of a stay of proceedings
1. The stay of proceedings shall take effect on the date indicated in the order to stay or, in the absence of such an indication, on the date of that order. The Court shall stipulate what effect the stay shall have on any existing orders.
2. Where the order to stay does not fix the length of the stay, it shall end on the date indicated in the order to resume proceedings or, in the absence of such indication, on the date of the order to resume.

3. While proceedings are stayed, time shall cease to run for the purposes of procedural periods. Time shall begin to run afresh for the purposes of procedural periods from the date on which the stay of proceedings comes to an end.

Rule 297 – Resumption of proceedings

Any decision referred to in Rule 296.2 ordering the resumption of proceedings before the end of the stay shall be made by order of the judge-rapporteur after hearing the parties. The judge-rapporteur may refer the matter to the panel.

Rule 298 – Accelerated proceedings before the European Patent Office

The Court may of its own motion or at the request of a party request that opposition proceedings or limitation proceedings (including any subsequent appeal proceedings) before the European Patent Office be accelerated in accordance with the proceedings of the European Patent Office. The Court may stay its proceedings in accordance with Rule 295(a) pending the outcome of such request and any subsequent accelerated proceedings.

CHAPTER 5 – TIME PERIODS

Rule 300 – Calculation of periods

Any period of time prescribed by the Agreement, the Statute, these Rules or any order of the Court for the taking of any procedural step shall be laid down in terms of full days, weeks, months or years and shall be reckoned as follows:

(a) computation shall start on the day following the day on which the relevant event occurred; in the case of service of a document, the relevant event shall be the receipt of that document in accordance with Part 5, Chapter 2;

(b) when a period is expressed as one year or a certain number of years, it shall expire in the relevant subsequent year in the month having the same name and on the day having the same number as the month and the day on which the said event occurred. If the relevant subsequent month has no day with the same number, the period shall expire on the last day of that month;

(c) when a period is expressed as one month or a certain number of months, it shall expire in the relevant subsequent month on the day which has the same number as the day on which the said event occurred. If the relevant subsequent month has no day with the same number, the period shall expire on the last day of that month;

(d) when a period is expressed as one week or a certain number of weeks, it shall expire in the relevant subsequent week on the day having the same name as the day on which the said event occurred;

(e) day shall mean a calendar day unless expressed as a working day;

(f) calendar days shall include official holidays of the Contracting Member State in which the division or the seat of the central division or its section concerned or the Court of Appeal is located, Saturdays and Sundays;

(g) working days shall not include official holidays of the Contracting Member State in which the division or the seat of the central division or its section concerned or the Court of Appeal is located, Saturdays and Sundays;

(h) periods shall not be suspended during the judicial vacations.

Rule 301 – Automatic extension of periods

1. If a period expires on a Saturday, Sunday or official holiday of the Contracting Member State in which the division or the seat of the central division or its section concerned or the Court of Appeal is located, it shall be extended until the end of the first following working day.

2. Paragraph 1 shall apply *mutatis mutandis* if documents filed in electronic form cannot be received by the Court.

CHAPTER 6 – PARTIES TO PROCEEDINGS

SECTION 1 – PLURALITY OF PARTIES

Rule 302 - Plurality of claimants or patents
1. The Court may order that proceedings commenced by a plurality of claimants or in respect of a plurality of patents be heard in separate proceedings.
2. Where the Court orders a separation of proceedings the Court shall decide on the payment of a new court fee or court fees in accordance with Part 6.
3. The Court may order that parallel infringement or revocation proceedings relating to the same patent or patents and before the same local or regional division or the central division or the Court of Appeal be heard together where it is in the interests of justice to do so.

Rule 303 - Plurality of defendants
1. Proceedings may be started against a plurality of defendants if the Court has competence in respect of all of them.
2. The Court may separate the proceedings into two or more separate proceedings against different defendants.
3. Where the Court orders a separation of proceedings under paragraph 2, the claimants in the new proceedings shall pay a new court fee in accordance with Part 6, unless the Court decides otherwise.

SECTION 2 – CHANGE IN PARTIES

Rule 305 - Change in parties
1. The Court may, on application by a party, order a person to:
- (a) be added as a party;
- (b) cease to be a party;
- (c) be substituted for a party.

2. The Court shall invite other parties to the proceedings to comment on the application, as soon as practicable after service of the application.
3. When ordering that a person shall become a party or shall cease to be a party, the Court may make appropriate orders as to payment of court fees and costs as regards such party.

Rule 306 - Consequences for the proceedings
1. Where the Court orders that a party be added, removed or substituted under Rule 305.1, it shall give directions to regulate the consequences as to case management.
2. The Court shall also determine the extent to which a new party is bound by the proceedings as then constituted.

SECTION 3 – DEATH, DEMISE OR INSOLVENCY OF A PARTY

Rule 310 - Death or demise of a party
1. If a party dies or ceases to exist during proceedings, the proceedings shall be stayed until such party is replaced by his successor. The Court may specify a period in this respect.
2. If there are more than two parties to the proceedings, the Court may decide that:
- (a) proceedings between the remaining parties be continued separately; and

(b) the stay shall only concern the proceedings regarding the party that no longer exists.
3. If the successor of the party that died or ceased to exist does not continue the proceedings of his own motion, within a period specified by the Court, any other party may apply to have the successor added to or substituted for a party.
4. The Court shall decide who shall be added or substituted as a party pursuant to Rule 305 and 306 shall apply *mutatis mutandis*.

Rule 311 – Insolvency of a party
1. If a party is declared insolvent under the law applicable to the insolvency proceedings the Court shall stay the proceedings up to three months. They may be stayed until the competent national authority or person dealing with the insolvency has decided whether to continue the proceedings or not. Where the competent national authority or person dealing with the insolvency decides not to continue the proceedings, the Court may decide, upon a reasoned request by the other party, that the proceedings should be continued in accordance with the applicable national insolvency law.
2. Proceedings may also be stayed at the request of a temporary administrator who has been appointed before a party is declared insolvent.
3. The claimant may withdraw the action against an insolvent defendant in accordance with Rule 265 and a defendant may withdraw a Counterclaim against an insolvent claimant. Such withdrawal shall not prejudice the action against other parties.
4. If proceedings are continued, the effect of a decision of the Court as regards the insolvent party in the action shall be determined by the law applicable to the insolvency proceedings.

SECTION 4 – TRANSFER OF PATENT

Rule 312 – Transfer of the patent or patent application during proceedings
1. If a patent or patent application is transferred, for one or more Contracting Member States, to another proprietor after proceedings have been started before the Court, the Court may authorise the new proprietor to be added as a party or substituted for a party pursuant to Rule 305 to the extent that the patent and the claims in the proceedings have been assigned to the new proprietor. Rule 306 shall apply *mutatis mutandis*.
2. If the new proprietor takes over the proceedings, no new court fee shall be payable, even if the new proprietor is represented by a new representative.
3. If the new proprietor chooses not to take over the proceedings, any decision in proceedings that have been recorded in the register shall be binding upon him.

SECTION 5 – INTERVENTION

Rule 313 – Application to intervene
1. An Application to intervene may be lodged at any stage of the proceedings before the Court of First Instance or the Court of Appeal by any person establishing a legal interest in the result of an action submitted to the Court (hereinafter 'the intervener').
2. An Application to intervene shall be admissible only if it is made in support, in whole or in part, of a claim, order or remedy sought by one of the parties and is made before the closure of the written procedure unless the Court of First Instance or Court of Appeal orders otherwise.
3. The intervener shall be represented in accordance with Article 48 of the Agreement.
4. The Application to intervene shall contain:
   (a) a reference to the action number of the file;
   (b) the names of the intervener and of the intervener's representative, as well as postal and electronic addresses for service and the names of the persons authorised to accept service;

(c) the claim, order or remedy in support of which intervention is sought by the intervener; and
(d) a statement of the facts establishing the right to intervene under paragraphs 1 and 2.

Rule 314 - Order on Application to intervene
The judge-rapporteur shall decide on the admissibility of the Application to intervene by way of order. The other parties shall be given an opportunity to be heard beforehand.

Rule 315 - Statement in intervention
1. If an Application to intervene is admissible, the judge-rapporteur or the presiding judge shall:
   (a) inform the parties to proceedings; and
   (b) specify a period within which the intervener may lodge a Statement in intervention.
2. The Registry shall as soon as practicable serve on the intervener any written pleading served by the parties. On a reasoned request by a party the Court may for the protection of confidential information order that a pleading or part of a pleading be disclosed only to certain named persons and subject to appropriate terms of non-disclosure.
3. The Statement in intervention shall contain:
   (a) a statement as to the issues involving the intervener and one or more of the parties, and their connection to the matters in dispute;
   (b) the arguments of law; and
   (c) the facts and evidence relied on.
4. The intervener shall be treated as a party, unless otherwise ordered by the Court.

Rule 316 - Invitation to intervene
1. The judge-rapporteur or the presiding judge may, of his own motion after hearing the parties, or on a reasoned request from a party, invite any person concerned by the outcome of the dispute to inform the Court, within a period to be specified, whether he wishes to intervene in the proceedings.
2. If the person wishes to intervene, he shall present his Application to intervene within one month of service of the invitation and his Statement in intervention within such further period to be specified by the judge-rapporteur or the presiding judge. Rules 313.3, .4, 314 and 315 shall apply *mutatis mutandis*.
3. An intervener shall be bound by the decision in the action.

Rule 316A - Forced intervention
1. A party who contends that the person should be bound by the decision in the action even if he refuses to intervene shall give reasons for this contention in its reasoned request. In such a case the invitation must include these reasons and must state that the party making the request contends that the person should be bound by the decision in the action even if that person refuses to intervene.
2. If the person invited to intervene pursuant to Rule 316.1 does not intervene but wishes to contend that he should not be bound by the decision in the action, he shall lodge a statement to that effect within the one month period referred to in Rule 316.2. If no such statement is lodged within the time specified he shall be bound by the decision in the action as between himself and any other party to the action and shall not be entitled to argue that the decision in the action was wrong or that the inviting party did not conduct the proceedings leading to the decision in the action properly. If a statement is lodged within the time specified then the Court shall decide whether the person invited to intervene shall be bound having heard the parties and the person invited to intervene. If the Court so decides, the person invited to intervene may present an Application to intervene within one month of service of the Court's decision. Rule 316.2 shall apply. If the person invited to intervene fails to present such an application, he shall be bound by the decision in the action.

Rule 317 – No appeal against an order on the Application to intervene
There shall be no appeal against an order refusing an Application to intervene.

SECTION 6 – RE-ESTABLISHMENT OF RIGHTS

Rule 320 – Re-establishment of rights
1. Where a party has failed to observe a time-limit set by these Rules or the Court for a cause which, despite all due care having been taken by the party, was outside his control and the non-observance of this time limit has had the direct consequence of causing the party to lose a right or means of redress, the relevant panel of the Court may upon the request of that party re-establish the right or means of redress.
2. The Application for Re-establishment of rights shall be lodged with the Registry within one month of the removal of the cause for non-observance of the time-limit but in any event within six months of the non-observed time-limit. Within that time-limit a fee shall be paid for a Request for Re-establishment of rights, in accordance with Part 6.
3. The Application shall:
   (a) state the grounds on which it is based and shall set out the facts on which it relies; and
   (b) contain the evidence relied on in the form of affidavits from all persons involved in the non-observance of the time-limit and the persons involved in establishing the precautionary measures of due care taken in order to avoid such cases of non-compliance.
4. The omitted act shall be performed or completed together with Application for Re-establishment within the time-limit mentioned in paragraph 2.
5. There shall be no grant of Re-establishment of rights in respect of the non-observance of the time limit mentioned in paragraphs 2 and 4 of this Rule.
6. The panel shall decide on the Application for Re-establishment of rights by way of order. The other parties shall be given an opportunity to be heard beforehand.
7. There shall be no right to appeal from an order rejecting an Application for Re-establishment of rights or from an order granting Re-establishment of rights.

CHAPTER 7 – MISCELLANEOUS PROVISIONS ON LANGUAGES

Rule 321 – Application by both parties to use of the language in which the patent was granted as language of the proceedings
1. At any time during the written procedure, any party may lodge an Application by both parties to use the language in which the patent was granted as language of the proceedings, in accordance with Article 49(3) of the Agreement. The Application shall state that both parties agree to use the language in which the patent was granted as the language of the proceedings.
2. As soon as practicable, the Registry shall forward the Application to the panel.
3. The panel shall, as soon as practicable, decide whether it approves the Application by both parties to use the language in which the patent was granted as the language of the proceedings. Where the panel does not approve the Application, the Registry shall as soon as practicable inform the parties who may request, within 10 days, that the action be referred to the central division and the action shall be transferred accordingly.
4. Where the action is transferred to the central division Rule 41 shall apply *mutatis mutandis*.

Relation with Agreement: Article 49(3)

Rule 322 – Proposal from the judge-rapporteur to use of the language in which the patent was granted as language of the proceedings
At any time during the written procedure and the interim procedure, the judge-rapporteur may, of his own motion or on a request by a party, after consulting the panel, propose to the parties that the language of the proceedings be changed to the language in which the patent was granted, in accordance with Article 49(4) of the Agreement. If the parties and panel agree the language of the proceedings shall be changed.

Relation with Agreement: Article 49(4)

Rule 323 – Application by one party to use the language in which the patent was granted as language of the proceedings
1. If a party wishes to use the language in which the patent was granted as language of the proceedings, in accordance with Article 49(5) of the Agreement, the party shall include such Application in the Statement of Claim, in the case of a claimant, or in the Statement of Defence, in the case of a defendant. The judge-rapporteur shall forward the Application to the President of the Court of First Instance.
2. The President shall invite the other party to indicate, within 10 days, its position on the use of the language in which the patent was granted as language of the proceedings.
3. The President, having consulted the panel of the division, may order that the language in which the patent was granted shall be the language of the proceedings and may make the order conditional on specific translation or interpretation arrangements.

Relation with Agreement: Article 49(5)

Rule 324 – Consequences where the language of the proceedings is changed in the course of the proceedings
An Application under Rule 321.1 or 323.1 shall specify whether existing pleadings and other documents should be translated and at whose cost. If the parties cannot agree the judge-rapporteur or the President of the Court of First Instance, as the case may be, shall decide in accordance with Rule 323.3.

CHAPTER 8 – CASE MANAGEMENT

Relation with Agreement: Article 43

Rule 331 – Responsibility for case management
1. During the written procedure and the interim procedure, case management shall be the responsibility of the judge-rapporteur subject to Rules 102 and 333.
2. The judge-rapporteur may refer a proposed order to the panel.
3. After the closure of the interim conference, case management shall be the responsibility of the presiding judge in consultation with the judge-rapporteur.
4. The Registry shall serve any case management orders on the parties as soon as practicable after the decision of the judge-rapporteur, presiding judge or panel.

Rule 332 – General principles of case management
Active case management includes:
(a) encouraging the parties to co-operate with each other during the proceedings;
(b) identifying the issues at an early stage;
(c) deciding promptly which issues need full investigation and disposing summarily of other issues;
(d) deciding the order in which issues are to be resolved;

(e) encouraging the parties to make use of the Centre and facilitating the use of the Centre;
(f) helping the parties to settle the whole or part of the action;
(g) fixing timetables or otherwise controlling the progress of the action;
(h) considering whether the likely benefits of taking a particular step justify the cost of taking it;
(i) dealing with as many aspects of the action as the Court can on the same occasion;
(j) dealing with the action without the parties needing to attend in person;
(k) making use of available technical means; and
(l) giving directions to ensure that the hearing of the action proceeds quickly and efficiently.

Rule 333 – Review of case management orders
1. Case management decisions or orders made by the judge-rapporteur or the presiding judge shall be reviewed by the panel, on a reasoned Application by a party.
2. An Application for the review of a case management order shall be lodged within 15 days of service of the order. The Application shall set out the grounds for review and the evidence, if any, in support of the grounds. The other party shall be given an opportunity to be heard.
3. The party seeking a review shall pay the fee for the review of a case management order, in accordance with Part 6. Rule 15.2 shall apply *mutatis mutandis*.
4. The panel shall as soon as practicable decide the Application for review and make any necessary revised case management order.
5. A decision of the panel on an Application for review is a procedural decision for the purposes of Rule 220.2.

Rule 334 – Case management powers
Except where the Agreement, the Statute or these Rules provide otherwise, the judge-rapporteur, the presiding judge or the panel may:
(a) extend or shorten the period for compliance with any rule or order [Rule 9.3];
(b) adjourn or bring forward the interim conference or the oral hearing;
(c) communicate with the parties to instruct them about wishes or requirements of the Court;
(d) direct a separate hearing of any issue;
(e) decide the order in which issues are to be decided;
(f) exclude an issue from consideration;
(g) dismiss or decide on a claim after a decision on a preliminary issue makes a decision on further issues irrelevant to the outcome of the action;
(h) dismiss a claim summarily if it has no prospect of succeeding;
(i) consolidate any matter or issue or order them to be heard together;
(j) make any order pursuant to Rules 103 to 109.

Rule 335 – Varying or revoking orders
The power of the Court to make a case management order includes a power to vary or revoke such order.

Rule 336 – Exercise of case management powers
The Court may exercise its case management powers on the application by a party or of its own motion, unless otherwise provided.

Rule 337 – Orders of the Court's own motion
Where the Court proposes to make an order of its own motion, it may do so but only after hearing the parties.

Rule 340 - Connection Joinder

1. In the interests of the proper administration of justice and of avoiding inconsistent decisions, where more than one action concerning the same patent (whether or not between the same parties) is pending before:

(a) different panels (whether in the same or different divisions); or

(b) different panels of the Court of Appeal,

the panels may by agreement, at any time, after hearing the parties, order that two or more actions shall, on account of the connection between them, be heard together. Article 33 of the Agreement shall be respected.

2. The actions may subsequently be disjoined.

CHAPTER 9 – RULES RELATING TO THE ORGANISATION OF THE COURT

Rule 341 - Precedence

1. With the exception of the President of the Court of Appeal and the President of the Court of First Instance, the judges shall rank in precedence according to their seniority in office.

2. Where there is equal seniority in office, precedence shall be determined by age.

3. Retiring judges who are reappointed shall retain their former precedence.

4. The Presidium may determine the presiding judge of a panel. In the absence of such a determination by the Presidium and unless otherwise agreed by the panel the most senior judge shall be the presiding judge.

Rule 342 - Dates, times and place of the sittings of the Court

1. The duration of judicial vacations shall be fixed by the President of the Court of Appeal, on a proposal from the Presidium. The dates and times of the sittings of the Court shall be decided by the presiding judge of the panel in question.

2. The Court may choose to hold one or more particular sittings in a place other than that in which it has its seat. Subject to any rules agreed by the relevant Contracting Member States pursuant to Article 7(5) of the Agreement where an action is pending before a regional division the judge-rapporteur or the presiding judge shall designate the place within the region for each hearing having regard to the residence or place of business of the defendant and all other relevant circumstances such as the facilities available, the financial means of the parties and the place of actual or threatened infringement.

Relation with Statute: Article 17

Rule 343 - Order in which actions are to be dealt with

1. The Court shall deal with the actions before it in the order in which they become ready for hearing in accordance with Rule 108.

2. The presiding judge of a panel may, after hearing the parties [Rule 264]:

(a) direct that a particular action be given priority and that time limits provided for in these Rules be shortened;

(b) defer an action to be dealt with later, in particular with a view to facilitating an amicable settlement of the dispute.

Rule 344 - Deliberations

1. The Court shall deliberate in closed session.

2. The presiding judge shall preside over the deliberations. Only those judges who were present at the oral hearing may take part in the deliberations on the decision.

3. The deliberation of the Court shall take place as soon as possible after the closure of the oral hearing.

Rule 345 – Composition of panels and assignment of actions

1. The President of the Court of First Instance or a judge to whom he has delegated this task in a division, the seat of the central division or one of its sections shall allocate the judges to the panels of the local and regional divisions, the seat of the central division and its sections.
2. The allocation shall be in conformity with Article 8 of the Agreement.
3. The actions pending in the division, the seat of the central division or one of its sections shall be assigned to the panels by the Registrar following an action-distribution-scheme established by the presiding judge of each local or regional division, the seat of the central division and its sections (being the judge appointed by the Presidium as the presiding judge) for the duration of one calendar year, preferably distributing the actions according to the date of receipt of the actions at the division or section.
4. Each panel may delegate to one or more judges of the panel:
   (a) the function of acting as a single judge; or
   (b) the function of acting for the panel in the procedures of Part 1 Chapter 4 (Procedure for the Determination of Damages and Compensation, including the procedure for the laying open of books) and Chapter 5 (Procedure for Cost Decisions). These functions may be delegated to the judge-rapporteur who has prepared the action for the oral hearing.
5. The President of the Court of First Instance or a judge to whom he has delegated this task in a division, the seat of the central division or one of its sections shall designate the judges assigned to each division, the seat of the central division and each of its sections as standing judges for urgent actions. The assignment may be limited to certain periods of time.
6. If all parties agree to having the action heard by a single judge, the presiding judge of the panel to which the action is allocated shall assign the action to a legally qualified judge of the panel.
7. Where paragraphs 1 to 6 apply to decisions by the presiding judge of the seat of the central division or one of its sections, the President of the Court of First Instance may of his own motion review that decision.
8. Paragraphs 1 to 6 shall apply *mutatis mutandis* to the Court of Appeal; the President of the Court of Appeal exercising the respective functions.

Relation with Statute: Article 19

Rule 346 – Application of Article 7 of the Statute

1. A party who believes to have reason to object to a judge taking part in proceedings pursuant to Article 7(4) of the Statute shall as soon as is reasonably practicable in the circumstances notify the President of the Court of First Instance or the President of the Court of Appeal wherever the case is pending that it objects to the judge taking part in the proceedings.
2. Any failure to notify an objection as soon as is reasonably practicable shall amount to a waiver of such objection.
3. The President concerned shall, after hearing the judge involved, decide whether the objection is valid pursuant to Article 7(2) and (4) of the Statute and considering the circumstances.
4. In case of any difficulty within the meaning of Article 7(5) of the Statute the President concerned shall refer the matter to the Presidium.
5. If it is decided that the objection is valid the judge concerned shall be replaced on the panel of judges allocated to the case concerned.
6. The panel assigned to the proceedings may decide to continue with the proceedings or to stay the proceedings pending the final decision of the President concerned or the Presidium. The President concerned or the Presidium may give instructions in the final decision as to the future conduct of the proceedings.

Relation with Statute: Article 7

CHAPTER 10 – DECISIONS AND ORDERS

Rule 350 - Decisions

1. Any decision shall contain:
   (a) the statement that it is a decision of the Court;
   (b) the date of its delivery;
   (c) the names of the presiding judge, the judge-rapporteur and other judges taking part in it;
   (d) the names of the parties and of the parties' representatives;
   (e) an indication of the claim, order or remedy sought by the parties;
   (f) a summary of the facts; and
   (g) the grounds for the decision.
2. The order of the Court consequential upon the decision (other than costs) including any order giving immediate effect to an injunction, shall be appended to the decision. The order shall comply with Rule 351.
3. Any dissenting opinion shall be attached to the Court's decision.
4. The decision of the Court of First Instance shall contain a summary of the requests and facts submitted by the parties and a statement of the facts and arguments on which the Court bases its decision.
5. All decisions shall be recorded in the register.

Relation with Statute: Article 35(4)

Rule 351 - Orders

1. Every order shall contain:
   (a) the statement that it is an order of the judge-rapporteur, of the standing judge, of the single judge, of the presiding judge, of a President of the Court or of the Court;
   (b) the date of its adoption;
   (c) the names of any judge taking part in its adoption;
   (d) the names of the parties and of the parties' representatives; and
   (e) the operative part of the order.
2. Where, in accordance with these Rules the Court grants leave to appeal an order the order shall in addition contain:
   (a) a statement of the forms of order sought by the parties;
   (b) a summary of the facts; and
   (c) the grounds for the order.
3. All orders shall be recorded in the register.

Rule 352 - Binding effect of decisions or orders subject to security

1. Decisions and orders may be subject to the rendering of a security (whether by deposit or bank guarantee or otherwise) by a party to the other party for legal costs and other expenses and compensation for any damage incurred or likely to be incurred by the other party if the decisions and orders are enforced and subsequently revoked.
2. The Court may upon the application of a party release a security by order.

Rule 353 - Rectification of decisions and orders

The Court may, by way of order, of its own motion or on application by a party made within one month of service of the decision or order to be rectified, after hearing the parties, rectify clerical mistakes, errors in calculation and obvious slips in the decision or order.

Rule 354 – Enforcement

1. Subject to Rule 118.8 and 352 decisions and orders of the Court shall be directly enforceable from their date of service in each Contracting Member State. Enforcement shall take place in accordance with the enforcement procedures and conditions governed by the law of the particular Contracting Member State where enforcement takes place.
2. Where during an action an enforceable decision or order of the Court is subsequently varied or revoked, the Court may order the party which has enforced such decision or order, upon the request of the party against whom the decision or order has been enforced, to provide appropriate compensation for any injury caused by the enforcement. Rule 125 shall apply *mutatis mutandis*. Where an enforceable decision or order has been made pursuant to a finding of infringement of a patent and, following the conclusion of the action, the patent is amended or revoked, the Court may order, upon the request of the party against whom the decision or order would be enforceable, that the decision or order ceases to be enforceable.
3. The Court's decisions and orders may provide for periodic penalty payments payable to the Court in the event that a party fails to comply with the terms of the order or an earlier order. The value of such payments shall be set by the Court having regard to the importance of the order in question.
4. If it is alleged that a party has failed to comply with the terms of the order of the Court, the first instance panel of the division in question may decide on penalty payments provided for in the order upon the request of the other party or of its own motion. The procedure foreseen in Rule 264 shall apply. After having heard both parties the Court may make an appropriate order which may be subject to an appeal pursuant to Rule 220.2.

Relation with Agreement: Article 82

CHAPTER 11 – DECISION BY DEFAULT

Rule 355 – Decision by default (Court of First Instance)

1. Upon request a decision by default may be given against a party where:
   (a) the Rules of Procedure so provide if a party fails to take a step within the time limit foreseen in these Rules or set by the Court; or
   (b) without prejudice to Rules 116 and 117, the party which was duly summoned fails to appear at an oral hearing.
2. A decision by default against the defendant of the claim or counterclaim may only be given where the facts put forward by the claimant justify the remedy sought and the procedural conduct of the defendant does not preclude to give such decision.
3. A decision by default against the defendant of the claim or counterclaim may only be given where the time limits for the defence to the claim or counterclaim have expired and thus, it is established that the service of the claim or counterclaim was effected in sufficient time to enable the defendant to enter a defence.
4. A decision by default shall be enforceable. The Court may, however:
   (a) grant a stay of enforcement until it has given its decision on any Application under Rule 356; or
   (b) make enforcement subject to the provision of security; this security shall be released if no Application is made or if the Application fails.

Rule 356 – Application to set aside a decision by default

1. A party against whom a decision by default has been given may lodge an Application to set aside that decision within one month of service of the decision.
2. The Application to set aside a decision by default shall contain the party's explanation for the default. It shall mention the date and number of the decision by default. The party shall pay a fee for the Appli-

cation to set aside the decision by default, in accordance with Part 6. In the case of Rule 355.1(a) the Application shall be accompanied by the step the party has failed to take.
3. If the provisions of paragraph 2 are met the Application shall be allowed unless a party has been put on notice in an earlier decision that a further decision by default shall be final. If the Application is allowed, a note of allowance shall be included in any publication of the decision by default.

Relation with Statute: Article 37

Rule 357 - Decision by default (Court of Appeal)
1. Rules 355 and 356 shall apply *mutatis mutandis*, in particular where a respondent on whom a Statement of appeal and a Statement of the grounds of appeal have been duly served fails to lodge a Statement of response or where a party fails to file a Reply to a Statement of Cross-Appeal or translations ordered by the judge-rapporteur.
2. When considering whether to give a decision by default, the Court of Appeal may consider the merits of the appeal.
3. Rules 355 and 356 shall apply *mutatis mutandis* where the appellant fails to correct the deficiencies or to pay the fee pursuant to Rule 229.4 or to lodge the translations pursuant to Rule 232.1 within the period specified.

CHAPTER 12 – ACTIONS BOUND TO FAIL OR MANIFESTLY INADMISSIBLE

Rule 360 - No need to adjudicate
If the Court finds that an action has become devoid of purpose and that there is no longer any need to adjudicate on it, it may at any time, on the application of a party or of its own motion, after giving the parties an opportunity to be heard, dispose of the action by way of order.

Rule 361 - Action manifestly bound to fail
Where it is clear that the Court has no jurisdiction to take cognisance of an action or of certain of the claims therein or where the action or defence is, in whole or in part, manifestly inadmissible or manifestly lacking any foundation in law, the Court may, after giving the parties an opportunity to be heard, give a decision by way of order.

Rule 362 - Absolute bar to proceeding with an action
The Court may at any time, on the application of a party or of its own motion, after giving the parties an opportunity to be heard, decide that there exists an absolute bar to proceeding with an action, for example because of the application of the principle of res judicata.

Rule 363 - Orders dismissing manifestly inadmissible claims
1. Orders under Rules 360, 361 and 362 shall be taken by the panel upon the recommendation of the judge-rapporteur.
2. Where the decision is taken by the Court of First Instance pursuant to Rules 360, 361 and 362 it is a final decision within the meaning of Rule 220.1(a).

CHAPTER 13 – SETTLEMENT

Rule 365 - Confirmation by the Court of a settlement
1. Where the parties have concluded their action by way of settlement, they shall inform the judge-rapporteur. The Court shall confirm the settlement by decision of the Court [Rule 11.2], if requested by the parties, and the decision may be enforced as a final decision of the Court.

2. At the request of the parties the Court may order that details of the settlement are confidential.
3. Subject to paragraph 2 the decision of the Court under paragraph 1 shall be entered on the register.
4. The judge-rapporteur shall give a decision as to costs in accordance with the terms of the settlement or, failing that, at his discretion.

Relation with Agreement: Article 79

PART 6 – FEES AND LEGAL AID

COURT FEES

Rule 370 - Court fees
1. Court fees provided for in these Rules shall be paid in accordance with the provisions contained in this Part and the table of fees adopted by the Administrative Committee pursuant to Article 36 (3) of the Agreement (hereinafter: table of fees).
2. A fixed fee shall be paid in accordance with Section I (fixed fees) of the table of fees for the following actions at the Court of First Instance:
(a) Infringement action [Rule 15],
(b) Counterclaim for infringement [Rule 53],
(c) Action for declaration of non-infringement [Rule 70],
(d) Action for compensation for licence of right [Rule 80.3],
(e) Application to determine damages [Rule 132].
3. In addition to the fixed fee a value-based fee shall be paid in accordance with Section II (value-based fees) of the table of fees for those actions at the Court of First Instance set out in paragraph 2, which exceed a value of 500,000 EUR.
4. For the following procedures and actions at the Court of First Instance a fee shall be paid in accordance with Section III (other procedures and actions) of the table of fees adopted by the Administrative Committee:
(a) Revocation action [Rule 46],
(b) Counterclaim for revocation [Rule 26],
(c) Application for provisional measures [Rule 206.5],
(d) Action against a decision of the European Patent Office [Rule 88.3, 97.2],
(e) Application to preserve evidence [Rule 192.5],
(f) Application for an order for inspection [Rule199.2],
(g) Application for an order to freeze assets [Rule 200.2],
(h) Filing a protective letter [Rule 207.3],
(i) Application to prolong the period of a protective letter to be kept on the register [Rule.207.9],
(j) Application for rehearing [Rule 250],
(k) Application for re-establishment of rights [Rule 320.2],
(l) Application to review a case management order [Rule 333.3],
(m) Application to set aside decision by default [Rule 356.2].
5. For the following procedures at the Court of Appeal a fixed fee and, where applicable, a value based fee shall be paid in accordance with Section IV. of the table of fees:
(a) Appeal pursuant to Rule 220.1 (a) and (b) [Rule 228],
(b) Interlocutory appeal pursuant to Rule 220.1(c), appeal with leave of the Court of First Instance pursuant to Rule 220.2 or allowance by the Court of Appeal pursuant to Rule 220.4 or appeal of a cost decision with leave of the Court of Appeal pursuant to Rule 221.4 [Rule 228],
(c) Application for leave to appeal against cost decision pursuant to Rule 221 [Rule 228],
(d) Request for discretionary review pursuant to Rule 220.3, [Rule 228],

(e) Application for re-establishment of rights [Rule 320.2],
(f) Application to review a case management order pursuant to Rule 220.2 [R. 333.3],
(g) Application to set aside decision by default pursuant to Rule 357 [Rule 356.2],
(h) Application for rehearing pursuant to Rule 245.2 [Rule 250].

6. The assessment of the value of the relevant action in paragraphs 3 and 5 shall reflect the objective interest pursued by the filing party at the time of filing the action. In deciding on the value, the Court may in particular take into account the guidelines laid down in a decision of the Administrative Committee for this purpose.

7. If an action has more than one claimant and/or more than one defendant or if an action concerns a plurality of patents only one fixed fee and, if applicable, one value-based fee shall apply.

8. Small enterprises and micro-enterprises are required to pay only 60 % of the fees provided for in paragraphs 2 to 5 above (hereinafter: regular fees) subject to the following:

(a) In the Statement of claim or Counterclaim or in the application for a procedure or an appeal the party shall lodge with the Registry a notification in an electronic form in the language of the proceedings. In this notification the party shall provide an affirmation that he fulfils either the criteria of a 'small enterprise' or a 'micro-enterprise' as defined in Title I of the Annex to the Recommendation of the European Commission n° 2003/361 of 6 May 2003.
(b) If the requirements referred to above have not been met Rule 16.3 to .5 shall apply *mutatis mutandis*.
(c) The Court may, of its own motion, order the party to supply further documentation including any document relating to that party's financial resources. The application shall be dealt with by the Court as soon as practicable.
(d) The Court may, at any time, of its own motion, and after having heard the party order payment of
  (i) the remainder of the regular fee, in the event that payment of 60 % of the regular fees is manifestly disproportionate and unreasonable having regard to the financial capacity of the party;
  (ii) the remainder of the regular fee plus an additional 50 % of that regular fee, if the affirmation provided by the party is found to be wholly or partially incorrect. An order for the payment of an additional fee pursuant to (i) and (ii) above shall state the reasons for such order.
(e) If the additional fee is not paid within the time limit set by the Court, a decision by default against the party shall be given by the Court pursuant to Rule 355.

9. Fixed and value-based fees may be reimbursed as follows:

(a) If the action is heard by a single judge [Rule 345.6.] the party liable for the Court fee will be reimbursed by 25 % of the fee.
(b) In case of the withdrawal of an action [Rule 265] the party liable for the Court fees will be reimbursed by:
  (i) 60 % if the action is withdrawn before the closure of the written procedure
  (ii) 40 % if the action is withdrawn before the closure of the interim procedure
  (iii) 20 % if the action is withdrawn before the closure of the oral procedure
(c) If the parties have concluded their action by way of settlement the party liable for the Court fees will be reimbursed by:
  (i) 60 % if the action is settled before the closure of the written procedure
  (ii) 40 % if the action is settled before the closure of the interim procedure
  (iii) 20 % if the action is settled before the closure of the oral procedure
(d) Only one of the reimbursements referred to in paragraph 9 (a), (b) and (c) will apply per action and party. Where more than one reimbursement is applicable, the larger will be applied for each party.

(e) In exceptional cases, having regard, in particular, to the stage of the proceedings and the procedural behaviour of the party, the Court may deny or decrease the reimbursement payable according to paragraph 9 (b) and (c) of the aforementioned provisions.

10. If the amount of Court fees threatens the economic existence of a party who is not a natural person, and has presented reasonably available and plausible evidence to support that the amount of Court fees threatens its economic existence, the Court may upon request by that party, wholly or partially reimburse the fixed and value-based fee. In reaching a decision the Court shall reflect on all circumstances of the case including the procedural behaviour of the party. Before making such a decision the Court may give the other party an opportunity to be heard.

11. The party seeking reimbursement under paragraphs 9 and 10 shall lodge a reasoned Application for reimbursement to the Court. The Court shall deal with the application without delay and if satisfied that the reimbursement is appropriate shall direct the Registrar to make the payment as soon as practicable.

Rule 371 – Time periods for paying court fees

1. The fixed fees provided for in Section I and Section IV of the table of fees and fees for other procedures and actions provided for in Section III of the table of fees shall be paid at the time of lodging the relevant pleading or application. The payment shall be made to one of the bank accounts indicated by the Court and it shall indicate the paying party or its representative together with the number of the patent involved and the number of the case.

2. Proof of payment shall be provided together with the relevant pleading or application.

3. In cases of urgency, where a payment in advance is not possible, the representative of the party in question shall pay the fixed fee within the period set by the Court and the Court may order that the relevant pleading or application shall be deemed lodged and effective when received by the Registry if payment of the fixed fee is made within such period.

4. The value-based fee provided for in Section II of the table of fees shall be paid according to the claimant's assessment of the value at the time of lodging the relevant pleading or application. In the event that a higher value is determined by the judge-rapporteur the remaining fees due shall be paid within 10 days of service of the order determining the value of the action in accordance with the Rules 22, 60, 74, and 133. Where the value is lower, the Court will reimburse overpaid fees.

5. Where an Application for legal aid has been lodged in accordance with Rule 377, the rules on the obligation as to the time when to pay the fees under paragraph 1 shall not apply.

Relation with Agreement: Article 70

LEGAL AID

Rule 375 – Aim and scope

1. In order to ensure effective access to justice, the Court may grant legal aid to a party (hereinafter 'the applicant').

2. Legal aid may be granted in respect of any proceedings before the Court.

Rule 376 – Costs eligible for legal aid

1. Subject to Article 71(3) of the Agreement, legal aid may cover, in whole or in part, the following costs:
   - (a) court fees;
   - (b) costs of legal assistance and representation regarding:
     - (i) pre-litigation advice with a view to reaching a settlement prior to commencing legal proceedings;
     - (ii) commencing and maintaining proceedings before the Court;

(iii) all costs relating to proceedings including the application for legal aid;
(iv) enforcement of decisions;

(c) other necessary costs related to the proceedings to be borne by a party, including costs of witnesses, experts, interpreters and translators and necessary travel, accommodation and subsistence costs of the applicant and his representative.

2. Subject to Article 71(3) of the Agreement, legal aid may also cover the costs awarded to the successful party, in the event that the applicant loses the action.

Rule 376A – Maximum amount to be paid for representation

1. For the costs of representation pursuant to Rule 376.1(b) the maximum level of legal aid that may be granted by the Court shall be the maximum amount of recoverable costs laid down in the decision of the Administrative Committee pursuant to Article 69(1) of the Agreement and Rule 152.2.

2. The Administrative Committee may define thresholds below the level set in paragraph 1 for the maximum level of legal aid for representation pursuant to Rule 376.1(b), taking into account necessary costs for legal representation in the Contracting Member States and the need to guarantee adequate access to justice.

Rule 377 – Conditions for granting legal aid

1. The applicant shall be entitled to apply for legal aid where:

(a) owing to his economic situation, he is wholly or partly unable to meet the costs referred to in Rule 376; and

(b) the action in respect of which the application for legal aid is made has a reasonable prospect of success, considering the applicant's procedural position; and

(c) the claimant applying for legal aid is entitled to bring actions under Article 47 of the Agreement.

2. The Administrative Committee may define thresholds above which legal aid applicants are deemed wholly or partly able to bear the costs of proceedings set out in Rule 376. These thresholds may not prevent applicants whose economic situation is above the thresholds from being granted legal aid if they prove that they are in fact unable to pay the costs of the proceedings referred to in Rule 376 as a result of the high level of the cost of living in the Contracting Member State of domicile or habitual residence.

3. When deciding on the grant of legal aid the Court shall, without prejudice to paragraph 1(a), consider all relevant circumstances including the importance of the action to the applicant and also the nature of the action when the application concerns a claim arising directly out of the applicant's trade or self-employed profession.

Rule 377A – Conditions regarding the financial situation of the applicant

1. When assessing a party's financial situation, his income and assets must be taken into account.

2. Income shall include all earnings in money or equivalent value after deducting all costs required by the applicant and dependent persons in order to cover their reasonable living expenses (disposable income).

3. The Administrative Committee shall define the deductions from income and assets to be taken into account when assessing the applicant's financial situation. It shall also define levels of monthly instalments to be paid by the applicant. All thresholds set by the Administrative Committee shall be adapted regularly to price and income indices.

Rule 378 – Application for legal aid

1. An application for legal aid may be lodged before or after proceedings have been started before the Court.

2. The Application for legal aid shall contain in a language of a Contracting Member State:

(a) the name of the applicant;
(b) postal and electronic addresses for service on the applicant and the names of the persons authorised to accept service;
(c) the name of the other party as well as postal and electronic addresses for service on the other party where available and the names of the persons authorised to accept service, if known;
(d) the action number of the action in respect of which the application is made or, where the application is lodged before the action has been brought, a brief description of the action;
(e) an indication of the value of the action and the costs to be covered by legal aid;
(f) where legal aid is requested for costs of legal assistance and representation, the name of the proposed representative;
(g) an indication of the applicant's financial resources, such as income, assets and capital, and of the applicant's family situation including an assessment of the resources of persons who are financially dependent on the applicant;
(h) where appropriate, a reasoned request for suspension of a time limit which would otherwise need to be observed until the date of notification of the order deciding on legal aid.

3. The application for legal aid must be supported by:
(a) evidence of the applicant's need for assistance, such as certificates attesting his income, assets and capital and family situation; and
(b) where the application is lodged before the action has been brought, an indication of the evidence in support of the action.

4. In the event of an appeal, a new application shall be lodged.
5. Rule 8 shall not apply.

Rule 378A – Type of proof

1. To be admissible, the application must contain a statement of the facts and legal situation, with specific mention of the evidence to be presented. The application must also contain a statement regarding the economic and financial situation of the applicant. The following documents shall be attached to the application:
(a) latest property and income declarations of the applicant;
(b) a document showing the personal monthly income for the previous year, or a declaration of unemployment delivered by the competent authorities, or a certificate proving that the applicant is receiving aid or financial support under a social welfare scheme;
(c) a certificate of composition of household;
(d) any other official document that can provide proof of the financial situation of the applicant.

2. Where appropriate, a certificate relating to the income of other members of the household of the applicant should also be attached to the application. The official documents shall not be older than 3 months. At the request of the Court, the applicant shall produce further documentation and, if so requested, an affidavit of the truthfulness of his statements, otherwise the application will not be admissible.

Rule 379 – Examination and decision

1. The Registry shall examine the formal admissibility of the application for legal aid and the conditions regarding the financial situation of the applicant pursuant to Rules 377.1(a), .2 and 377A.
2. If the requirements referred to in Rules 377.1(a), .2, 377A, 378 and 378A have not been met, the applicant shall, as soon as practicable, be invited to correct the deficiencies within 14 days.
3. If the requirements referred to in Rules 377.1(a), .2, 377A, 378 and 378A have been met or the applicant fails to correct a deficiency, the decision on such application shall be taken, by way of order, by the judge-rapporteur or, where the application is lodged before the action has been brought, by the standing judge.

4. Before making a decision on an application for legal aid, the Court shall invite the other party to submit written observations unless it is already apparent from the information submitted that the conditions referred to in Rule 377.1(b) have not been met. Documents regarding the economic and financial situation of the applicant shall be made accessible to the other party only where the applicant has consented or the applicant's refusal of consent is unreasonable or in the view of the Court the other party has a right to information on the economic or financial situation of the applicant.
5. An order refusing legal aid shall state the reasons on which it is based.
6. An order granting legal aid may provide for:
   (a) an exemption, wholly or partly, from Court fees;
   (b) an interim amount to be paid to enable the applicant and/or the representative of the applicant to meet any request of the judge-rapporteur or standing judge prior to making a final order;
   (c) an amount to be paid to the representative of the applicant or a limit which the representative's disbursements and fees may not exceed;
   (d) a contribution to be made by the applicant to the costs referred to in Rule 376.1(c).
7. Legal aid may be granted only for the period from receipt of the application with the Court.
8. Where the legal aid covers, in whole or in part, the costs of legal assistance and representation the order granting legal aid shall designate the representative of the applicant.
9. On a request by the designated representative, the Court may order that an amount shall be paid by way of advance.
10. Where requested by the applicant in accordance with Rule 378.2(h), the Court shall decide on the suspension of any time limit.

Rule 379A – Alteration of economic situation
The applicant shall inform the Court promptly of any alteration in his economic situation.

Rule 380 – Withdrawal of legal aid
1. If the economic situation of the applicant which has led to the grant of legal aid according to Rule 377.1(a) alters during the proceedings, the Court may at any time, of his own motion or on a reasoned request by the other party, withdraw wholly or partly legal aid but only after having heard the applicant.
2. The Court may withdraw wholly or partly legal aid if the applicant:
   (a) by inaccurately representing the circumstances of the case, has misrepresented its prospects of success, which are determinative for the approval of assistance with Court costs; or
   (b) has grossly negligently made false statements as to his personal or economic circumstances; or
   (c) has not immediately informed the Court of a considerable improvement to his financial circumstances;
   (d) has been in arrears for longer than three months with the payment of a monthly instalment or with the payment of any other amount.
3. An order withdrawing legal aid shall state the reasons on which it is based.

Rule 381 – Appeal
1. An order wholly or partly refusing or withdrawing legal aid may be appealed to the Court of Appeal. The appeal shall be filed with the Court of Appeal within a period of one month after receiving the order and satisfy the provisions of Rules 377 to 379. The President of the Court of Appeal shall appoint a panel which shall decide on the appeal having heard the applicant.
2. An application for legal aid to appeal a decision of the Court of First Instance shall be filed with the Court of Appeals and shall satisfy the provisions of Rules 377 to 379. The Application for legal aid to bring an appeal against a decision of the Court of First Instance shall be filed within the time limit

provided for the appeal as specified in Rule 224 and should, where possible, be accompanied by the appeal itself. The Application shall be assigned according to Rule 345.8.

Rule 382 – Recovery

1. Where the Court has ordered another party to pay the costs of the applicant for legal aid, that other party shall be required to refund to the Court any sums advanced by way of legal aid. In the event of a shortfall between the costs so ordered and the sums advanced by way of legal aid the applicant may be required to meet such shortfall from any damages or compensation awarded by the Court or from any sum received by way of settlement.

2. In the event of withdrawal of legal aid under Rule 380, the applicant may be required to refund to the Court any sums advanced by way of legal aid.

2. UPC Agreement

AGREEMENT ON A UNIFIED PATENT COURT 2013/C 175/01

THE CONTRACTING MEMBER STATES,

CONSIDERING that cooperation amongst the Member States of the European Union in the field of patents contributes significantly to the integration process in Europe, in particular to the establishment of an internal market within the European Union characterised by the free movement of goods and services and the creation of a system ensuring that competition in the internal market is not distorted;

CONSIDERING that the fragmented market for patents and the significant variations between national court systems are detrimental for innovation, in particular for small and medium-sized enterprises which have difficulties to enforce their patents and to defend themselves against unfounded claims and claims relating to patents which should be revoked;

CONSIDERING that the European Patent Convention ('EPC') which has been ratified by all Member States of the European Union provides for a single procedure for granting European patents by the European Patent Office;

CONSIDERING that by virtue of Regulation (EU) No 1257/2012,[1] patent proprietors can request unitary effect of their European patents so as to obtain unitary patent protection in the Member States of the European Union participating in the enhanced cooperation;

WISHING to improve the enforcement of patents and the defence against unfounded claims and patents which should be revoked and to enhance legal certainty by setting up a Unified Patent Court for litigation relating to the infringement and validity of patents;

CONSIDERING that the Unified Patent Court should be devised to ensure expeditious and high quality decisions, striking a fair balance between the interests of right holders and other parties and taking into account the need for proportionality and flexibility;

CONSIDERING that the Unified Patent Court should be a court common to the Contracting Member States and thus part of their judicial system, with exclusive competence in respect of European patents with unitary effect and European patents granted under the provisions of the EPC;

CONSIDERING that the Court of Justice of the European Union is to ensure the uniformity of the Union legal order and the primacy of European Union law;

RECALLING the obligations of the Contracting Member States under the Treaty on European Union (TEU) and the Treaty on the Functioning of the European Union (TFEU), including the obligation of sincere cooperation as set out in Article 4(3) TEU and the obligation to ensure through the Unified

1 Regulation (EU) No 1257/2012 of the European Parliament and of the Council of 17 December 2012 implementing enhanced cooperation in the area of the creation of unitary patent protection (OJ L 361, 31.12.2012, p. 1) including any subsequent amendments.

Patent Court the full application of, and respect for, Union law in their respective territories and the judicial protection of an individual's rights under that law;

CONSIDERING that, as any national court, the Unified Patent Court must respect and apply Union law and, in collaboration with the Court of Justice of the European Union as guardian of Union law, ensure its correct application and uniform interpretation; the Unified Patent Court must in particular cooperate with the Court of Justice of the European Union in properly interpreting Union law by relying on the latter's case law and by requesting preliminary rulings in accordance with Article 267 TFEU;

CONSIDERING that the Contracting Member States should, in line with the case law of the Court of Justice of the European Union on non-contractual liability, be liable for damages caused by infringements of Union law by the Unified Patent Court, including the failure to request preliminary rulings from the Court of Justice of the European Union;

CONSIDERING that infringements of Union law by the Unified Patent Court, including the failure to request preliminary rulings from the Court of Justice of the European Union, are directly attributable to the Contracting Member States and infringement proceedings can therefore be brought under Article 258, 259 and 260 TFEU against any Contracting Member State to ensure the respect of the primacy and proper application of Union law;

RECALLING the primacy of Union law, which includes the TEU, the TFEU, the Charter of Fundamental Rights of the European Union, the general principles of Union law as developed by the Court of Justice of the European Union, and in particular the right to an effective remedy before a tribunal and a fair and public hearing within a reasonable time by an independent and impartial tribunal, the case law of the Court of Justice of the European Union and secondary Union law;

CONSIDERING that this Agreement should be open to accession by any Member State of the European Union; Member States which have decided not to participate in the enhanced cooperation in the area of the creation of unitary patent protection may participate in this Agreement in respect of European patents granted for their respective territory;

CONSIDERING that this Agreement should enter into force on 1 January 2014 or on the first day of the fourth month after the 13th deposit, provided that the Contracting Member States that will have deposited their instruments of ratification or accession include the three States in which the highest number of European patents was in force in the year preceding the year in which the signature of the Agreement takes place, or on the first day of the fourth month after the date of entry into force of the amendments to Regulation (EU) No 1215/2012[2] concerning its relationship with this Agreement, whichever is the latest,

HAVE AGREED AS FOLLOWS:

2 Regulation (EU) No 1215/2012 of the European Parliament and of the Council of 12 December 2012 on jurisdiction and the recognition and enforcement of judgments in civil and commercial matters (OJ L 351, 20.12.2012, p. 1) including any subsequent amendments.

PART I GENERAL AND INSTITUTIONAL PROVISIONS

CHAPTER I GENERAL PROVISIONS

Article 1 Unified Patent Court

A Unified Patent Court for the settlement of disputes relating to European patents and European patents with unitary effect is hereby established.

The Unified Patent Court shall be a court common to the Contracting Member States and thus subject to the same obligations under Union law as any national court of the Contracting Member States.

Article 2 Definitions

For the purposes of this Agreement:

(a) 'Court' means the Unified Patent Court created by this Agreement.
(b) 'Member State' means a Member State of the European Union.
(c) 'Contracting Member State' means a Member State party to this Agreement.
(d) 'EPC' means the Convention on the Grant of European Patents of 5 October 1973, including any subsequent amendments.
(e) 'European patent' means a patent granted under the provisions of the EPC, which does not benefit from unitary effect by virtue of Regulation (EU) No 1257/2012.
(f) 'European patent with unitary effect' means a patent granted under the provisions of the EPC which benefits from unitary effect by virtue of Regulation (EU) No 1257/2012.
(g) 'Patent' means a European patent and/or a European patent with unitary effect.
(h) 'Supplementary protection certificate' means a supplementary protection certificate granted under Regulation (EC) No 469/2009[3] or under Regulation (EC) No 1610/96.[4]
(i) 'Statute' means the Statute of the Court as set out in Annex I, which shall be an integral part of this Agreement.
(j) 'Rules of Procedure' means the Rules of Procedure of the Court, as established in accordance with Article 41.

Article 3 Scope of application

This Agreement shall apply to any:

(a) European patent with unitary effect;
(b) supplementary protection certificate issued for a product protected by a patent;
(c) European patent which has not yet lapsed at the date of entry into force of this Agreement or was granted after that date, without prejudice to Article 83; and
(d) European patent application which is pending at the date of entry into force of this Agreement or which is filed after that date, without prejudice to Article 83.

Article 4 Legal status

1. The Court shall have legal personality in each Contracting Member State and shall enjoy the most extensive legal capacity accorded to legal persons under the national law of that State.

---

3 Regulation (EC) No 469/2009 of the European Parliament and of the Council of 6 May 2009 concerning the supplementary protection certificate for medicinal products (OJ L 152, 16.6.2009, p. 1) including any subsequent amendments.

4 Regulation (EC) No 1610/96 of the European Parliament and of the Council of 23 July 1996 concerning the creation of a supplementary certificate for plant protection products (OJ L 198, 8.8.1996, p. 30) including any subsequent amendments.

2. The Court shall be represented by the President of the Court of Appeal who shall be elected in accordance with the Statute.

Article 5 Liability

1. The contractual liability of the Court shall be governed by the law applicable to the contract in question in accordance with Regulation (EC) No 593/2008[5] (Rome I), where applicable, or failing that in accordance with the law of the Member State of the court seized.
2. The non-contractual liability of the Court in respect of any damage caused by it or its staff in the performance of their duties, to the extent that it is not a civil and commercial matter within the meaning of Regulation (EC) No 864/2007[6] (Rome II), shall be governed by the law of the Contracting Member State in which the damage occurred. This provision is without prejudice to the application of Article 22.
3. The court with jurisdiction to settle disputes under paragraph 2 shall be a court of the Contracting Member State in which the damage occurred.

CHAPTER II INSTITUTIONAL PROVISIONS

Article 6 The Court

1. The Court shall comprise a Court of First Instance, a Court of Appeal and a Registry.
2. The Court shall perform the functions assigned to it by this Agreement.

Article 7 The Court of First Instance

1. The Court of First Instance shall comprise a central division as well as local and regional divisions.
2. The central division shall have its seat in Paris, with sections in London and Munich. The cases before the central division shall be distributed in accordance with Annex II, which shall form an integral part of this Agreement.
3. A local division shall be set up in a Contracting Member State upon its request in accordance with the Statute. A Contracting Member State hosting a local division shall designate its seat.
4. An additional local division shall be set up in a Contracting Member State upon its request for every one hundred patent cases per calendar year that have been commenced in that Contracting Member State during three successive years prior to or subsequent to the date of entry into force of this Agreement. The number of local divisions in one Contracting Member State shall not exceed four.
5. A regional division shall be set up for two or more Contracting Member States, upon their request in accordance with the Statute. Such Contracting Member States shall designate the seat of the division concerned. The regional division may hear cases in multiple locations.

Article 8 Composition of the panels of the Court of First Instance

1. Any panel of the Court of First Instance shall have a multinational composition. Without prejudice to paragraph 5 of this Article and to Article 33(3)(a), it shall sit in a composition of three judges.
2. Any panel of a local division in a Contracting Member State where, during a period of three successive years prior or subsequent to the entry into force of this Agreement, less than fifty patent cases per calendar year on average have been commenced shall sit in a composition of one legally qualified judge who is a national of the Contracting Member State hosting the local division concerned and two legally

5 Regulation (EC) No 593/2008 of the European Parliament and of the Council of 17 June 2008 on the law applicable to contractual obligations (Rome I) (OJ L 177, 4.7.2008, p. 6) including any subsequent amendments.

6 Regulation (EC) No 864/2007 of the European Parliament and of the Council of 11 July 2007 on the law applicable to non-contractual obligations (Rome II) (OJ L 199, 31.7.2007, p. 40) including any subsequent amendments.

qualified judges who are not nationals of the Contracting Member State concerned and are allocated from the Pool of Judges in accordance with Article 18(3) on a case by case basis.
3. Notwithstanding paragraph 2, any panel of a local division in a Contracting Member State where, during a period of three successive years prior or subsequent to the entry into force of this Agreement, fifty or more patent cases per calendar year on average have been commenced, shall sit in a composition of two legally qualified judges who are nationals of the Contracting Member State hosting the local division concerned and one legally qualified judge who is not a national of the Contracting Member State concerned and is allocated from the Pool of Judges in accordance with Article 18(3). Such third judge shall serve at the local division on a long term basis, where this is necessary for the efficient functioning of divisions with a high work load.
4. Any panel of a regional division shall sit in a composition of two legally qualified judges chosen from a regional list of judges, who shall be nationals of the Contracting Member States concerned, and one legally qualified judge who shall not be a national of the Contracting Member States concerned and who shall be allocated from the Pool of Judges in accordance with Article 18(3).
5. Upon request by one of the parties, any panel of a local or regional division shall request the President of the Court of First Instance to allocate from the Pool of Judges in accordance with Article 18(3) an additional technically qualified judge with qualifications and experience in the field of technology concerned. Moreover, any panel of a local or regional division may, after having heard the parties, submit such request on its own initiative, where it deems this appropriate.
In cases where such a technically qualified judge is allocated, no further technically qualified judge may be allocated under Article 33(3)(a).
6. Any panel of the central division shall sit in a composition of two legally qualified judges who are nationals of different Contracting Member States and one technically qualified judge allocated from the Pool of Judges in accordance with Article 18(3) with qualifications and experience in the field of technology concerned. However, any panel of the central division dealing with actions under Article 32(1)(i) shall sit in a composition of three legally qualified judges who are nationals of different Contracting Member States.
7. Notwithstanding paragraphs 1 to 6 and in accordance with the Rules of Procedure, parties may agree to have their case heard by a single legally qualified judge.
8. Any panel of the Court of First Instance shall be chaired by a legally qualified judge.

Article 9 The Court of Appeal
1. Any panel of the Court of Appeal shall sit in a multinational composition of five judges. It shall sit in a composition of three legally qualified judges who are nationals of different Contracting Member States and two technically qualified judges with qualifications and experience in the field of technology concerned. Those technically qualified judges shall be assigned to the panel by the President of the Court of Appeal from the pool of judges in accordance with Article 18.
2. Notwithstanding paragraph 1, a panel dealing with actions under Article 32(1)(i) shall sit in a composition of three legally qualified judges who are nationals of different Contracting Member States.
3. Any panel of the Court of Appeal shall be chaired by a legally qualified judge.
4. The panels of the Court of Appeal shall be set up in accordance with the Statute.
5. The Court of Appeal shall have its seat in Luxembourg.

Article 10 The Registry
1. A Registry shall be set up at the seat of the Court of Appeal. It shall be managed by the Registrar and perform the functions assigned to it in accordance with the Statute. Subject to conditions set out in this Agreement and the Rules of Procedure, the register kept by the Registry shall be public.
2. Sub-registries shall be set up at all divisions of the Court of First Instance.

3. The Registry shall keep records of all cases before the Court. Upon filing, the sub-registry concerned shall notify every case to the Registry.
4. The Court shall appoint the Registrar in accordance with Article 22 of the Statute and lay down the rules governing the Registrar's service.

Article 11 Committees
An Administrative Committee, a Budget Committee and an Advisory Committee shall be set up in order to ensure the effective implementation and operation of this Agreement. They shall in particular exercise the duties foreseen by this Agreement and the Statute.

Article 12 The Administrative Committee
1. The Administrative Committee shall be composed of one representative of each Contracting Member State. The European Commission shall be represented at the meetings of the Administrative Committee as observer.
2. Each Contracting Member State shall have one vote.
3. The Administrative Committee shall adopt its decisions by a majority of three quarters of the Contracting Member States represented and voting, except where this Agreement or the Statute provides otherwise.
4. The Administrative Committee shall adopt its rules of procedure.
5. The Administrative Committee shall elect a chairperson from among its members for a term of three years. That term shall be renewable.

Article 13 The Budget Committee
1. The Budget Committee shall be composed of one representative of each Contracting Member State.
2. Each Contracting Member State shall have one vote.
3. The Budget Committee shall take its decisions by a simple majority of the representatives of the Contracting Member States. However, a majority of three-quarters of the representatives of Contracting Member States shall be required for the adoption of the budget.
4. The Budget Committee shall adopt its rules of procedure.
5. The Budget Committee shall elect a chairperson from among its members for a term of three years. That term shall be renewable.

Article 14 The Advisory Committee
1. The Advisory Committee shall:
- (a) assist the Administrative Committee in the preparation of the appointment of judges of the Court;
- (b) make proposals to the Presidium referred to in Article 15 of the Statute on the guidelines for the training framework for judges referred to in Article 19; and
- (c) deliver opinions to the Administrative Committee concerning the requirements for qualifications referred to in Article 48(2).

2. The Advisory Committee shall comprise patent judges and practitioners in patent law and patent litigation with the highest recognised competence. They shall be appointed, in accordance with the procedure laid down in the Statute, for a term of six years. That term shall be renewable.
3. The composition of the Advisory Committee shall ensure a broad range of relevant expertise and the representation of each of the Contracting Member States. The members of the Advisory Committee shall be completely independent in the performance of their duties and shall not be bound by any instructions.
4. The Advisory Committee shall adopt its rules of procedure.

5. The Advisory Committee shall elect a chairperson from among its members for a term of three years. That term shall be renewable.

CHAPTER III JUDGES OF THE COURT

Article 15 Eligibility criteria for the appointment of judges

1. The Court shall comprise both legally qualified judges and technically qualified judges. Judges shall ensure the highest standards of competence and shall have proven experience in the field of patent litigation.
2. Legally qualified judges shall possess the qualifications required for appointment to judicial offices in a Contracting Member State.
3. Technically qualified judges shall have a university degree and proven expertise in a field of technology. They shall also have proven knowledge of civil law and procedure relevant in patent litigation.

Article 16 Appointment procedure

1. The Advisory Committee shall establish a list of the most suitable candidates to be appointed as judges of the Court, in accordance with the Statute.
2. On the basis of that list, the Administrative Committee shall appoint the judges of the Court acting by common accord.
3. The implementing provisions for the appointment of judges are set out in the Statute.

Article 17 Judicial independence and impartiality

1. The Court, its judges and the Registrar shall enjoy judicial independence. In the performance of their duties, the judges shall not be bound by any instructions.
2. Legally qualified judges, as well as technically qualified judges who are full-time judges of the Court, may not engage in any other occupation, whether gainful or not, unless an exception is granted by the Administrative Committee.
3. Notwithstanding paragraph 2, the exercise of the office of judges shall not exclude the exercise of other judicial functions at national level.
4. The exercise of the office of technically qualified judges who are part-time judges of the Court shall not exclude the exercise of other functions provided there is no conflict of interest.
5. In case of a conflict of interest, the judge concerned shall not take part in proceedings. Rules governing conflicts of interest are set out in the Statute.

Article 18 Pool of Judges

1. A Pool of Judges shall be established in accordance with the Statute.
2. The Pool of Judges shall be composed of all legally qualified judges and technically qualified judges from the Court of First Instance who are full-time or part-time judges of the Court. The Pool of Judges shall include at least one technically qualified judge per field of technology with the relevant qualifications and experience. The technically qualified judges from the Pool of Judges shall also be available to the Court of Appeal.
3. Where so provided by this Agreement or the Statute, the judges from the Pool of Judges shall be allocated to the division concerned by the President of the Court of First Instance. The allocation of judges shall be based on their legal or technical expertise, linguistic skills and relevant experience. The allocation of judges shall guarantee the same high quality of work and the same high level of legal and technical expertise in all panels of the Court of First Instance.

Article 19 Training framework

1. A training framework for judges, the details of which are set out in the Statute, shall be set up in order to improve and increase available patent litigation expertise and to ensure a broad geographic distribution of such specific knowledge and experience. The facilities for that framework shall be situated in Budapest.

2. The training framework shall in particular focus on:
   (a) internships in national patent courts or divisions of the Court of First Instance hearing a substantial number of patent litigation cases;
   (b) improvement of linguistic skills;
   (c) technical aspects of patent law;
   (d) the dissemination of knowledge and experience in civil procedure for technically qualified judges;
   (e) the preparation of candidate-judges.

3. The training framework shall provide for continuous training. Regular meetings shall be organised between all judges of the Court in order to discuss developments in patent law and to ensure the consistency of the Court's case law.

CHAPTER IV THE PRIMACY OF UNION LAW, LIABILITY AND RESPONSIBILITY OF THE CONTRACTING MEMBER STATES

Article 20 Primacy of and respect for Union law

The Court shall apply Union law in its entirety and shall respect its primacy.

Article 21 Requests for preliminary rulings

As a court common to the Contracting Member States and as part of their judicial system, the Court shall cooperate with the Court of Justice of the European Union to ensure the correct application and uniform interpretation of Union law, as any national court, in accordance with Article 267 TFEU in particular. Decisions of the Court of Justice of the European Union shall be binding on the Court.

Article 22 Liability for damage caused by infringements of Union law

1. The Contracting Member States are jointly and severally liable for damage resulting from an infringement of Union law by the Court of Appeal, in accordance with Union law concerning non-contractual liability of Member States for damage caused by their national courts breaching Union law.

2. An action for such damages shall be brought against the Contracting Member State where the claimant has its residence or principal place of business or, in the absence of residence or principal place of business, place of business, before the competent authority of that Contracting Member State. Where the claimant does not have its residence, or principal place of business or, in the absence of residence or principal place of business, place of business in a Contracting Member State, the claimant may bring such an action against the Contracting Member State where the Court of Appeal has its seat, before the competent authority of that Contracting Member State.

The competent authority shall apply the *lex fori*, with the exception of its private international law, to all questions not regulated by Union law or by this Agreement. The claimant shall be entitled to obtain the entire amount of damages awarded by the competent authority from the Contracting Member State against which the action was brought.

3. The Contracting Member State that has paid damages is entitled to obtain proportional contribution, established in accordance with the method laid down in Article 37(3) and (4), from the other Contracting Member States. The detailed rules governing the Contracting Member States' contribution under this paragraph shall be determined by the Administrative Committee.

Article 23 Responsibility of the Contracting Member States
Actions of the Court are directly attributable to each Contracting Member State individually, including for the purposes of Articles 258, 259 and 260 TFEU, and to all Contracting Member States collectively.

CHAPTER V SOURCES OF LAW AND SUBSTANTIVE LAW

Article 24 Sources of law
1. In full compliance with Article 20, when hearing a case brought before it under this Agreement, the Court shall base its decisions on:
(a) Union law, including Regulation (EU) No 1257/2012 and Regulation (EU) No 1260/2012;[7]
(b) this Agreement;
(c) the EPC;
(d) other international agreements applicable to patents and binding on all the Contracting Member States; and
(e) national law.
2. To the extent that the Court shall base its decisions on national law, including where relevant the law of non-contracting States, the applicable law shall be determined:
(a) by directly applicable provisions of Union law containing private international law rules, or
(b) in the absence of directly applicable provisions of Union law or where the latter do not apply, by international instruments containing private international law rules; or
(c) in the absence of provisions referred to in points (a) and (b), by national provisions on private international law as determined by the Court.
3. The law of non-contracting States shall apply when designated by application of the rules referred to in paragraph 2, in particular in relation to Articles 25 to 28, 54, 55, 64, 68 and 72.

Article 25 Right to prevent the direct use of the invention
A patent shall confer on its proprietor the right to prevent any third party not having the proprietor's consent from the following:
(a) making, offering, placing on the market or using a product which is the subject-matter of the patent, or importing or storing the product for those purposes;
(b) using a process which is the subject-matter of the patent or, where the third party knows, or should have known, that the use of the process is prohibited without the consent of the patent proprietor, offering the process for use within the territory of the Contracting Member States in which that patent has effect;
(c) offering, placing on the market, using, or importing or storing for those purposes a product obtained directly by a process which is the subject-matter of the patent.

Article 26 Right to prevent the indirect use of the invention
1. A patent shall confer on its proprietor the right to prevent any third party not having the proprietor's consent from supplying or offering to supply, within the territory of the Contracting Member States in which that patent has effect, any person other than a party entitled to exploit the patented invention, with means, relating to an essential element of that invention, for putting it into effect therein, when the third party knows, or should have known, that those means are suitable and intended for putting that invention into effect.

---

7 Council Regulation (EU) No 1260/2012 of 17 December 2012 implementing enhanced cooperation in the area of the creation of unitary patent protection with regard to the applicable translation arrangements (OJ L 361, 31.12.2012, p. 89) including any subsequent amendments.

2. Paragraph 1 shall not apply when the means are staple commercial products, except where the third party induces the person supplied to perform any of the acts prohibited by Article 25.
3. Persons performing the acts referred to in Article 27(a) to (e) shall not be considered to be parties entitled to exploit the invention within the meaning of paragraph 1.

Article 27 Limitations of the effects of a patent
The rights conferred by a patent shall not extend to any of the following:
(a) acts done privately and for non-commercial purposes;
(b) acts done for experimental purposes relating to the subject-matter of the patented invention;
(c) the use of biological material for the purpose of breeding, or discovering and developing other plant varieties;
(d) the acts allowed pursuant to Article 13(6) of Directive 2001/82/EC[8] or Article 10(6) of Directive 2001/83/EC[9] in respect of any patent covering the product within the meaning of either of those Directives;
(e) the extemporaneous preparation by a pharmacy, for individual cases, of a medicine in accordance with a medical prescription or acts concerning the medicine so prepared;
(f) the use of the patented invention on board vessels of countries of the International Union for the Protection of Industrial Property (Paris Union) or members of the World Trade Organisation, other than those Contracting Member States in which that patent has effect, in the body of such vessel, in the machinery, tackle, gear and other accessories, when such vessels temporarily or accidentally enter the waters of a Contracting Member State in which that patent has effect, provided that the invention is used there exclusively for the needs of the vessel;
(g) the use of the patented invention in the construction or operation of aircraft or land vehicles or other means of transport of countries of the International Union for the Protection of Industrial Property (Paris Union) or members of the World Trade Organisation, other than those Contracting Member States in which that patent has effect, or of accessories to such aircraft or land vehicles, when these temporarily or accidentally enter the territory of a Contracting Member State in which that patent has effect;
(h) the acts specified in Article 27 of the Convention on International Civil Aviation of 7 December 1944,[10] where these acts concern the aircraft of a country party to that Convention other than a Contracting Member State in which that patent has effect;
(i) the use by a farmer of the product of his harvest for propagation or multiplication by him on his own holding, provided that the plant propagating material was sold or otherwise commercialised to the farmer by or with the consent of the patent proprietor for agricultural use. The extent and the conditions for this use correspond to those under Article 14 of Regulation (EC) No 2100/94;[11]
(j) the use by a farmer of protected livestock for an agricultural purpose, provided that the breeding stock or other animal reproductive material were sold or otherwise commercialised to the farmer by or with the consent of the patent proprietor. Such use includes making the animal or other animal reproductive material available for the purposes of pursuing the farmer's agricultural activity,

---

8 Directive 2001/82/EC of the European Parliament and of the Council of 6 November 2001 on the Community code relating to veterinary medicinal products (OJ L 311, 28.11.2001, p. 1) including any subsequent amendments.

9 Directive 2001/83/EC of the European Parliament and of the Council of 6 November 2001 on the Community code relating to medicinal products for human use (OJ L 311, 28.11.2001, p. 67) including any subsequent amendments.

10 International Civil Aviation Organization (ICAO), 'Chicago Convention', Document 7300/9 (9th edition, 2006).

11 Council Regulation (EC) No 2100/94 of 27 July 1994 on Community plant variety rights (OJ L 227, 1.9.1994, p. 1) including any subsequent amendments.

but not the sale thereof within the framework of, or for the purpose of, a commercial reproductive activity;

(k) the acts and the use of the obtained information as allowed under Articles 5 and 6 of Directive 2009/24/EC,[12] in particular, by its provisions on decompilation and interoperability; and

(l) the acts allowed pursuant to Article 10 of Directive 98/44/EC.[13]

Article 28 Right based on prior use of the invention

Any person, who, if a national patent had been granted in respect of an invention, would have had, in a Contracting Member State, a right based on prior use of that invention or a right of personal possession of that invention, shall enjoy, in that Contracting Member State, the same rights in respect of a patent for the same invention.

Article 29 Exhaustion of the rights conferred by a European patent

The rights conferred by a European patent shall not extend to acts concerning a product covered by that patent after that product has been placed on the market in the European Union by, or with the consent of, the patent proprietor, unless there are legitimate grounds for the patent proprietor to oppose further commercialisation of the product.

Article 30 Effects of supplementary protection certificates

A supplementary protection certificate shall confer the same rights as conferred by the patent and shall be subject to the same limitations and the same obligations.

CHAPTER VI INTERNATIONAL JURISDICTION AND COMPETENCE

Article 31 International jurisdiction

The international jurisdiction of the Court shall be established in accordance with Regulation (EU) No 1215/2012 or, where applicable, on the basis of the Convention on jurisdiction and the recognition and enforcement of judgments in civil and commercial matters (Lugano Convention).[14]

Article 32 Competence of the Court

1. The Court shall have exclusive competence in respect of:
   (a) actions for actual or threatened infringements of patents and supplementary protection certificates and related defences, including counterclaims concerning licences;
   (b) actions for declarations of non-infringement of patents and supplementary protection certificates;
   (c) actions for provisional and protective measures and injunctions;
   (d) actions for revocation of patents and for declaration of invalidity of supplementary protection certificates;
   (e) counterclaims for revocation of patents and for declaration of invalidity of supplementary protection certificates;
   (f) actions for damages or compensation derived from the provisional protection conferred by a published European patent application;

12 Directive 2009/24/EC of the European Parliament and of the Council of 23 April 2009 on the legal protection of computer programs (OJ L 111, 5.5.2009, p. 16) including any subsequent amendments.

13 Directive 98/44/EC of the European Parliament and of the Council of 6 July 1998 on the legal protection of biotechnological inventions (OJ L 213, 30.7.1998, p. 13) including any subsequent amendments.

14 Convention on jurisdiction and the recognition and enforcement of judgments in civil and commercial matters, done at Lugano on 30 October 2007, including any subsequent amendments.

(g) actions relating to the use of the invention prior to the granting of the patent or to the right based on prior use of the invention;
(h) actions for compensation for licences on the basis of Article 8 of Regulation (EU) No 1257/2012; and
(i) actions concerning decisions of the European Patent Office in carrying out the tasks referred to in Article 9 of Regulation (EU) No 1257/2012.

2. The national courts of the Contracting Member States shall remain competent for actions relating to patents and supplementary protection certificates which do not come within the exclusive competence of the Court.

Article 33 Competence of the divisions of the Court of First Instance

1. Without prejudice to paragraph 7 of this Article, actions referred to in Article 32(1)(a), (c), (f) and (g) shall be brought before:
(a) the local division hosted by the Contracting Member State where the actual or threatened infringement has occurred or may occur, or the regional division in which that Contracting Member State participates; or
(b) the local division hosted by the Contracting Member State where the defendant or, in the case of multiple defendants, one of the defendants has its residence, or principal place of business, or in the absence of residence or principal place of business, its place of business, or the regional division in which that Contracting Member State participates. An action may be brought against multiple defendants only where the defendants have a commercial relationship and where the action relates to the same alleged infringement.

Actions referred to in Article 32(1)(h) shall be brought before the local or regional division in accordance with point (b) of the first subparagraph.

Actions against defendants having their residence, or principal place of business or, in the absence of residence or principal place of business, their place of business, outside the territory of the Contracting Member States shall be brought before the local or regional division in accordance with point (a) of the first subparagraph or before the central division.

If the Contracting Member State concerned does not host a local division and does not participate in a regional division, actions shall be brought before the central division.

2. If an action referred to in Article 32(1)(a), (c), (f), (g) or (h) is pending before a division of the Court of First Instance, any action referred to in Article 32(1)(a), (c), (f), (g) or (h) between the same parties on the same patent may not be brought before any other division.

If an action referred to in Article 32(1)(a) is pending before a regional division and the infringement has occurred in the territories of three or more regional divisions, the regional division concerned shall, at the request of the defendant, refer the case to the central division.

In case an action between the same parties on the same patent is brought before several different divisions, the division first seized shall be competent for the whole case and any division seized later shall declare the action inadmissible in accordance with the Rules of Procedure.

3. A counterclaim for revocation as referred to in Article 32(1)(e) may be brought in the case of an action for infringement as referred to in Article 32(1)(a). The local or regional division concerned shall, after having heard the parties, have the discretion either to:
(a) proceed with both the action for infringement and with the counterclaim for revocation and request the President of the Court of First Instance to allocate from the Pool of Judges in accordance with Article 18(3) a technically qualified judge with qualifications and experience in the field of technology concerned.
(b) refer the counterclaim for revocation for decision to the central division and suspend or proceed with the action for infringement; or
(c) with the agreement of the parties, refer the case for decision to the central division.

4. Actions referred to in Article 32(1)(b) and (d) shall be brought before the central division. If, however, an action for infringement as referred to in Article 32(1)(a) between the same parties relating to the same patent has been brought before a local or a regional division, these actions may only be brought before the same local or regional division.
5. If an action for revocation as referred to in Article 32(1)(d) is pending before the central division, an action for infringement as referred to in Article 32(1)(a) between the same parties relating to the same patent may be brought before any division in accordance with paragraph 1 of this Article or before the central division. The local or regional division concerned shall have the discretion to proceed in accordance with paragraph 3 of this Article.
6. An action for declaration of non-infringement as referred to in Article 32(1)(b) pending before the central division shall be stayed once an infringement action as referred to in Article 32(1)(a) between the same parties or between the holder of an exclusive licence and the party requesting a declaration of non-infringement relating to the same patent is brought before a local or regional division within three months of the date on which the action was initiated before the central division.
7. Parties may agree to bring actions referred to in Article 32(1)(a) to (h) before the division of their choice, including the central division.
8. Actions referred to in Article 32(1)(d) and (e) can be brought without the applicant having to file notice of opposition with the European Patent Office.
9. Actions referred to in Article 32(1)(i) shall be brought before the central division.
10. A party shall inform the Court of any pending revocation, limitation or opposition proceedings before the European Patent Office, and of any request for accelerated processing before the European Patent Office. The Court may stay its proceedings when a rapid decision may be expected from the European Patent Office.

Article 34 Territorial scope of decisions
Decisions of the Court shall cover, in the case of a European patent, the territory of those Contracting Member States for which the European patent has effect.

CHAPTER VII PATENT MEDIATION AND ARBITRATION

Article 35 Patent mediation and arbitration centre
1. A patent mediation and arbitration centre ('the Centre') is hereby established. It shall have its seats in Ljubljana and Lisbon.
2. The Centre shall provide facilities for mediation and arbitration of patent disputes falling within the scope of this Agreement. Article 82 shall apply *mutatis mutandis* to any settlement reached through the use of the facilities of the Centre, including through mediation. However, a patent may not be revoked or limited in mediation or arbitration proceedings.
3. The Centre shall establish Mediation and Arbitration Rules.
4. The Centre shall draw up a list of mediators and arbitrators to assist the parties in the settlement of their dispute.

PART II FINANCIAL PROVISIONS

Article 36 Budget of the Court
1. The budget of the Court shall be financed by the Court's own financial revenues and, at least in the transitional period referred to in Article 83 as necessary, by contributions from the Contracting Member States. The budget shall be balanced.
2. The Court's own financial revenues shall comprise court fees and other revenues.

3. Court fees shall be fixed by the Administrative Committee. They shall consist of a fixed fee, combined with a value-based fee above a pre-defined ceiling. The Court fees shall be fixed at such a level as to ensure a right balance between the principle of fair access to justice, in particular for small and medium-sized enterprises, micro-entities, natural persons, non-profit organisations, universities and public research organisations and an adequate contribution of the parties for the costs incurred by the Court, recognising the economic benefits to the parties involved, and the objective of a self-financing Court with balanced finances. The level of the Court fees shall be reviewed periodically by the Administrative Committee. Targeted support measures for small and medium-sized enterprises and micro entities may be considered.
4. If the Court is unable to balance its budget out of its own resources, the Contracting Member States shall remit to it special financial contributions.

Article 37 Financing of the Court
1. The operating costs of the Court shall be covered by the budget of the Court, in accordance with the Statute.
Contracting Member States setting up a local division shall provide the facilities necessary for that purpose. Contracting Member States sharing a regional division shall provide jointly the facilities necessary for that purpose. Contracting Member States hosting the central division, its sections or the Court of Appeal shall provide the facilities necessary for that purpose. During an initial transitional period of seven years starting from the date of the entry into force of this Agreement, the Contracting Member States concerned shall also provide administrative support staff, without prejudice to the Statute of that staff.
2. On the date of entry into force of this Agreement, the Contracting Member States shall provide the initial financial contributions necessary for the setting up of the Court.
3. During the initial transitional period of seven years, starting from the date of the entry into force of this Agreement, the contribution by each Contracting Member State having ratified or acceded to the Agreement before the entry into force thereof shall be calculated on the basis of the number of European patents having effect in the territory of that State on the date of entry into force of this Agreement and the number of European patents with respect to which actions for infringement or for revocation have been brought before the national courts of that State in the three years preceding entry into force of this Agreement.
During the same initial transitional period of seven years, for Member States which ratify, or accede to, this Agreement after the entry into force thereof, the contributions shall be calculated on the basis of the number of European patents having effect in the territory of the ratifying or acceding Member State on the date of the ratification or accession and the number of European patents with respect to which actions for infringement or for revocation have been brought before the national courts of the ratifying or acceding Member State in the three years preceding the ratification or accession.
4. After the end of the initial transitional period of seven years, by which the Court is expected to have become self-financing, should contributions by the Contracting Member States become necessary, they shall be determined in accordance with the scale for the distribution of annual renewal fees for European patents with unitary effect applicable at the time the contribution becomes necessary.

Article 38 Financing of the training framework for judges
The training framework for judges shall be financed by the budget of the Court.

Article 39 Financing of the Centre
The operating costs of the Centre shall be financed by the budget of the Court.

PART III ORGANISATION AND PROCEDURAL PROVISIONS

CHAPTER I GENERAL PROVISIONS

Article 40 Statute
1. The Statute shall lay down the details of the organisation and functioning of the Court.
2. The Statute is annexed to this Agreement. The Statute may be amended by decision of the Administrative Committee, on the basis of a proposal of the Court or a proposal of a Contracting Member State after consultation with the Court. However, such amendments shall not contradict or alter this Agreement.
3. The Statute shall guarantee that the functioning of the Court is organised in the most efficient and cost-effective manner and shall ensure equitable access to justice.

Article 41 Rules of Procedure
1. The Rules of Procedure shall lay down the details of the proceedings before the Court. They shall comply with this Agreement and the Statute.
2. The Rules of Procedure shall be adopted by the Administrative Committee on the basis of broad consultations with stakeholders. The prior opinion of the European Commission on the compatibility of the Rules of Procedure with Union law shall be requested.
The Rules of Procedure may be amended by a decision of the Administrative Committee, on the basis of a proposal from the Court and after consultation with the European Commission. However, such amendments shall not contradict or alter this Agreement or the Statute.
3. The Rules of Procedure shall guarantee that the decisions of the Court are of the highest quality and that proceedings are organised in the most efficient and cost effective manner. They shall ensure a fair balance between the legitimate interests of all parties. They shall provide for the required level of discretion of judges without impairing the predictability of proceedings for the parties.

Article 42 Proportionality and fairness
1. The Court shall deal with litigation in ways which are proportionate to the importance and complexity thereof.
2. The Court shall ensure that the rules, procedures and remedies provided for in this Agreement and in the Statute are used in a fair and equitable manner and do not distort competition.

Article 43 Case management
The Court shall actively manage the cases before it in accordance with the Rules of Procedure without impairing the freedom of the parties to determine the subject-matter of, and the supporting evidence for, their case.

Article 44 Electronic procedures
The Court shall make best use of electronic procedures, such as the electronic filing of submissions of the parties and stating of evidence in electronic form, as well as video conferencing, in accordance with the Rules of Procedure.

Article 45 Public proceedings
The proceedings shall be open to the public unless the Court decides to make them confidential, to the extent necessary, in the interest of one of the parties or other affected persons, or in the general interest of justice or public order.

Article 46 Legal capacity

Any natural or legal person, or any body equivalent to a legal person entitled to initiate proceedings in accordance with its national law, shall have the capacity to be a party to the proceedings before the Court.

Article 47 Parties

1. The patent proprietor shall be entitled to bring actions before the Court.
2. Unless the licensing agreement provides otherwise, the holder of an exclusive licence in respect of a patent shall be entitled to bring actions before the Court under the same circumstances as the patent proprietor, provided that the patent proprietor is given prior notice.
3. The holder of a non-exclusive licence shall not be entitled to bring actions before the Court, unless the patent proprietor is given prior notice and in so far as expressly permitted by the licence agreement.
4. In actions brought by a licence holder, the patent proprietor shall be entitled to join the action before the Court.
5. The validity of a patent cannot be contested in an action for infringement brought by the holder of a licence where the patent proprietor does not take part in the proceedings. The party in an action for infringement wanting to contest the validity of a patent shall have to bring actions against the patent proprietor.
6. Any other natural or legal person, or any body entitled to bring actions in accordance with its national law, who is concerned by a patent, may bring actions in accordance with the Rules of Procedure.
7. Any natural or legal person, or any body entitled to bring actions in accordance with its national law and who is affected by a decision of the European Patent Office in carrying out the tasks referred to in Article 9 of Regulation (EU) No 1257/2012 is entitled to bring actions under Article 32(1)(i).

Article 48 Representation

1. Parties shall be represented by lawyers authorised to practise before a court of a Contracting Member State.
2. Parties may alternatively be represented by European Patent Attorneys who are entitled to act as professional representatives before the European Patent Office pursuant to Article 134 of the EPC and who have appropriate qualifications such as a European Patent Litigation Certificate.
3. The requirements for qualifications pursuant to paragraph 2 shall be established by the Administrative Committee. A list of European Patent Attorneys entitled to represent parties before the Court shall be kept by the Registrar.
4. Representatives of the parties may be assisted by patent attorneys, who shall be allowed to speak at hearings of the Court in accordance with the Rules of Procedure.
5. Representatives of the parties shall enjoy the rights and immunities necessary for the independent exercise of their duties, including the privilege from disclosure in proceedings before the Court in respect of communications between a representative and the party or any other person, under the conditions laid down in the Rules of Procedure, unless such privilege is expressly waived by the party concerned.
6. Representatives of the parties shall be obliged not to misrepresent cases or facts before the Court either knowingly or with good reasons to know.
7. Representation in accordance with paragraphs 1 and 2 of this Article shall not be required in proceedings under Article 32(1)(i).

CHAPTER II LANGUAGE OF PROCEEDINGS

Article 49 Language of proceedings at the Court of First Instance

1. The language of proceedings before any local or regional division shall be an official European Union language which is the official language or one of the official languages of the Contracting Member State hosting the relevant division, or the official language(s) designated by Contracting Member States sharing a regional division.
2. Notwithstanding paragraph 1, Contracting Member States may designate one or more of the official languages of the European Patent Office as the language of proceedings of their local or regional division.
3. The parties may agree on the use of the language in which the patent was granted as the language of proceedings, subject to approval by the competent panel. If the panel does not approve their choice, the parties may request that the case be referred to the central division.
4. With the agreement of the parties the competent panel may, on grounds of convenience and fairness, decide on the use of the language in which the patent was granted as the language of proceedings.
5. At the request of one of the parties and after having heard the other parties and the competent panel, the President of the Court of First Instance may, on grounds of fairness and taking into account all relevant circumstances, including the position of parties, in particular the position of the defendant, decide on the use of the language in which the patent was granted as language of proceedings. In this case the President of the Court of First Instance shall assess the need for specific translation and interpretation arrangements.
6. The language of proceedings at the central division shall be the language in which the patent concerned was granted.

Article 50 Language of proceedings at the Court of Appeal

1. The language of proceedings before the Court of Appeal shall be the language of proceedings before the Court of First Instance.
2. Notwithstanding paragraph 1 the parties may agree on the use of the language in which the patent was granted as the language of proceedings.
3. In exceptional cases and to the extent deemed appropriate, the Court of Appeal may decide on another official language of a Contracting Member State as the language of proceedings for the whole or part of the proceedings, subject to agreement by the parties.

Article 51 Other language arrangements

1. Any panel of the Court of First Instance and the Court of Appeal may, to the extent deemed appropriate, dispense with translation requirements.
2. At the request of one of the parties, and to the extent deemed appropriate, any division of the Court of First Instance and the Court of Appeal shall provide interpretation facilities to assist the parties concerned at oral proceedings.
3. Notwithstanding Article 49(6), in cases where an action for infringement is brought before the central division, a defendant having its residence, principal place of business or place of business in a Member State shall have the right to obtain, upon request, translations of relevant documents in the language of the Member State of residence, principal place of business or, in the absence of residence or principal place of business, place of business, in the following circumstances:
   (a) jurisdiction is entrusted to the central division in accordance with Article 33(1) third or fourth subparagraph, and

(b) the language of proceedings at the central division is a language which is not an official language of the Member State where the defendant has its residence, principal place of business or, in the absence of residence or principal place of business, place of business, and
(c) the defendant does not have proper knowledge of the language of the proceedings.

CHAPTER III PROCEEDINGS BEFORE THE COURT

Article 52 Written, interim and oral procedures

1. The proceedings before the Court shall consist of a written, an interim and an oral procedure, in accordance with the Rules of Procedure. All procedures shall be organized in a flexible and balanced manner.
2. In the interim procedure, after the written procedure and if appropriate, the judge acting as Rapporteur, subject to a mandate of the full panel, shall be responsible for convening an interim hearing. That judge shall in particular explore with the parties the possibility for a settlement, including through mediation, and/or arbitration, by using the facilities of the Centre referred to in Article 35.
3. The oral procedure shall give parties the opportunity to explain properly their arguments. The Court may, with the agreement of the parties, dispense with the oral hearing.

Article 53 Means of evidence

1. In proceedings before the Court, the means of giving or obtaining evidence shall include in particular the following:
(a) hearing the parties;
(b) requests for information;
(c) production of documents;
(d) hearing witnesses;
(e) opinions by experts;
(f) inspection;
(g) comparative tests or experiments;
(h) sworn statements in writing (affidavits).
2. The Rules of Procedure shall govern the procedure for taking such evidence. Questioning of witnesses and experts shall be under the control of the Court and be limited to what is necessary.

Article 54 Burden of proof

Without prejudice to Article 24(2) and (3), the burden of the proof of facts shall be on the party relying on those facts.

Article 55 Reversal of burden of proof

1. Without prejudice to Article 24(2) and (3), if the subject-matter of a patent is a process for obtaining a new product, the identical product when produced without the consent of the patent proprietor shall, in the absence of proof to the contrary, be deemed to have been obtained by the patented process.
2. The principle set out in paragraph 1 shall also apply where there is a substantial likelihood that the identical product was made by the patented process and the patent proprietor has been unable, despite reasonable efforts, to determine the process actually used for such identical product.
3. In the adduction of proof to the contrary, the legitimate interests of the defendant in protecting its manufacturing and trade secrets shall be taken into account.

CHAPTER IV POWERS OF THE COURT

Article 56 The general powers of the Court

1. The Court may impose such measures, procedures and remedies as are laid down in this Agreement and may make its orders subject to conditions, in accordance with the Rules of Procedure.
2. The Court shall take due account of the interest of the parties and shall, before making an order, give any party the opportunity to be heard, unless this is incompatible with the effective enforcement of such order.

Article 57 Court experts

1. Without prejudice to the possibility for the parties to produce expert evidence, the Court may at any time appoint court experts in order to provide expertise for specific aspects of the case. The Court shall provide such expert with all information necessary for the provision of the expert advice.
2. To this end, an indicative list of experts shall be drawn up by the Court in accordance with the Rules of Procedure. That list shall be kept by the Registrar.
3. The court experts shall guarantee independence and impartiality. Rules governing conflicts of interest applicable to judges set out in Article 7 of the Statute shall by analogy apply to court experts.
4. Expert advice given to the Court by court experts shall be made available to the parties which shall have the possibility to comment on it.

Article 58 Protection of confidential information

To protect the trade secrets, personal data or other confidential information of a party to the proceedings or of a third party, or to prevent an abuse of evidence, the Court may order that the collection and use of evidence in proceedings before it be restricted or prohibited or that access to such evidence be restricted to specific persons.

Article 59 Order to produce evidence

1. At the request of a party which has presented reasonably available evidence sufficient to support its claims and has, in substantiating those claims, specified evidence which lies in the control of the opposing party or a third party, the Court may order the opposing party or a third party to present such evidence, subject to the protection of confidential information. Such order shall not result in an obligation of self-incrimination.
2. At the request of a party the Court may order, under the same conditions as specified in paragraph 1, the communication of banking, financial or commercial documents under the control of the opposing party, subject to the protection of confidential information.

Article 60 Order to preserve evidence and to inspect premises

1. At the request of the applicant which has presented reasonably available evidence to support the claim that the patent has been infringed or is about to be infringed the Court may, even before the commencement of proceedings on the merits of the case, order prompt and effective provisional measures to preserve relevant evidence in respect of the alleged infringement, subject to the protection of confidential information.
2. Such measures may include the detailed description, with or without the taking of samples, or the physical seizure of the infringing products, and, in appropriate cases, the materials and implements used in the production and/or distribution of those products and the documents relating thereto.
3. The Court may, even before the commencement of proceedings on the merits of the case, at the request of the applicant who has presented evidence to support the claim that the patent has been infringed or is about to be infringed, order the inspection of premises. Such inspection of premises shall be conducted by a person appointed by the Court in accordance with the Rules of Procedure.

4. At the inspection of the premises the applicant shall not be present itself but may be represented by an independent professional practitioner whose name has to be specified in the Court's order.
5. Measures shall be ordered, if necessary without the other party having been heard, in particular where any delay is likely to cause irreparable harm to the proprietor of the patent, or where there is a demonstrable risk of evidence being destroyed.
6. Where measures to preserve evidence or inspect premises are ordered without the other party in the case having been heard, the parties affected shall be given notice, without delay and at the latest immediately after the execution of the measures. A review, including a right to be heard, shall take place upon request of the parties affected with a view to deciding, within a reasonable period after the notification of the measures, whether the measures are to be modified, revoked or confirmed.
7. The measures to preserve evidence may be subject to the lodging by the applicant of adequate security or an equivalent assurance intended to ensure compensation for any prejudice suffered by the defendant as provided for in paragraph 9.
8. The Court shall ensure that the measures to preserve evidence are revoked or otherwise cease to have effect, at the defendant's request, without prejudice to the damages which may be claimed, if the applicant does not bring, within a period not exceeding 31 calendar days or 20 working days, whichever is the longer, action leading to a decision on the merits of the case before the Court.
9. Where the measures to preserve evidence are revoked, or where they lapse due to any act or omission by the applicant, or where it is subsequently found that there has been no infringement or threat of infringement of the patent, the Court may order the applicant, at the defendant's request, to provide the defendant with appropriate compensation for any damage suffered as a result of those measures.

Article 61 Freezing orders
1. At the request of the applicant which has presented reasonably available evidence to support the claim that the patent has been infringed or is about to be infringed the Court may, even before the commencement of proceedings on the merits of the case, order a party not to remove from its jurisdiction any assets located therein, or not to deal in any assets, whether located within its jurisdiction or not.
2. Article 60(5) to (9) shall apply by analogy to the measures referred to in this Article.

Article 62 Provisional and protective measures
1. The Court may, by way of order, grant injunctions against an alleged infringer or against an intermediary whose services are used by the alleged infringer, intended to prevent any imminent infringement, to prohibit, on a provisional basis and subject, where appropriate, to a recurring penalty payment, the continuation of the alleged infringement or to make such continuation subject to the lodging of guarantees intended to ensure the compensation of the right holder.
2. The Court shall have the discretion to weigh up the interests of the parties and in particular to take into account the potential harm for either of the parties resulting from the granting or the refusal of the injunction.
3. The Court may also order the seizure or delivery up of the products suspected of infringing a patent so as to prevent their entry into, or movement, within the channels of commerce. If the applicant demonstrates circumstances likely to endanger the recovery of damages, the Court may order the precautionary seizure of the movable and immovable property of the alleged infringer, including the blocking of the bank accounts and of other assets of the alleged infringer.
4. The Court may, in respect of the measures referred to in paragraphs 1 and 3, require the applicant to provide any reasonable evidence in order to satisfy itself with a sufficient degree of certainty that the applicant is the right holder and that the applicant's right is being infringed, or that such infringement is imminent.
5. Article 60(5) to (9) shall apply by analogy to the measures referred to in this Article.

Article 63 Permanent injunctions

1. Where a decision is taken finding an infringement of a patent, the Court may grant an injunction against the infringer aimed at prohibiting the continuation of the infringement. The Court may also grant such injunction against an intermediary whose services are being used by a third party to infringe a patent.
2. Where appropriate, non-compliance with the injunction referred to in paragraph 1 shall be subject to a recurring penalty payment payable to the Court.

Article 64 Corrective measures in infringement proceedings

1. Without prejudice to any damages due to the injured party by reason of the infringement, and without compensation of any sort, the Court may order, at the request of the applicant, that appropriate measures be taken with regard to products found to be infringing a patent and, in appropriate cases, with regard to materials and implements principally used in the creation or manufacture of those products.
2. Such measures shall include:
   (a) a declaration of infringement;
   (b) recalling the products from the channels of commerce;
   (c) depriving the product of its infringing property;
   (d) definitively removing the products from the channels of commerce; or
   (e) the destruction of the products and/or of the materials and implements concerned.
3. The Court shall order that those measures be carried out at the expense of the infringer, unless particular reasons are invoked for not doing so.
4. In considering a request for corrective measures pursuant to this Article, the Court shall take into account the need for proportionality between the seriousness of the infringement and the remedies to be ordered, the willingness of the infringer to convert the materials into a non-infringing state, as well as the interests of third parties.

Article 65 Decision on the validity of a patent

1. The Court shall decide on the validity of a patent on the basis of an action for revocation or a counterclaim for revocation.
2. The Court may revoke a patent, either entirely or partly, only on the grounds referred to in Articles 138(1) and 139(2) of the EPC.
3. Without prejudice to Article 138(3) of the EPC, if the grounds for revocation affect the patent only in part, the patent shall be limited by a corresponding amendment of the claims and revoked in part.
4. To the extent that a patent has been revoked it shall be deemed not to have had, from the outset, the effects specified in Articles 64 and 67 of the EPC.
5. Where the Court, in a final decision, revokes a patent, either entirely or partly, it shall send a copy of the decision to the European Patent Office and, with respect to a European patent, to the national patent office of any Contracting Member State concerned.

Article 66 Powers of the Court concerning decisions of the European Patent Office

1. In actions brought under Article 32(1)(i), the Court may exercise any power entrusted on the European Patent Office in accordance with Article 9 of Regulation (EU) No 1257/2012, including the rectification of the Register for unitary patent protection.
2. In actions brought under Article 32(1)(i) the parties shall, by way of derogation from Article 69, bear their own costs.

Article 67 Power to order the communication of information

1. The Court may, in response to a justified and proportionate request of the applicant and in accordance with the Rules of Procedure, order an infringer to inform the applicant of:
   (a) the origin and distribution channels of the infringing products or processes;
   (b) the quantities produced, manufactured, delivered, received or ordered, as well as the price obtained for the infringing products; and
   (c) the identity of any third person involved in the production or distribution of the infringing products or in the use of the infringing process.
2. The Court may, in accordance with the Rules of Procedure, also order any third party who:
   (a) was found in the possession of the infringing products on a commercial scale or to be using an infringing process on a commercial scale;
   (b) was found to be providing on a commercial scale services used in infringing activities; or
   (c) was indicated by the person referred to in points (a) or (b) as being involved in the production, manufacture or distribution of the infringing products or processes or in the provision of the services,

to provide the applicant with the information referred to in paragraph 1.

Article 68 Award of damages

1. The Court shall, at the request of the injured party, order the infringer who knowingly, or with reasonable grounds to know, engaged in a patent infringing activity, to pay the injured party damages appropriate to the harm actually suffered by that party as a result of the infringement.
2. The injured party shall, to the extent possible, be placed in the position it would have been in if no infringement had taken place. The infringer shall not benefit from the infringement. However, damages shall not be punitive.
3. When the Court sets the damages:
   (a) it shall take into account all appropriate aspects, such as the negative economic consequences, including lost profits, which the injured party has suffered, any unfair profits made by the infringer and, in appropriate cases, elements other than economic factors, such as the moral prejudice caused to the injured party by the infringement; or
   (b) as an alternative to point (a), it may, in appropriate cases, set the damages as a lump sum on the basis of elements such as at least the amount of the royalties or fees which would have been due if the infringer had requested authorisation to use the patent in question.
4. Where the infringer did not knowingly, or with reasonable grounds to know, engage in the infringing activity, the Court may order the recovery of profits or the payment of compensation.

Article 69 Legal costs

1. Reasonable and proportionate legal costs and other expenses incurred by the successful party shall, as a general rule, be borne by the unsuccessful party, unless equity requires otherwise, up to a ceiling set in accordance with the Rules of Procedure.
2. Where a party succeeds only in part or in exceptional circumstances, the Court may order that costs be apportioned equitably or that the parties bear their own costs.
3. A party should bear any unnecessary costs it has caused the Court or another party.
4. At the request of the defendant, the Court may order the applicant to provide adequate security for the legal costs and other expenses incurred by the defendant which the applicant may be liable to bear, in particular in the cases referred to in Articles 59 to 62.

Article 70 Court fees

1. Parties to proceedings before the Court shall pay court fees.

2. Court fees shall be paid in advance, unless the Rules of Procedure provide otherwise. Any party which has not paid a prescribed court fee may be excluded from further participation in the proceedings.

Article 71 Legal aid

1. A party who is a natural person and who is unable to meet the costs of the proceedings, either wholly or in part, may at any time apply for legal aid. The conditions for granting of legal aid shall be laid down in the Rules of Procedure.
2. The Court shall decide whether legal aid should be granted in full or in part, or whether it should be refused, in accordance with the Rules of Procedure.
3. On a proposal from the Court, the Administrative Committee shall set the level of legal aid and the rules on bearing the costs thereof.

Article 72 Period of limitation

Without prejudice to Article 24(2) and (3), actions relating to all forms of financial compensation may not be brought more than five years after the date on which the applicant became aware, or had reasonable grounds to become aware, of the last fact justifying the action.

CHAPTER V APPEALS

Article 73 Appeal

1. An appeal against a decision of the Court of First Instance may be brought before the Court of Appeal by any party which has been unsuccessful, in whole or in part, in its submissions, within two months of the date of the notification of the decision.
2. An appeal against an order of the Court of First Instance may be brought before the Court of Appeal by any party which has been unsuccessful, in whole or in part, in its submissions:
   - (a) for the orders referred to in Articles 49(5), 59 to 62 and 67 within 15 calendar days of the notification of the order to the applicant;
   - (b) for other orders than the orders referred to in point (a):
     - (i) together with the appeal against the decision, or
     - (ii) where the Court grants leave to appeal, within 15 days of the notification of the Court's decision to that effect.
3. The appeal against a decision or an order of the Court of First Instance may be based on points of law and matters of fact.
4. New facts and new evidence may only be introduced in accordance with the Rules of Procedure and where the submission thereof by the party concerned could not reasonably have been expected during proceedings before the Court of First Instance.

Article 74 Effects of an appeal

1. An appeal shall not have suspensive effect unless the Court of Appeal decides otherwise at the motivated request of one of the parties. The Rules of Procedure shall guarantee that such a decision is taken without delay.
2. Notwithstanding paragraph 1, an appeal against a decision on actions or counterclaims for revocation and on actions based on Article 32(1)(i) shall always have suspensive effect.
3. An appeal against an order referred to in Articles 49(5), 59 to 62 or 67 shall not prevent the continuation of the main proceedings. However, the Court of First Instance shall not give a decision in the main proceedings before the decision of the Court of Appeal concerning an appealed order has been given.

Article 75 Decision on appeal and referral back

1. If an appeal pursuant to Article 73 is well-founded, the Court of Appeal shall revoke the decision of the Court of First Instance and give a final decision. The Court of Appeal may in exceptional cases and in accordance with the Rules of Procedure refer the case back to the Court of First Instance for decision.
2. Where a case is referred back to the Court of First Instance pursuant to paragraph 1, the Court of First Instance shall be bound by the decision of the Court of Appeal on points of law.

CHAPTER VI DECISIONS

Article 76 Basis for decisions and right to be heard

1. The Court shall decide in accordance with the requests submitted by the parties and shall not award more than is requested.
2. Decisions on the merits may only be based on grounds, facts and evidence, which were submitted by the parties or introduced into the procedure by an order of the Court and on which the parties have had an opportunity to present their comments.
3. The Court shall evaluate evidence freely and independently.

Article 77 Formal requirements

1. Decisions and orders of the Court shall be reasoned and shall be given in writing in accordance with the Rules of Procedure.
2. Decisions and orders of the Court shall be delivered in the language of proceedings.

Article 78 Decisions of the Court and dissenting opinions

1. Decisions and orders of the Court shall be taken by a majority of the panel, in accordance with the Statute. In case of equal votes, the vote of the presiding judge shall prevail.
2. In exceptional circumstances, any judge of the panel may express a dissenting opinion separately from the decision of the Court.

Article 79 Settlement

The parties may, at any time in the course of proceedings, conclude their case by way of settlement, which shall be confirmed by a decision of the Court. A patent may not be revoked or limited by way of settlement.

Article 80 Publication of decisions

The Court may order, at the request of the applicant and at the expense of the infringer, appropriate measures for the dissemination of information concerning the Court's decision, including displaying the decision and publishing it in full or in part in public media.

Article 81 Rehearing

1. A request for rehearing after a final decision of the Court may exceptionally be granted by the Court of Appeal in the following circumstances:
   (a) on discovery of a fact by the party requesting the rehearing, which is of such a nature as to be a decisive factor and which, when the decision was given, was unknown to the party requesting the rehearing; such request may only be granted on the basis of an act which was held, by a final decision of a national court, to constitute a criminal offence; or
   (b) in the event of a fundamental procedural defect, in particular when a defendant who did not appear before the Court was not served with the document initiating the proceedings or an

equivalent document in sufficient time and in such a way as to enable him to arrange for the defence.

2. A request for a rehearing shall be filed within 10 years of the date of the decision but not later than two months from the date of the discovery of the new fact or of the procedural defect. Such request shall not have suspensive effect unless the Court of Appeal decides otherwise.

3. If the request for a rehearing is well-founded, the Court of Appeal shall set aside, in whole or in part, the decision under review and re-open the proceedings for a new trial and decision, in accordance with the Rules of Procedure.

4. Persons using patents which are the subject-matter of a decision under review and who act in good faith should be allowed to continue using such patents.

Article 82 Enforcement of decisions and orders

1. Decisions and orders of the Court shall be enforceable in any Contracting Member State. An order for the enforcement of a decision shall be appended to the decision by the Court.

2. Where appropriate, the enforcement of a decision may be subject to the provision of security or an equivalent assurance to ensure compensation for any damage suffered, in particular in the case of injunctions.

3. Without prejudice to this Agreement and the Statute, enforcement procedures shall be governed by the law of the Contracting Member State where the enforcement takes place. Any decision of the Court shall be enforced under the same conditions as a decision given in the Contracting Member State where the enforcement takes place.

4. If a party does not comply with the terms of an order of the Court, that party may be sanctioned with a recurring penalty payment payable to the Court. The individual penalty shall be proportionate to the importance of the order to be enforced and shall be without prejudice to the party's right to claim damages or security.

PART IV TRANSITIONAL PROVISIONS

Article 83 Transitional regime

1. During a transitional period of seven years after the date of entry into force of this Agreement, an action for infringement or for revocation of a European patent or an action for infringement or for declaration of invalidity of a supplementary protection certificate issued for a product protected by a European patent may still be brought before national courts or other competent national authorities.

2. An action pending before a national court at the end of the transitional period shall not be affected by the expiry of this period.

3. Unless an action has already been brought before the Court, a proprietor of or an applicant for a European patent granted or applied for prior to the end of the transitional period under paragraph 1 and, where applicable, paragraph 5, as well as a holder of a supplementary protection certificate issued for a product protected by a European patent, shall have the possibility to opt out from the exclusive competence of the Court. To this end they shall notify their opt-out to the Registry by the latest one month before expiry of the transitional period. The opt-out shall take effect upon its entry into the register.

4. Unless an action has already been brought before a national court, proprietors of or applicants for European patents or holders of supplementary protection certificates issued for a product protected by a European patent who made use of the opt-out in accordance with paragraph 3 shall be entitled to withdraw their opt-out at any moment. In this event they shall notify the Registry accordingly. The withdrawal of the opt-out shall take effect upon its entry into the register.

5. Five years after the entry into force of this Agreement, the Administrative Committee shall carry out a broad consultation with the users of the patent system and a survey on the number of European

patents and supplementary protection certificates issued for products protected by European patents with respect to which actions for infringement or for revocation or declaration of invalidity are still brought before the national courts pursuant to paragraph 1, the reasons for this and the implications thereof. On the basis of this consultation and an opinion of the Court, the Administrative Committee may decide to prolong the transitional period by up to seven years.

PART V FINAL PROVISIONS

Article 84 Signature, ratification and accession

1. This Agreement shall be open for signature by any Member State on 19 February 2013.
2. This Agreement shall be subject to ratification in accordance with the respective constitutional requirements of the Member States. Instruments of ratification shall be deposited with the General Secretariat of the Council of the European Union (hereinafter referred to as 'the depositary').
3. Each Member State having signed this Agreement shall notify the European Commission of its ratification of the Agreement at the time of the deposit of its ratification instrument pursuant to Article 18(3) of Regulation (EU) No 1257/2012.
4. This Agreement shall be open to accession by any Member State. Instruments of accession shall be deposited with the depositary.

Article 85 Functions of the depositary

1. The depositary shall draw up certified true copies of this Agreement and shall transmit them to the governments of all signatory or acceding Member States.
2. The depositary shall notify the governments of the signatory or acceding Member States of:
   (a) any signature;
   (b) the deposit of any instrument of ratification or accession;
   (c) the date of entry into force of this Agreement.
3. The depositary shall register this Agreement with the Secretariat of the United Nations.

Article 86 Duration of the Agreement

This Agreement shall be of unlimited duration.

Article 87 Revision

1. Either seven years after the entry into force of this Agreement or once 2 000 infringement cases have been decided by the Court, whichever is the later point in time, and if necessary at regular intervals thereafter, a broad consultation with the users of the patent system shall be carried out by the Administrative Committee on the functioning, efficiency and cost-effectiveness of the Court and on the trust and confidence of users of the patent system in the quality of the Court's decisions. On the basis of this consultation and an opinion of the Court, the Administrative Committee may decide to revise this Agreement with a view to improving the functioning of the Court.
2. The Administrative Committee may amend this Agreement to bring it into line with an international treaty relating to patents or Union law.
3. A decision of the Administrative Committee taken on the basis of paragraphs 1 and 2 shall not take effect if a Contracting Member State declares within twelve months of the date of the decision, on the basis of its relevant internal decision-making procedures, that it does not wish to be bound by the decision. In this case, a Review Conference of the Contracting Member States shall be convened.

Article 88 Languages of the Agreement

1. This Agreement is drawn up in a single original in the English, French and German languages, each text being equally authentic.

2. The texts of this Agreement drawn up in official languages of Contracting Member States other than those specified in paragraph 1 shall, if they have been approved by the Administrative Committee, be considered as official texts. In the event of divergences between the various texts, the texts referred to in paragraph 1 shall prevail.

Article 89 Entry into force
1. This Agreement shall enter into force on 1 January 2014 or on the first day of the fourth month after the deposit of the thirteenth instrument of ratification or accession in accordance with Article 84, including the three Member States in which the highest number of European patents had effect in the year preceding the year in which the signature of the Agreement takes place or on the first day of the fourth month after the date of entry into force of the amendments to Regulation (EU) No 1215/2012 concerning its relationship with this Agreement, whichever is the latest.
2. Any ratification or accession after the entry into force of this Agreement shall take effect on the first day of the fourth month after the deposit of the instrument of ratification or accession.
In witness whereof the undersigned, being duly authorised thereto, have signed this Agreement,

Done at Brussels on 19 February 2013 in English, French and German, all three texts being equally authentic, in a single copy which shall be deposited in the archives of the General Secretariat of the Council of the European Union.

ANNEX I STATUTE OF THE UNIFIED PATENT COURT

Article 1 Scope of the Statute
This Statute contains institutional and financial arrangements for the Unified Patent Court as established under Article 1 of the Agreement.

CHAPTER I JUDGES

Article 2 Eligibility of judges
1. Any person who is a national of a Contracting Member State and fulfils the conditions set out in Article 15 of the Agreement and in this Statute may be appointed as a judge.
2. Judges shall have a good command of at least one official language of the European Patent Office.
3. Experience with patent litigation which has to be proven for the appointment pursuant to Article 15(1) of the Agreement may be acquired by training under Article 11(4)(a) of this Statute.

Article 3 Appointment of judges
1. Judges shall be appointed pursuant to the procedure set out in Article 16 of the Agreement.
2. Vacancies shall be publicly advertised and shall indicate the relevant eligibility criteria as set out in Article 2. The Advisory Committee shall give an opinion on candidates' suitability to perform the duties of a judge of the Court. The opinion shall comprise a list of most suitable candidates. The list shall contain at least twice as many candidates as there are vacancies. Where necessary, the Advisory Committee may recommend that, prior to the decision on the appointment, a candidate judge receive training in patent litigation pursuant to Article 11(4)(a).
3. When appointing judges, the Administrative Committee shall ensure the best legal and technical expertise and a balanced composition of the Court on as broad a geographical basis as possible among nationals of the Contracting Member States.
4. The Administrative Committee shall appoint as many judges as are needed for the proper functioning of the Court. The Administrative Committee shall initially appoint the necessary number of judges

for setting up at least one panel in each of the divisions of the Court of First Instance and at least two panels in the Court of Appeal.
5. The decision of the Administrative Committee appointing full-time or part-time legally qualified judges and full-time technically qualified judges shall state the instance of the Court and/or the division of the Court of First Instance for which each judge is appointed and the field(s) of technology for which a technically qualified judge is appointed.
6. Part-time technically qualified judges shall be appointed as judges of the Court and shall be included in the Pool of Judges on the basis of their specific qualifications and experience. The appointment of these judges to the Court shall ensure that all fields of technology are covered.

Article 4 Judges' term of office
1. Judges shall be appointed for a term of six years, beginning on the date laid down in the instrument of appointment. They may be re-appointed.
2. In the absence of any provision regarding the date, the term shall begin on the date of the instrument of appointment.

Article 5 Appointment of the members of the Advisory Committee
1. Each Contracting Member State shall propose a member of the Advisory Committee who fulfils the requirements set out in Article 14(2) of the Agreement.
2. The members of the Advisory Committee shall be appointed by the Administrative Committee acting by common accord.

Article 6 Oath
Before taking up their duties judges shall, in open court, take an oath to perform their duties impartially and conscientiously and to preserve the secrecy of the deliberations of the Court.

Article 7 Impartiality
1. Immediately after taking their oath, judges shall sign a declaration by which they solemnly undertake that, both during and after their term of office, they shall respect the obligations arising therefrom, in particular the duty to behave with integrity and discretion as regards the acceptance, after they have ceased to hold office, of certain appointments or benefits.
2. Judges may not take part in the proceedings of a case in which they:
  (a) have taken part as adviser;
  (b) have been a party or have acted for one of the parties;
  (c) have been called upon to pronounce as a member of a court, tribunal, board of appeal, arbitration or mediation panel, a commission of inquiry or in any other capacity;
  (d) have a personal or financial interest in the case or in relation to one of the parties; or
  (e) are related to one of the parties or the representatives of the parties by family ties.
3. If, for some special reason, a judge considers that he or she should not take part in the judgement or examination of a particular case, that judge shall so inform the President of the Court of Appeal accordingly or, in the case of judges of the Court of First Instance, the President of the Court of First Instance. If, for some special reason, the President of the Court of Appeal or, in the case of judges of the Court of First Instance, the President of the Court of First Instance considers that a judge should not sit or make submissions in a particular case, the President of the Court of Appeal or the President of the Court of First Instance shall justify this in writing and notify the judge concerned accordingly.
4. Any party to an action may object to a judge taking part in the proceedings on any of the grounds listed in paragraph 2 or where the judge is suspected, with good reason, of partiality.

5. Any difficulty arising as to the application of this Article shall be settled by decision of the Presidium, in accordance with the Rules of Procedure. The judge concerned shall be heard but shall not take part in the deliberations.

Article 8 Immunity of judges
1. The judges shall be immune from legal proceedings. After they have ceased to hold office, they shall continue to enjoy immunity in respect of acts performed by them in relation to their official capacity.
2. The Presidium may waive the immunity.
3. Where immunity has been waived and criminal proceedings are instituted against a judge, that judge shall be tried, in any of the Contracting Member States, only by the court competent to judge the members of the highest national judiciary.
4. The Protocol on the privileges and immunities of the European Union shall apply to the judges of the Court, without prejudice to the provisions relating to immunity from legal proceedings of judges which are set out in this Statute.

Article 9 End of duties
1. Apart from replacement after expiry of a judge's term pursuant to Article 4, or death, the duties of a judge shall end when that judge resigns.
2. Where a judge resigns, the letter of resignation shall be addressed to the President of the Court of Appeal or, in the case of judges of the Court of First Instance, the President of the Court of First Instance for transmission to the Chairman of the Administrative Committee.
3. Save where Article 10 applies, a judge shall continue to hold office until that judge's successor takes up his or her duties.
4. Any vacancy shall by filled by the appointment of a new judge for the remainder of his or her predecessor's term.

Article 10 Removal from office
1. A judge may be deprived of his or her office or of other benefits only if the Presidium decides that that judge no longer fulfils the requisite conditions or meets the obligations arising from his or her office. The judge concerned shall be heard but shall not take part in the deliberations.
2. The Registrar of the Court shall communicate this decision to the Chairman of the Administrative Committee.
3. In the case of a decision depriving a judge of his or her office, a vacancy shall arise upon that notification.

Article 11 Training
1. Appropriate and regular training of judges shall be provided for within the training framework set up under Article 19 of the Agreement. The Presidium shall adopt Training Regulations ensuring the implementation and overall coherence of the training framework.
2. The training framework shall provide a platform for the exchange of expertise and a forum for discussion, in particular by:
   (a) organising courses, conferences, seminars, workshops and symposia;
   (b) cooperating with international organisations and education institutes in the field of intellectual property; and
   (c) promoting and supporting further vocational training.
3. An annual work programme and training guidelines shall be drawn up, which shall include for each judge an annual training plan identifying that judge's main training needs in accordance with the Training Regulations.
4. The training framework shall in addition:

(a) ensure appropriate training for candidate-judges and newly appointed judges of the Court;
(b) support projects aimed at facilitating cooperation between representatives, patent attorneys and the Court.

Article 12 Remuneration
The Administrative Committee shall set the remuneration of the President of the Court of Appeal, the President of the Court of First Instance, the judges, the Registrar, the Deputy-Registrar and the staff.

CHAPTER II ORGANISATIONAL PROVISIONS

SECTION 1 COMMON PROVISIONS

Article 13 President of the Court of Appeal
1. The President of the Court of Appeal shall be elected by all judges of the Court of Appeal for a term of three years, from among their number. The President of the Court of Appeal may be re-elected twice.
2. The elections of the President of the Court of Appeal shall be by secret ballot. A judge obtaining an absolute majority shall be elected. If no judge obtains an absolute majority, a second ballot shall be held and the judge obtaining the most votes shall be elected.
3. The President of the Court of Appeal shall direct the judicial activities and the administration of the Court of Appeal and chair the Court of Appeal sitting as a full Court.
4. If the office of the President of the Court of Appeal falls vacant before the date of expiry of his or her term, a successor shall be elected for the remainder thereof.

Article 14 President of the Court of First Instance
1. The President of the Court of First Instance shall be elected by all judges of the Court of First Instance who are full-time judges, for a term of three years, from among their number. The President of the Court of First Instance may be re-elected twice.
2. The first President of the Court of First Instance shall be a national of the Contracting Member State hosting the seat of the central division.
3. The President of the Court of First Instance shall direct the judicial activities and the administration of the Court of First Instance.
4. Article 13(2) and (4), shall by analogy apply to the President of the Court of First Instance.

Article 15 Presidium
1. The Presidium shall be composed of the President of the Court of Appeal, who shall act as chairperson, the President of the Court of First Instance, two judges of the Court of Appeal elected from among their number, three judges of the Court of First Instance who are full-time judges of the Court elected from among their number, and the Registrar as a non-voting member.
2. The Presidium shall exercise its duties in accordance with this Statute. It may, without prejudice to its own responsibility, delegate certain tasks to one of its members.
3. The Presidium shall be responsible for the management of the Court and shall in particular:
(a) draw up proposals for the amendment of the Rules of Procedure in accordance with Article 41 of the Agreement and proposals regarding the Financial Regulations of the Court;
(b) prepare the annual budget, the annual accounts and the annual report of the Court and submit them to the Budget Committee;
(c) establish the guidelines for the training programme for judges and supervise the implementation thereof;
(d) take decisions on the appointment and removal of the Registrar and the Deputy-Registrar;
(e) lay down the rules governing the Registry including the sub-registries;

(f) give an opinion in accordance with Article 83(5) of the Agreement.

4. Decisions of the Presidium referred to in Articles 7, 8, 10 and 22 shall be taken without the participation of the Registrar.

5. The Presidium can take valid decisions only when all members are present or duly represented. Decisions shall be taken by a majority of the votes.

Article 16 Staff

1. The officials and other servants of the Court shall have the task of assisting the President of the Court of Appeal, the President of the Court of First Instance, the judges and the Registrar. They shall be responsible to the Registrar, under the authority of the President of the Court of Appeal and the President of the Court of First Instance.

2. The Administrative Committee shall establish the Staff Regulations of officials and other servants of the Court.

Article 17 Judicial vacations

1. After consulting the Presidium, the President of the Court of Appeal shall establish the duration of judicial vacations and the rules on observing official holidays.

2. During the period of judicial vacations, the functions of the President of the Court of Appeal and of the President of the Court of First Instance may be exercised by any judge invited by the respective President to that effect. In cases of urgency, the President of the Court of Appeal may convene the judges.

3. The President of the Court of Appeal or the President of the Court of First Instance may, in proper circumstances, grant leave of absence to respectively judges of the Court of Appeal or judges of the Court of First Instance.

SECTION 2 THE COURT OF FIRST INSTANCE

Article 18 Setting up and discontinuance of a local or regional division

1. A request from one or more Contracting Member States for the setting up of a local or regional division shall be addressed to the Chairman of the Administrative Committee. It shall indicate the seat of the local or regional division.

2. The decision of the Administrative Committee setting up a local or regional division shall indicate the number of judges for the division concerned and shall be public.

3. The Administrative Committee shall decide to discontinue a local or regional division at the request of the Contracting Member State hosting the local division or the Contracting Member States participating in the regional division. The decision to discontinue a local or regional division shall state the date after which no new cases may be brought before the division and the date on which the division will cease to exist.

4. As from the date on which a local or regional division ceases to exist, the judges assigned to that local or regional division shall be assigned to the central division, and cases still pending before that local or regional division together with the sub-registry and all of its documentation shall be transferred to the central division.

Article 19 Panels

1. The allocation of judges and the assignment of cases within a division to its panels shall be governed by the Rules of Procedure. One judge of the panel shall be designated as the presiding judge, in accordance with the Rules of Procedure.

2. The panel may delegate, in accordance with the Rules of Procedure, certain functions to one or more of its judges.

3. A standing judge for each division to hear urgent cases may be designated in accordance with the Rules of Procedure.
4. In cases where a single judge in accordance with Article 8(7) of the Agreement, or a standing judge, in accordance with paragraph 3 of this Article, hears a case that judge shall carry out all functions of a panel.
5. One judge of the panel shall act as Rapporteur, in accordance with the Rules of Procedure.

Article 20 Pool of Judges
1. A list with the names of the judges included in the Pool of Judges shall be drawn up by the Registrar. In relation to each judge, the list shall at least indicate the linguistic skills, the field of technology and experience of, as well as the cases previously handled by, that judge.
2. A request addressed to the President of the Court of First Instance to assign a judge from the Pool of Judges shall indicate, in particular, the subject-matter of the case, the official language of the European Patent Office used by the judges of the panel, the language of the proceedings and the field of technology required.

SECTION 3 THE COURT OF APPEAL

Article 21 Panels
1. The allocation of judges and the assignment of cases to panels shall be governed by the Rules of Procedure. One judge of the panel shall be appointed as the presiding judge, in accordance with the Rules of Procedure.
2. When a case is of exceptional importance, and in particular when the decision may affect the unity and consistency of the case law of the Court, the Court of Appeal may decide, on the basis of a proposal from the presiding judge, to refer the case to the full Court.
3. The panel may delegate, in accordance with the Rules of Procedure, certain functions to one or more of its judges.
4. One judge of the panel shall act as Rapporteur, in accordance with the Rules of Procedure.

SECTION 4 THE REGISTRY

Article 22 Appointment and removal from office of the Registrar
1. The Presidium shall appoint the Registrar of the Court for a term of six years. The Registrar may be re-appointed.
2. Two weeks before the date fixed for appointing the Registrar, the President of the Court of Appeal shall inform the Presidium of the applications which have been submitted for the post.
3. Before taking up his or her duties, the Registrar shall take oath before the Presidium to perform the duties of the Registrar impartially and conscientiously.
4. The Registrar may be removed from office only if the Registrar no longer meets the obligations arising from his or her office. The Presidium shall take its decision after having heard the Registrar.
5. If the office of the Registrar falls vacant before the date of expiry of the term thereof, the Presidium shall appoint a new Registrar for a term of six years.
6. If the Registrar is absent or prevented from attending or where such post is vacant, the President of the Court of Appeal after having consulted the Presidium shall designate a member of the staff of the Court to carry out the duties of the Registrar.

Article 23 Duties of the Registrar
1. The Registrar shall assist the Court, the President of the Court of Appeal, the President of the Court of First Instance and the judges in the performance of their functions. The Registrar shall be responsi-

ble for the organisation and activities of the Registry under the authority of the President of the Court of Appeal.
2. The Registrar shall in particular be responsible for:
   (a) keeping the register which shall include records of all cases before the Court;
   (b) keeping and administering lists drawn up in accordance with Articles 18, 48(3) and 57(2) of the Agreement;
   (c) keeping and publishing a list of notifications and withdrawals of opt-outs in accordance with Article 83 of the Agreement;
   (d) publishing the decisions of the Court, subject to the protection of confidential information;
   (e) publishing annual reports with statistical data; and
   (f) ensuring that the information on opt-outs in accordance with Article 83 of the Agreement is notified to the European Patent Office.

Article 24 Keeping of the register
1. Detailed rules for keeping the register of the Court shall be prescribed in the Rules governing the Registry, adopted by the Presidium.
2. The rules on access to documents of the Registry shall be provided for in the Rules of Procedure.

Article 25 Sub-registries and Deputy-Registrar
1. A Deputy-Registrar shall be appointed for a term of six years by the Presidium. The Deputy-Registrar may be re-appointed.
2. Article 22(2) to (6) shall apply by analogy.
3. The Deputy-Registrar shall be responsible for the organisation and activities of sub-registries under the authority of the Registrar and the President of the Court of First Instance. The duties of the Deputy-Registrar shall in particular include:
   (a) keeping records of all cases before the Court of First Instance;
   (b) notifying every case before the Court of First Instance to the Registry.
4. The Deputy-Registrar shall also provide administrative and secretarial assistance to the divisions of the Court of First Instance.

CHAPTER III FINANCIAL PROVISIONS

Article 26 Budget
1. The budget shall be adopted by the Budget Committee on a proposal from the Presidium. It shall be drawn up in accordance with the generally accepted accounting principles laid down in the Financial Regulations, established in accordance with Article 33.
2. Within the budget, the Presidium may, in accordance with the Financial Regulations, transfer funds between the various headings or subheadings.
3. The Registrar shall be responsible for the implementation of the budget in accordance with the Financial Regulations.
4. The Registrar shall annually make a statement on the accounts of the preceding financial year relating to the implementation of the budget which shall be approved by the Presidium.

Article 27 Authorisation for expenditure
1. The expenditure entered in the budget shall be authorised for the duration of one accounting period unless the Financial Regulations provide otherwise.
2. In accordance with the Financial Regulations, any appropriations, other than those relating to staff costs, which are unexpended at the end of the accounting period may be carried forward, but not beyond the end of the following accounting period.

3. Appropriations shall be set out under different headings according to type and purpose of the expenditure, and subdivided, to the extent necessary, in accordance with the Financial Regulations.

Article 28 Appropriations for unforeseeable expenditure
1. The budget of the Court may include appropriations for unforeseeable expenditure.
2. The employment of these appropriations by the Court shall be subject to the prior approval of the Budget Committee.

Article 29 Accounting period
The accounting period shall commence on 1 January and end on 31 December.

Article 30 Preparation of the budget
The Presidium shall submit the draft budget of the Court to the Budget Committee no later than the date prescribed in the Financial Regulations.

Article 31 Provisional budget
1. If, at the beginning of the accounting period, the budget has not been adopted by the Budget Committee, expenditure may be effected on a monthly basis per heading or other division of the budget, in accordance with the Financial Regulations, up to one-twelfth of the budget appropriations for the preceding accounting period, provided that the appropriations thus made available to the Presidium do not exceed one-twelfth of those provided for in the draft budget.
2. The Budget Committee may, subject to the observance of the other provisions laid down in paragraph 1, authorise expenditure in excess of one-twelfth of the budget appropriations for the preceding accounting period.

Article 32 Auditing of accounts
1. The annual financial statements of the Court shall be examined by independent auditors. The auditors shall be appointed and if necessary dismissed by the Budget Committee.
2. The audit, which shall be based on professional auditing standards and shall take place, if necessary, in situ, shall ascertain that the budget has been implemented in a lawful and proper manner and that the financial administration of the Court has been conducted in accordance with the principles of economy and sound financial management. The auditors shall draw up a report after the end of each accounting period containing a signed audit opinion.
3. The Presidium shall submit to the Budget Committee the annual financial statements of the Court and the annual budget implementation statement for the preceding accounting period, together with the auditors' report.
4. The Budget Committee shall approve the annual accounts together with the auditors' report and shall discharge the Presidium in respect of the implementation of the budget.

Article 33 Financial Regulations
1. The Financial Regulations shall be adopted by the Administrative Committee. They shall be amended by the Administrative Committee on a proposal from the Court.
2. The Financial Regulations shall lay down in particular:
   (a) arrangements relating to the establishment and implementation of the budget and for the rendering and auditing of accounts;
   (b) the method and procedure whereby the payments and contributions, including the initial financial contributions provided for in Article 37 of the Agreement are to be made available to the Court;

(c) the rules concerning the responsibilities of authorising and accounting officers and the arrangements for their supervision; and
(d) the generally accepted accounting principles on which the budget and the annual financial statements are to be based.

CHAPTER IV PROCEDURAL PROVISIONS

Article 34 Secrecy of deliberations
The deliberations of the Court shall be and shall remain secret.

Article 35 Decisions
1. When a panel sits in composition of an even number of judges, decisions of the Court shall be taken by a majority of the panel. In case of equal vote, the vote of the presiding judge shall prevail.
2. In the event of one of the judges of a panel being prevented from attending, a judge from another panel may be called upon to sit in accordance with the Rules of Procedure.
3. In cases where this Statute provides that the Court of Appeal shall take a decision sitting as a full court, such decision shall be valid only if it is taken by at least 3/4 of the judges comprising the full court.
4. Decisions of the Court shall contain the names of the judges deciding the case.
5. Decisions shall be signed by the judges deciding the case, by the Registrar for decisions of the Court of Appeal, and by the Deputy-Registrar for decisions of the Court of First Instance. They shall be read in open court.

Article 36 Dissenting opinions
A dissenting opinion expressed separately by a judge of a panel in accordance with Article 78 of the Agreement shall be reasoned, given in writing and shall be signed by the judge expressing this opinion.

Article 37 Decision by default
1. At the request of a party to an action, a decision by default may be given in accordance with the Rules of Procedure, where the other party, after having been served with a document instituting proceedings or with an equivalent document, fails to file written submissions in defence or fails to appear at the oral hearing. An objection may be lodged against that decision within one month of it being notified to the party against which the default decision has been given.
2. The objection shall not have the effect of staying enforcement of the decision by default unless the Court decides otherwise.

Article 38 Questions referred to the Court of Justice of the European Union
1. The procedures established by the Court of Justice of the European Union for referrals for preliminary rulings within the European Union shall apply.
2. Whenever the Court of First Instance or the Court of Appeal has decided to refer to the Court of Justice of the European Union a question of interpretation of the Treaty on European Union or of the Treaty on the Functioning of the European Union or a question on the validity or interpretation of acts of the institutions of the European Union, it shall stay its proceedings.

ANNEX II

DISTRIBUTION OF CASES WITHIN THE CENTRAL DIVISION[15]

LONDON Section	PARIS Seat	MUNICH Section
	President's Office	
(A) Human necessities	(B) Performing operations, transporting	(F) Mechanical engineering, lighting, heating, weapons, blasting
(C) Chemistry, metallurgy	(D) Textiles, paper	
	(E) Fixed constructions	
	(G) Physics	
	(H) Electricity	

15 The classification into 8 sections (A to H) is based on the International Patent Classification of the World Intellectual Property Organisation (http://www.wipo.int/classifications/ipc/en).

3. Set-up of local and regional divisions of the Court of First Instance of the Unified Patent Court

Decision of the Administrative Committee of 8 July 2022 on the set-up of local and regional divisions of the court of First Instance of the Unified Patent Court

THE ADMINISTRATIVE COMMITTEE OF THE UNIFIED PATENT COURT

HAVING REGARD to the Agreement on a Unified Patent Court and in particular Article 7(3), (4) and (5) and Article 8(1) to (4) thereof;

HAVING REGARD to the Statute of the Unified Patent Court and in particular Article 18(1) and (2) thereof;

HAS DECIDED AS FOLLOWS:

I. SET-UP OF LOCAL AND REGIONAL DIVISIONS OF THE COURT OF FIRST INSTANCE OF THE UNIFIED PATENT COURT

1. Local divisions of the Court of First Instance of the Unified Patent Court shall be established at the following locations, with the indicated number of judges for the division concerned:
   (a) in Vienna, Austria – 1 Legally Qualified Judge
   (b) in Brussels, Belgium – 1 Legally Qualified Judge
   (c) in Copenhagen, Denmark – 1 Legally Qualified Judge
   (d) In Helsinki, Finland – 1 Legally Qualified Judge
   (e) in Paris, France – 2 Legally Qualified Judges
   (f) in Düsseldorf, Germany – 2 Legally Qualified Judges
   (g) in Hamburg, Germany – 2 Legally Qualified Judges
   (h) in Mannheim, Germany – 2 Legally Qualified Judges
   (i) in Munich, Germany – 2 Legally Qualified Judges
   (j) in Milan, Italy – 2 Legally Qualified Judges
   (k) in Lisbon, Portugal – 1 Legally Qualified Judge
   (l) in Ljubljana, Slovenia – 1 Legally Qualified Judge
   (m) in The Hague, The Netherlands – 2 Legally Qualified Judges
2. The following regional division of the Court of First Instance of the Unified Patent Court shall be established, with the indicated number of judges for the division concerned:
   (a) Nordic-Baltic regional division, mainly located in Stockholm – 2 Legally Qualified Judges

II. ENTRY INTO FORCE

This decision shall enter into force on 8 July 2022.

Done at Luxembourg on 8 July 2022

For the Administrative Committee

The Chairman

4. Rules on the European Patent Litigation Certificate and other appropriate qualifications

Decision of the Administrative Committee of 22 February 2022

Rules on the European Patent Litigation Certificate and other appropriate qualifications pursuant to article 48(2) of the agreement on a Unified Patent Court

THE ADMINISTRATIVE COMMITTEE OF THE UNIFIED PATENT COURT HAS DECIDED AS FOLLOWS:

PART I – EUROPEAN PATENT LITIGATION CERTIFICATE

Rule 1 - European Patent Litigation Certificate
The European Patent Litigation Certificate (hereinafter referred to as Certificate) may be acquired in accordance with the provisions laid down in this Part.

Rule 2 - European Patent Litigation Course
The Certificate may be issued by universities and other non-profit educational bodies of higher or professional education established in a Member State of the European Union as well as by the Unified Patent Court's Training Centre in Budapest (hereinafter referred to as Training Centre) to European Patent Attorneys[1] entitled to act as professional representatives before the European Patent Office pursuant to Article 134 of the European Patent Convention (hereinafter referred to as European Patent Attorneys) who have successfully completed a course on European patent litigation accredited pursuant to Rules 6 – 8 (hereinafter referred to as Course).

Rule 3 - Content of the Course
1. The curriculum of the Course shall cover:
   (a) a general introduction into law, including main aspects of European law;
   (b) basic knowledge of private law, including contract law, company law and tort law, in both common and continental law, and private international law;
   (c) the role, organisation and patent-related case law of the Court of Justice of the European Union, including case law on supplementary protection certificates;
   (d) enforcement of patents, providing knowledge of Directive 2004/48 (EC) on the enforcement of intellectual property rights and relevant case law of the Court of Justice of the European Union;
   (e) unitary patent protection, providing advanced knowledge of Regulations 1257/2012 (EU) implementing enhanced cooperation in the area of the creation of unitary patent protection and 1260/2012 (EU) implementing enhanced cooperation in the area of the creation of unitary patent protection with regard to the applicable translation arrangements, as well as the Rules relating to unitary patent protection;
   (f) a comparative overview on patent infringement proceedings and revocation of patents in Contracting Member States;
   (g) the operation of the Unified Patent Court, providing advanced knowledge of the Agreement on the Unified Patent Court and the Unified Patent Court's Statute;

1 Words importing the masculine gender shall include the feminine and vice versa.

(h) litigation before the Unified Patent Court, providing advanced knowledge of procedures, litigation and advocacy skills, practice and case management before the Unified Patent Court, with special regard to the Rules of Procedure of the Unified Patent Court.

2. The Course shall focus in particular on the contents mentioned in points (e)-(h) of paragraph (1) and include practical exercise on litigation and negotiation.

Rule 4 - Duration of the Course and examination requirements

1. The minimum duration of the Course shall be 120 hours of lectures and practical training.
2. The Course shall be concluded by both a written and oral examination.

Rule 5 - Course languages and e-learning

1. The Course may be provided in any official language of a Member State of the European Union.
2. E-learning facilities are encouraged as an integral part of the Course. However, practical training always requires personal participation.

Rule 6 - Accreditation requirement

Universities and other non-profit educational bodies of higher or professional education established in a Member State of the European Union may offer the Course subject to accreditation by the Administrative Committee.

Rule 7 - Request for accreditation

The request for accreditation of the Course shall be filed with the Unified Patent Court in one of the official languages of the European Patent Office and shall contain:

(a) the curriculum of the Course envisaged;
(b) information concerning the requirements under Rules 4 and 5;
(c) information concerning the requestor's status;
(d) information concerning the number of hours for each topic of the Course;
(e) names and titles of the selected teachers;
(f) draft scheme of examination, defining the objectives and the method of examination, including the number and duration of written and oral exams.

Rule 8 - Examination of the request and decision

1. The request for accreditation shall be decided upon by the Administrative Committee on the basis of an opinion of the Advisory Committee.
2. If the requirements under Rules 3 - 6 are met and the request for accreditation complies with Rule 7, the Advisory Committee shall give an opinion in favour of accreditation to the Administrative Committee.
3. If the requirements under Rules 3 - 6 are not met or if the request for accreditation fails to comply with Rule 7, the Advisory Committee shall give a negative opinion on the request.

In this event, the Administrative Committee shall communicate the Advisory Committee's opinion to the requestor and invite him, according to the nature of the objection, to correct the deficiencies noted or to submit comments within a non-extendable period of two months. If the deficiencies are not corrected in due time, the Administrative Committee shall refuse the request. If the requestor corrects the deficiencies or submits comments, the Administrative Committee shall consult the Advisory Committee once again and decide on the request on the basis of the second opinion of the Advisory Committee.

4. Accreditation is granted for five academic years following the date of the notification of the decision on accreditation. The request for the prolongation of the accreditation for another five years may be

filed one year before the expiry of the five-year period at the earliest. Rule 7 and Rule 8(1)-(3) shall apply *mutatis mutandis*.

Rule 9 – Reports
Participating educational bodies are required to report every year to the Unified Patent Court on the curriculum, results and statistics of the accredited Course. The Administrative Committee takes note of this report.

Rule 10 – Training Centre
1. The Training Centre, by offering the necessary infrastructural and organisational assets, shall assist the educational bodies that wish to provide a Course at the seat of the Training Centre as well. It may also facilitate e-learning options.
2. The Training Centre may also offer the Course in compliance with Rules 3-5. In this case, Rule 9 applies to the Training Centre as well.

PART II – OTHER APPROPRIATE QUALIFICATIONS

Rule 11 – Law diplomas
European Patent Attorneys holding a bachelor or master degree in law according to relevant educational standards in a Member State of the European Union or who have passed an equivalent state exam in law of a Member State of the European Union shall be deemed to have appropriate qualifications pursuant to Article 48(2) of the Agreement on a Unified Patent Court and may apply for registration on the list of entitled representatives.

Rule 12 – Other qualifications during a transitional period
1. During a period of one year from the entry into force of the Agreement on a Unified Patent Court, any of the following shall also be deemed as appropriate qualifications for a European Patent Attorney pursuant to Article 48(2) of the Agreement on a Unified Patent Court:
- (a) the successful completion of one of the following courses or the grant of one of the following certificates:
  - (i) Centre d'Études Internationales de la Propriété Intellectuelle, courses leading to the Diploma on Patent litigation in Europe or to the Diploma of international studies in industrial property (specialized in patents);
  - (ii) FernUniversität in Hagen, course "Law for Patent Attorneys" and its predecessor, the course "Kandidatenkurs Fischbachau";
  - (iii) Humboldt Universität zu Berlin, course "Zusatzstudium Gewerblicher Rechtsschutz";
  - (iv) Nottingham Law School, course "Intellectual Property Litigation and Advocacy";
  - (v) Queen Mary University of London, courses "Certificate in Intellectual Property Law" or "MSc Management of Intellectual Property";
  - (vi) Intellectual Property Regulation Board, "Intellectual Property Litigation Certificate";
  - (vii) Intellectual Property Regulation Board, "Higher Courts Litigation Certificate";
  - (viii) Intellectual Property Regulation Board, "Higher Courts Advocacy Certificate";
  - (ix) Stichting Beroepsopleiding Octrooigemachtigden, course "Beroepsopleiding Octrooigemachtigden";
  - (x) Hungarian Intellectual Property Office, course "Advanced Course in Intellectual Property";
  - (xi) University of Milano, course "Corso di Perfezionamento in Brevettistica";

(xii) Politecnico di Milano, "Certificato di superamento dell'esame conclusivo del Corso di Proprietà Industriale – Brevetti";
(xiii) University of Warsaw, course "Podyplomowe Studium Prawa Własności Przemysłowej";

or

(b) having represented a party on his own without the assistance of a lawyer admitted to the relevant court or having acted as a judge in at least three patent infringement actions, initiated before a national court of a Contracting Member State within the five years preceding the application for registration.

2. Paragraph 1(a) applies to the courses and certificates mentioned under (iv) to (viii) to the extent that they have been successfully completed or granted until 31 December 2020.

PART III – REGISTRATION

Rule 13 – Entry on the list of representatives based on the Certificate

The European Patent Attorney wishing to represent parties before the Unified Patent Court shall lodge the Certificate with the Registrar. He shall thereafter be registered on the list of entitled representatives under Article 48(3) of the Agreement on a Unified Patent Court (hereinafter referred to as List).

Rule 14 – Request for recognition of other appropriate qualifications

1. Requests for recognition of other appropriate qualifications shall be filed with the Registrar in one of the official languages of the European Patent Office.
2. In case of requests filed pursuant to Rule 11 or 12(1)(a), the request for recognition of other appropriate qualifications shall contain a copy of the respective diploma, certificate or other respective proof.
3. In case of requests filed pursuant to Rule 12(1)(b), the request shall include all details necessary to identify the infringement actions the European Patent Attorney intends to rely on such as:
   (a) name of the parties;
   (b) court seized with the action;
   (c) date of commencement of the proceedings.

Reasonably available evidence to support the request, such as a copy of the power of attorney, shall be submitted.

Rule 15 – Examination of and decision on the request for recognition of other appropriate qualifications

1. The request for recognition of other appropriate qualifications shall be examined by the Registrar. The Registrar may, if he deems it necessary, consult the Advisory Committee for an opinion.
2. If the requirements contained in Rules 11 or 12 are met and the request for recognition of other appropriate qualifications complies with Rule 14, the Registrar shall enter the requestor on the List.
3. If the request for recognition of other appropriate qualifications complies with Rule 14, but the requirements under Rules 11 or 12 are not met, the Registrar shall reject the request.
4. If the request for recognition of appropriate qualification fails to comply with the requirements of Rule 14, the Registrar shall invite the requestor to correct the deficiencies noted within a non-extendable period of two months. If the deficiencies are not corrected in due time, the Registrar shall reject the request.

Rule 16 – Effect of entries

1. Subject to paragraph 2, 3 and 4 of this Rule, registrations of European Patent Attorneys on the List shall be permanent, including registrations under the transitional provisions pursuant to Rule 12.
2. Registration on the List shall cease to have effect in the event that the registered representative ceases to be a registered European Patent Attorney on the list of European Patent Attorneys maintained by

the European Patent Office. The Registrar will strike the name off the List, upon request or ex-officio. In case the European Patent Attorney is re-entered on the list maintained by the European Patent Office, he shall, upon his request, be re-entered by the Registrar on the List.
3. Where the requirements for the entry are not met or no longer met the Registrar shall strike the name of an entitled representative from the List. He shall take due note of a final decision of the Unified Patent Court in case of a challenge of the registration in a procedure. Furthermore, the Registrar shall strike the name of an entitled representative from the List upon decision of a competent court or authority establishing that the registration has been obtained by fraud; a conviction is not necessary.
4. The Registrar will strike the name of an entitled representative from the List upon his request to this effect.

PART IV – REVIEW

Rule 17 – Decisions subject to review
Decisions of the Registrar referred to in Rules 15 and 16 may be challenged in accordance with the following provisions.

Rule 18 – Formalities of the petition for review
The petition for review shall be filed in writing with the Registrar in one of the official languages of the European Patent Office, within one month of the notification of the challenged decision. It shall indicate the reasons for setting aside the decision of the Registrar.

Rule 19 – Revision by the Registrar
1. If the Registrar considers the petition for review to be admissible and well founded, he shall rectify his decision.
2. If the Registrar does not rectify his decision within one month of receipt of the petition for review, he shall forward it to the President of the Court of Appeal who shall decide on the petition for review.

Rule 20 – Decision by the President of the Court of Appeal
If the petition for review is admissible, the President of the Court of Appeal shall examine whether the appeal is allowable. If the petition for review is allowable, he shall alter the Registrar's decision. If the petition for review is not allowable, he shall reject it.

PART V – NOTIFICATION AND ENTRY INTO FORCE

Rule 21 – Notification
Decisions of the Administrative Committee, the Registrar and the President of the Court of Appeal shall be notified.

Rule 22 – Entry into force
This Decision shall enter into force on 15 June 2022.

Done at on

For the Administrative Committee
The Chairman

5. Rules relating to Unitary Patent Protection

SELECT COMMITTEE OF THE ADMINISTRATIVE COUNCIL

Rules relating to Unitary Patent Protection as adopted by decision of the Select Committee of the Administrative Council of the European Patent Organisation of 15 December 2015 and as last amended by decision of the Select Committee of the Administrative Council of 23 March 2022

Rules relating to Regulation (EU) No 1257/2012 of the European Parliament and of the Council of 17 December 2012 implementing enhanced cooperation in the area of the creation of unitary patent protection and to Council Regulation (EU) No 1260/2012 of 17 December 2012 implementing enhanced cooperation in the area of the creation of unitary patent protection with regard to the applicable translation arrangements[1]
(hereinafter 'Rules relating to Unitary Patent Protection')

PART I INSTITUTIONAL PROVISIONS

CHAPTER I SUBJECT MATTER

Rule 1 Subject matter
(1) The participating Member States hereby entrust the European Patent Office with the tasks referred to in Article 9, paragraph 1, Regulation (EU) No 1257/2012. In carrying out these tasks, the European Patent Office shall apply the present Rules and shall be bound by decisions handed down by the Unified Patent Court in actions brought under Article 32, paragraph 1(i), Agreement on a Unified Patent Court.[2]
(2) In case of conflict between the provisions of the present Rules and Union law, including Regulation (EU) No 1257/2012[3] and Regulation (EU) No 1260/2012,[4] the provisions of Union law shall prevail.

CHAPTER II SELECT COMMITTEE OF THE ADMINISTRATIVE COUNCIL

Rule 2 Competences and duties
(1) The Select Committee of the Administrative Council shall be competent to amend
- (a) the present Rules;
- (b) the Rules relating to Fees for Unitary Patent Protection;
- (c) other rules or decisions of a financial or budgetary nature;
- (d) its Rules of Procedure.

(2) The Select Committee of the Administrative Council shall ensure the governance and supervision of the activities related to the tasks entrusted to the European Patent Office in accordance with Rule 1, paragraph 1.

---

1 Adopted by decision of the Select Committee of the Administrative Council SC/D 1/15 of 15.12.2015 (OJ EPO 2016, A39), which will enter into force on the date of application of Regulations (EU) No 1257/2012 and No 1260/2012.
2 Published in OJ EPO 2013, 287.
3 Published in OJ EPO 2013, 111.
4 Published in OJ EPO 2013, 132.

CHAPTER III FUNCTIONS AND POWERS OF THE PRESIDENT OF THE EUROPEAN PATENT OFFICE AND SPECIAL DEPARTMENTS OF THE EUROPEAN PATENT OFFICE

Rule 3 Functions and powers of the President of the European Patent Office
The Unitary Patent Protection Division referred to in Rule 4 shall be managed by the President of the European Patent Office, who shall be responsible for its activities to the Select Committee of the Administrative Council. To this end, Article 10, paragraphs 2 and 3, EPC shall apply *mutatis mutandis.*

Rule 4 Unitary Patent Protection Division
(1) A Unitary Patent Protection Division is hereby established within the European Patent Office as a special department within the meaning of Article 143, paragraph 2, EPC.
(2) The tasks entrusted to the European Patent Office in accordance with Rule 1, paragraph 1, shall be carried out under the responsibility of the Unitary Patent Protection Division.
(3) Decisions of the Unitary Patent Protection Division shall be taken by one legally qualified member.
(4) The President of the European Patent Office may entrust to employees who are not legally qualified members the execution of duties falling to the Unitary Patent Protection Division and involving no legal difficulties.

PART II PROCEDURES TO BE CARRIED BY THE EUROPEAN PATENT OFFICE UNDER REGULATIONS (EU) NO 1257/2012 AND NO 1260/2012

CHAPTER I THE REQUEST FOR UNITARY EFFECT

Rule 5 General
(1) At the request of the proprietor of the European patent, unitary effect shall be registered by the European Patent Office in the Register for unitary patent protection.
(2) Unitary effect shall be registered only if the European patent has been granted with the same set of claims in respect of all the participating Member States.

Rule 6 Requirements of the request for unitary effect
(1) The request for unitary effect shall be filed with the European Patent Office no later than one month after publication of the mention of grant of the European patent in the European Patent Bulletin.
(2) The request for unitary effect shall be filed in writing in the language of the proceedings and shall contain:

- (a) particulars of the proprietor of the European patent making the request (hereinafter 'the requester') as provided for in Rule 41, paragraph 2(c), EPC;
- (b) the number of the European patent to which unitary effect shall be attributed;
- (c) where the requester has appointed a representative, particulars as provided for in Rule 41, paragraph 2(d), EPC;
- (d) a translation of the European patent as required under Article 6, paragraph 1, Regulation (EU) No 1260/2012, as follows:
  - where the language of the proceedings is French or German, a full translation of the specification of the European patent into English; or
  - where the language of the proceedings is English, a full translation of the specification of the European patent into any other official language of the European Union.

Rule 7 Examination of the request by the European Patent Office

(1) If the requirements under Rule 5, paragraph 2, are met and the request for unitary effect complies with Rule 6, the European Patent Office shall register the unitary effect in the Register for unitary patent protection and communicate the date of this registration to the requester.
(2) If the requirements under Rule 5, paragraph 2, are not met or the request for unitary effect does not comply with Rule 6, paragraph 1, the European Patent Office shall reject the request.
(3) If the requirements under Rule 5, paragraph 2, are met and the request for unitary effect complies with Rule 6, paragraph 1, but fails to comply with the requirements of Rule 6, paragraph 2, the European Patent Office shall invite the requester to correct the deficiencies noted within a non-extendable period of one month. If the deficiencies are not corrected in due time, the European Patent Office shall reject the request.

CHAPTER II COMPENSATION SCHEME

Rule 8 Definition and beneficiaries

(1) Proprietors of European patents with unitary effect for which the European patent application was filed in an official language of the European Union other than English, French or German shall be entitled to compensation for translation costs if their residence or principal place of business is in a member state of the European Union and they are an entity or a natural person referred to in paragraph 2.
(2) Compensation for translation costs shall be granted, on request, to a patent proprietor falling within one of the following categories:

- (a) small and medium-sized enterprises as defined in European Commission recommendation 2003/361/EC dated 6 May 2003;
- (b) natural persons; or
- (c) non-profit organisations as defined in Article 2, paragraph 1(14) of Regulation (EU) No 1290/2013, universities and public research organisations.

(3) If the patent has multiple proprietors, compensation will be granted only if each proprietor fulfils the conditions referred to in paragraphs 1 and 2.
(4) If the European patent application or the European patent was transferred before a request for unitary effect was filed, compensation will be granted only if both the initial applicant and the proprietor of the patent fulfil the conditions referred to in paragraphs 1 and 2.
(5) The compensation scheme provided for in paragraph 1 shall also apply to Euro-PCT applications originally filed at a receiving office in an official language of the European Union other than English, French or German.

Rule 9 Request for compensation

(1) The proprietor of a European patent who wishes to benefit from compensation under Rule 8 shall file a request for it together with the request for unitary effect referred to in Rule 6.
(2) The request for compensation for translation costs shall contain a declaration that the proprietor of the European patent is an entity or a natural person referred to in Rule 8, paragraph 2.

Rule 10 Examination of the request and grant of compensation

(1) After the European Patent Office has registered the unitary effect of the European patent in the Register for unitary patent protection and has examined the request for compensation, it shall inform the patent proprietor whether that request has been granted or rejected.
(2) Once granted, compensation shall not be rescinded, even if, as a result of changed circumstances, the proprietor no longer qualifies for it under Rule 8.

(3) Should the Office have reason to doubt the veracity of the declaration filed under Rule 9, paragraph 2, it shall invite the patent proprietor to provide evidence that he fulfils the requirements of Rule 8, paragraph 2. Articles 113(1) and 114 EPC shall apply.
(4) If the Office finds that the compensation was granted on the basis of a false declaration, it shall invite the patent proprietor to pay, together with the next renewal fee falling due, an additional fee composed of the amount of the compensation paid and an administrative fee as laid down in the Rules relating to Fees for Unitary Patent Protection. If this additional fee is not paid in due time, the European patent with unitary effect shall lapse under Rule 14.

Rule 11 Level of compensation
Reimbursement of translation costs shall be made up to a ceiling and paid in the form of a lump sum, in accordance with the Rules relating to Fees for Unitary Patent Protection. The ceiling shall be fixed on the basis of the average length of a European patent and the average translation cost per page, taking account of the average reduction granted under Rule 6 EPC.

CHAPTER III LICENCES OF RIGHT

Rule 12 Filing of the statement by the patent proprietor
(1) The proprietor of a European patent with unitary effect may file a statement with the European Patent Office that he is prepared to allow any person to use the invention as a licensee in return for appropriate consideration. In that case, the renewal fees for the European patent with unitary effect which fall due after receipt of the statement shall be reduced; the amount of the reduction shall be fixed in the Rules relating to Fees for Unitary Patent Protection. The statement shall be entered in the Register for unitary patent protection.
(2) The statement referred to in paragraph 1 may be withdrawn at any time by a communication to this effect to the European Patent Office. Such withdrawal shall not take effect until the amount by which the renewal fees were reduced is paid to the European Patent Office.
(3) The statement referred to in paragraph 1 may not be filed as long as an exclusive licence is recorded in the Register for unitary patent protection or a request for the recording of such a licence is pending before the European Patent Office.
(4) No request for recording an exclusive licence in the Register for unitary patent protection shall be admissible after the statement referred to in paragraph 1 has been filed, unless that statement is withdrawn.

CHAPTER IV RENEWAL FEES

Rule 13 Payment of renewal fees for European patents with unitary effect
(1) Renewal fees for European patents with unitary effect and additional fees for their late payment shall be paid to the European Patent Office. Those fees shall be due in respect of the years following the year in which the mention of the grant of the European patent which benefits from unitary effect is published in the European Patent Bulletin.
(2) A renewal fee for the European patent with unitary effect in respect of the coming year shall be due on the last day of the month containing the anniversary of the date of filing of the European patent application which led to the European patent with unitary effect. Renewal fees may not be validly paid more than three months before they fall due.
(3) If a renewal fee is not paid in due time, the fee may still be paid within six months of the due date, provided that an additional fee is also paid within that period.

(4) A renewal fee in respect of a European patent with unitary effect falling due under paragraph 2 within three months of the notification of the communication referred to in Rule 7(1) may still be paid within that period without the additional fee referred to in paragraph 3.
(5) A renewal fee for a European patent with unitary effect which would have fallen due under paragraph 2 in the period starting on the date of publication of the mention of the grant of the European patent in the European Patent Bulletin up to and including the date of the notification of the communication referred to in Rule 7(1) shall be due on that latter date. This fee may still be paid within three months of that latter date without the additional fee referred to in paragraph 3.
(6) Rule 51, paragraphs 4 and 5, EPC shall apply mutatis mutandis.

CHAPTER V LAPSE

Rule 14 Lapse

(1) A European patent with unitary effect shall lapse:
- (a) 20 years after the date of filing of the European patent application;
- (b) if a renewal fee and, where applicable, any additional fee have not been paid in due time.

(2) The lapse of a European patent with unitary effect for failure to pay a renewal fee and any additional fee within the due period shall be deemed to have occurred on the date on which the renewal fee was due.

PART III INFORMATION TO THE PUBLIC

CHAPTER I REGISTER FOR UNITARY PATENT PROTECTION

Rule 15 Establishment of the Register for unitary patent protection

(1) The Register for unitary patent protection provided for in Article 9, paragraph 1(b), Regulation (EU) No 1257/2012 is hereby established as a special part of the European Patent Register kept by the European Patent Office under Article 127 EPC.
(2) Entries in the Register for unitary patent protection shall be made in the three official languages of the European Patent Office. In case of doubt, the entry in the language of the proceedings shall be authentic.

Rule 16 Entries in the Register for unitary patent protection

(1) The Register for unitary patent protection shall contain the following entries:
- (a) date of publication of the mention of the grant of the European patent;
- (b) date of filing of the request for unitary effect for the European patent;
- (c) particulars of the representative of the proprietor of the European patent as provided for in Rule 41, paragraph 2(d), EPC; in the case of several representatives, only the particulars of the representative first named, followed by the words 'and others' and, in the case of an association referred to in Rule 152, paragraph 11, EPC, only the name and address of the association;
- (d) date and purport of the decision on the registration of unitary effect for the European patent;
- (e) date of registration of the unitary effect of the European patent;
- (f) date of effect of the European patent with unitary effect pursuant to Article 4, paragraph 1, Regulation (EU) No 1257/2012;
- (g) participating Member States in which the European patent with unitary effect has unitary effect pursuant to Article 18, paragraph 2, Regulation (EU) No 1257/2012;
- (h) particulars of the proprietor of the European patent with unitary effect as provided for in Rule 41, paragraph 2(c), EPC;

(i)[5] family name, given names and country and place of residence of the inventor designated by the applicant for or proprietor of the patent, unless he has waived his right to be mentioned under Rule 20, paragraph 1, EPC;
(j) rights and transfer of such rights relating to the European patent with unitary effect where the present Rules provide that they shall be recorded at the request of an interested party;
(k) licensing commitments undertaken by the proprietor of the European patent with unitary effect in international standardisation bodies pursuant to Article 9, paragraph 1(c), Regulation (EU) No 1257/2012, where the proprietor requested their registration;
(l) date of filing and date of withdrawal of the statement provided for in Rule 12;
(m) date of lapse of the European patent with unitary effect;
(n) data as to the payment of renewal fees for the European patent with unitary effect, including, where applicable, data on the payment of an additional fee pursuant to Rule 13, paragraph 3;
(o) a record of the information communicated to the European Patent Office concerning proceedings before the Unified Patent Court;
(p) a record of the information communicated to the European Patent Office by the central industrial property offices, courts and other competent authorities of the participating Member States;
(q) date and purport of the decision on the validity of a European patent with unitary effect taken by the Unified Patent Court;
(r) date of receipt of a request for re-establishment of rights;
(s) refusal of a request for re-establishment of rights;
(t) date of re-establishment of rights;
(u) dates of interruption and resumption of proceedings;
(v) date of issuance, date of expiry and date and purport of the decision on the validity of a supplementary protection certificate for a product protected by the European patent with unitary effect as well as the participating Member State issuing it;
(w)[6] information regarding a place of business of the applicant on the date of filing of the application for the European patent pursuant to Article 7, paragraph 1(b), Regulation (EU) No 1257/2012, which may be provided by the proprietor of the European patent together with the request for unitary effect referred to in Rule 6.
(x)[7] information regarding the residence or principal place of business of the applicant on the date of filing of the application for the European patent pursuant to Article 7, paragraph 1(a), Regulation (EU) No 1257/2012.

(2) The President of the European Patent Office may decide that entries additional to those referred to in paragraph 1 shall be made in the Register for unitary patent protection.

5 Amended by decision of the Select Committee of the Administrative Council SC/D 3/21 of 16.12.2021 (OJ EPO 2022, A39), which will enter into force on the date of application of Regulations (EU) No 1257/2012 and No 1260/2012.

6 Amended by decision of the Select Committee of the Administrative Council SC/D 1/22 of 23.03.2022 (OJ EPO 2022, A40), which will enter into force on the date of application of Regulations (EU) No 1257/2012 and No 1260/2012.

7 Inserted by decision of the Select Committee of the Administrative Council SC/D 3/21 of 16.12.2021 (OJ EPO 2022, A39), which will enter into force on the date of application of Regulations (EU) No 1257/2012 and No 1260/2012.

CHAPTER II PUBLICATIONS

Rule 17 European Patent Bulletin and Official Journal of the European Patent Office
(1) The European Patent Bulletin referred to in Article 129(a) EPC shall contain, as a special part, the particulars the publication of which is prescribed by the present Rules, the Chairperson of the Select Committee of the Administrative Council or the President of the European Patent Office.
(2) The Official Journal referred to in Article 129(b) EPC shall contain, as a special part, notices and information of a general character issued by the Select Committee of the Administrative Council or by the President of the European Patent Office, as well as any other information relevant to the implementation of unitary patent protection.

Rule 18 Publication of translations
The President of the European Patent Office shall determine the form of the publication of the translations referred to in Rule 6, paragraph 2(d), and the data to be included.

Rule 19 Inclusion of decisions of the Unified Patent Court in the files
The European Patent Office shall include a copy of any decision of the Unified Patent Court forwarded to it by the Court and relating to European patents with unitary effect, including those decisions referred to in Rule 1, in the files relating to the European patent with unitary effect, where it shall be open to inspection.

PART IV COMMON PROVISIONS

Rule 20 Common provisions governing procedure
(1) The following provisions of the EPC, as amended, shall apply mutatis mutandis: Article 14, paragraphs 1, 3 and 7; Article 113, paragraph 1; Articles 114, 117, 119, 120, 125; Article 128, paragraph 4; Articles 131, 133; Article 134, paragraphs 1, 5 and 8.
(2) The following provisions of the Implementing Regulations to the EPC, as amended, shall apply mutatis mutandis:

- (a) Rules 1 and 2; unless otherwise provided Rule 3, paragraph 1, first sentence; Rule 3, paragraph 3; Rules 4 and 5;
- (b) Rules 22 to 24;
- (c) Rule 50, paragraphs 2 and 3;
- (d) Rule 111, paragraph 1; Rules 112 and 113;
- (e) Rule 115; Rule 116, paragraph 1; Rules 117 to 124;
- (f) Rules 125 to 130;
- (g) Rule 131; Rule 133, paragraph 1, subject to the proviso that the document referred to in that provision has been received no later than one month after expiry of the period; Rule 134;
- (h) Rule 139, first sentence, and Rule 140;
- (i) Rule 142;
- (j) Rules 144 to 147;
- (k) Rules 148 to 150;
- (l) Rules 151 to 153.

(3) When applying the provisions referred to in paragraphs 1 and 2 mutatis mutandis, the term 'Contracting States' shall be understood as meaning the Contracting States to the EPC, except in Article 125 EPC, where it shall be understood as meaning the participating Member States.
(4) Where the present Rules, including the provisions of the EPC applicable mutatis mutandis under the present Rules, refer to 'a period to be specified', this period shall be specified by the European

Patent Office. Unless otherwise provided, a period specified by the European Patent Office shall be neither less than one month nor more than four months.

Rule 21 Oral proceedings

(1) Oral proceedings shall take place either at the instance of the European Patent Office if it considers this to be expedient or at the request of any party to the proceedings. However, the European Patent Office may reject a request for further oral proceedings where the parties and the subject of the proceedings are the same.

(2) Nevertheless, in the procedure concerning the request for unitary effect, oral proceedings shall take place before the Unitary Patent Protection Division at the request of the proprietor of the European patent only where the Unitary Patent Protection Division considers this to be expedient.

(3) Oral proceedings before the Unitary Patent Protection Division shall not be public.

Rule 22 Re-establishment of rights

(1) A proprietor of a European patent or of a European patent with unitary effect who, in spite of all due care required by the circumstances having been taken, was unable to observe a time limit vis-à-vis the European Patent Office shall have his rights re-established upon request if the non-observance of this time limit has the direct consequence of causing the European patent with unitary effect to lapse according to Rule 14, paragraph 1(b), or the loss of any other right or means of redress.

(2) Any request for re-establishment of rights under paragraph 1 shall be filed in writing within two months of the removal of the cause of non-compliance with the period, but at the latest within one year of expiry of the unobserved time limit. However, a request for re-establishment of rights in respect of the period specified in Rule 6, paragraph 1, shall be filed within two months of expiry of that period. The request for re-establishment of rights shall not be deemed to have been filed until the fee prescribed in the Rules relating to Fees for Unitary Patent Protection has been paid.

(3) The request shall state the grounds on which it is based and shall set out the facts on which it relies. The omitted act shall be completed within the relevant period for filing the request according to paragraph 2.

(4) The European Patent Office shall grant the request, provided that the conditions laid down in the present Rule are met. Otherwise, it shall reject the request.

(5) If the request is granted, the legal consequences of the failure to observe the time limit shall be deemed not to have ensued.

(6) Re-establishment of rights shall be ruled out in respect of the time limit for requesting re-establishment of rights and in respect of the period referred to in Rule 7, paragraph 3.

(7) Any person who, in one or several participating Member States, has in good faith used or made effective and serious preparations for using an invention which is the subject of a European patent with unitary effect in the period between the loss of rights referred to in paragraph 1 and publication in the Register for unitary patent protection of the mention of re-establishment of those rights, may without payment continue such use in the course of his business or for the needs thereof.

Rule 23 Form of decisions

Decisions of the European Patent Office against which actions can be brought before the Unified Patent Court in accordance with Article 32, paragraph 1(i), Agreement on a Unified Patent Court shall be reasoned and shall be accompanied by a communication pointing out the possibility of bringing an action before the Unified Patent Court. The parties may not invoke the omission of the communication.

Rule 24 Interlocutory revision

If the European Patent Office is informed by the Unified Patent Court that an application to annul or alter a decision of the European Patent Office is admissible and if the European Patent Office considers that the application is well founded, it shall, within two months of the date of receipt of the application,

(a) rectify the contested decision in accordance with the order or remedy sought by the claimant and

(b) inform the Unified Patent Court that the decision has been rectified.

6. Rules relating to Fees for Unitary Patent Protection

SELECT COMMITTEE OF THE ADMINISTRATIVE COUNCIL

Rules relating to Fees for Unitary Patent Protection (RFeesUPP) as adopted by decision of the Select Committee of the Administrative Council of the European Patent Organisation of 15 December 2015[1]

Article 1 General

The fees due to be paid to the European Patent Office, the compensation for translation costs to be paid to proprietors of a European patent with unitary effect by the European Patent Office, as provided for in the Rules relating to Unitary Patent Protection, and the fees and expenses which the President of the European Patent Office lays down pursuant to Article 5 shall be levied or paid in accordance with the provisions contained in Articles 2 to 6.

Article 2 Fees provided for in the Rules relating to Unitary Patent Protection

(1) The fees due to be paid to the European Patent Office shall be as follows:

1. Renewal fees for the European patent with unitary effect (Rule 13, paragraph 1, Rules relating to Unitary Patent Protection), calculated in each case from the date of filing of the application

	EUR
for the 2nd year	35
for the 3rd year	105
for the 4th year	145
for the 5th year	315
for the 6th year	475
for the 7th year	630
for the 8th year	815
for the 9th year	990
for the 10th year	1 175
for the 11th year	1 460
for the 12th year	1 775
for the 13th year	2 105
for the 14th year	2 455
for the 15th year	2 830
for the 16th year	3 240
for the 17th year	3 640
for the 18th year	4 055
for the 19th year	4 455
for the 20th year	4 855
2. Additional fee for belated payment of a renewal fee (Rule 13, paragraph 3, relating to Unitary Patent Protection)	50% of the belated renewal fee

1 Adopted by decision of the Select Committee of the Administrative Council SC/D 2/15 of 15.12.2015 (OJ EPO 2016, A40), which will enter into force on the date of application of Regulations (EU) No 1257/2012 and No 1260/2012.

(2) The fee for re-establishment of rights (Rule 22, paragraph 2, relating to Unitary Patent Protection) shall be payable in the amount laid down in Article 2, paragraph 1, item 13, of the Rules relating to Fees under the EPC, as amended.

Article 3 Reduction of renewal fees
The reduction of the renewal fees for the European patent with unitary effect laid down in Rule 12, paragraph 1, relating to Unitary Patent Protection shall be 15%.

Article 4 Compensation for translation costs
(1) The amount of the lump sum provided for in Rule 11 relating to Unitary Patent Protection shall be EUR 500.
(2) The administrative fee provided for in Rule 10, paragraph 4, relating to Unitary Patent Protection shall be 50% of the lump sum referred to in paragraph 1.

Article 5 Fees, expenses and prices laid down by the President of the European Patent Office
The administrative fees provided for in the Rules relating to Unitary Patent Protection and the fees and expenses charged for any services rendered by the European Patent Office other than those specified in the present Rules shall be payable in the amounts laid down by the President of the European Patent Office pursuant to Article 3 of the Rules relating to Fees under the EPC.

Article 6 Common provisions governing procedure
The following provisions of the Rules relating to Fees under the EPC, as amended, shall apply *mutatis mutandis*: Articles 4 to 8, Article 12 and Article 13.

Article 7 Review of renewal fee level and report on specific entities
No later than five years from the date of application of Regulation (EU) No 1257/2012, and every five years thereafter,
(a) the European Patent Office shall submit a report to the Select Committee of the Administrative Council assessing the financial impact of the European patent with unitary effect on the budget of the European Patent Organisation and on the renewal fee income of the participating Member States and, where necessary, make an appropriate proposal for adjusting the level of renewal fees;
(b) the European Patent Office shall, after consultation of the European Commission, submit a report to the Select Committee of the Administrative Council on the use of the European patent with unitary effect by specific entities, such as small and medium-sized enterprises, and, where necessary, make proposals with a view to improving their access to the European patent with unitary effect.

7. EU Regulation No 1257/2012

Regulation (EU) No 1257/2012 of the European parliament and of the Council of 17 December 2012 implementing enhanced cooperation in the area of the creation of unitary patent protection

THE EUROPEAN PARLIAMENT AND THE COUNCIL OF THE EUROPEAN UNION,

Having regard to the Treaty on the Functioning of the European Union and in particular the first paragraph of Article 118 thereof,

Having regard to Council Decision 2011/167/EU of 10 March 2011 authorising enhanced cooperation in the area of the creation of unitary patent protection,[1]

Having regard to the proposal from the European Commission,

After transmission of the draft legislative act to the national parliaments,

Acting in accordance with the ordinary legislative procedure,[2]

Whereas:

(1) The creation of the legal conditions enabling undertakings to adapt their activities in manufacturing and distributing products across national borders and providing them with greater choice and more opportunities contributes to the attainment of the objectives of the Union set out in Article 3(3) of the Treaty on European Union. Uniform patent protection within the internal market, or at least a significant part thereof, should feature amongst the legal instruments which undertakings have at their disposal.

(2) Pursuant to the first paragraph of Article 118 of the Treaty on the Functioning of the European Union (TFEU), measures to be taken in the context of the establishment and functioning of the internal market include the creation of uniform patent protection throughout the Union and the establishment of centralised Union-wide authorisation, coordination and supervision arrangements.

(3) On 10 March 2011, the Council adopted Decision 2011/167/EU authorising enhanced cooperation between Belgium, Bulgaria, the Czech Republic, Denmark, Germany, Estonia, Ireland, Greece, France, Cyprus, Latvia, Lithuania, Luxembourg, Hungary, Malta, the Netherlands, Austria, Poland, Portugal, Romania, Slovenia, Slovakia, Finland, Sweden and the United Kingdom (hereinafter 'participating Member States') in the area of the creation of unitary patent protection.

(4) Unitary patent protection will foster scientific and technological advances and the functioning of the internal market by making access to the patent system easier, less costly and legally secure. It will also improve the level of patent protection by making it possible to obtain uniform patent protection in the participating Member States and eliminate costs and complexity for undertakings throughout the Union. It should be available to proprietors of a European patent from both

1 OJ L 76, 22.3.2011, p. 53.

2 Position of the European Parliament of 11 December 2012 (not yet published in the Official Journal) and decision of the Council of 17 December 2012.

the participating Member States and from other States, regardless of their nationality, residence or place of establishment.

(5) The Convention on the Grant of European Patents of 5 October 1973, as revised on 17 December 1991 and on 29 November 2000 (hereinafter 'EPC'), established the European Patent Organisation and entrusted it with the task of granting European patents. This task is carried out by the European Patent Office (hereinafter 'EPO'). A European patent granted by the EPO should, at the request of the patent proprietor, benefit from unitary effect by virtue of this Regulation in the participating Member States. Such a patent is hereinafter referred to as a 'European patent with unitary effect'.

(6) In accordance with Part IX of the EPC a group of Contracting States to the EPC may provide that European patents granted for those States have a unitary character. This Regulation constitutes a special agreement within the meaning of Article 142 of the EPC, a regional patent treaty within the meaning of Article 45(1) of the Patent Cooperation Treaty of 19 June 1970 as last modified on 3 February 2001 and a special agreement within the meaning of Article 19 of the Convention for the Protection of Industrial Property, signed in Paris on 20 March 1883 and last amended on 28 September 1979.

(7) Unitary patent protection should be achieved by attributing unitary effect to European patents in the post-grant phase by virtue of this Regulation and in respect of all the participating Member States. The main feature of a European patent with unitary effect should be its unitary character, i.e. providing uniform protection and having equal effect in all the participating Member States. Consequently, a European patent with unitary effect should only be limited, transferred or revoked, or lapse, in respect of all the participating Member States. It should be possible for a European patent with unitary effect to be licensed in respect of the whole or part of the territories of the participating Member States. To ensure the uniform substantive scope of protection conferred by unitary patent protection, only European patents that have been granted for all the participating Member States with the same set of claims should benefit from unitary effect. Finally, the unitary effect attributed to a European patent should have an accessory nature and should be deemed not to have arisen to the extent that the basic European patent has been revoked or limited.

(8) In accordance with the general principles of patent law and Article 64(1) of the EPC, unitary patent protection should take effect retroactively in the participating Member States as from the date of publication of the mention of the grant of the European patent in the European Patent Bulletin. Where unitary patent protection takes effect, the participating Member States should ensure that the European patent is deemed not to have taken effect on their territory as a national patent, so as to avoid any duplication of patent protection.

(9) The European patent with unitary effect should confer on its proprietor the right to prevent any third party from committing acts against which the patent provides protection. This should be ensured through the establishment of a Unified Patent Court. In matters not covered by this Regulation or by Council Regulation (EU) No 1260/2012 of 17 December 2012 implementing enhanced cooperation in the area of unitary patent protection with regard to the applicable translation arrangements, the provisions of the EPC, the Agreement on a Unified Patent Court, including its provisions defining the scope of that right and its limitations, and national law, including rules of private international law, should apply.

(10) Compulsory licences for European patents with unitary effect should be governed by the laws of the participating Member States as regards their respective territories.

(11) In its report on the operation of this Regulation, the Commission should evaluate the functioning of the applicable limitations and, where necessary, make appropriate proposals, taking account of the contribution of the patent system to innovation and technological progress, the legitimate

interests of third parties and overriding interests of society. The Agreement on a Unified Patent Court does not preclude the European Union from exercising its powers in this field.

(12) In accordance with the case-law of the Court of Justice of the European Union, the principle of the exhaustion of rights should also be applied to European patents with unitary effect. Therefore, rights conferred by a European patent with unitary effect should not extend to acts concerning the product covered by that patent which are carried out within the participating Member States after that product has been placed on the market in the Union by the patent proprietor.

(13) The regime applicable to damages should be governed by the laws of the participating Member States, in particular the provisions implementing Article 13 of Directive 2004/48/EC of the European Parliament and of the Council of 29 April 2004 on the enforcement of intellectual property rights.[3]

(14) As an object of property, a European patent with unitary effect should be dealt with in its entirety, and in all the participating Member States, as a national patent of the participating Member State determined in accordance with specific criteria such as the applicant's residence, principal place of business or place of business.

(15) In order to promote and facilitate the economic exploitation of an invention protected by a European patent with unitary effect, the proprietor of that patent should be able to offer it to be licensed in return for appropriate consideration. To that end, the patent proprietor should be able to file a statement with the EPO that he is prepared to grant a license in return for appropriate consideration. In that case, the patent proprietor should benefit from a reduction of the renewal fees as from the EPO's receipt of such statement.

(16) The group of Member States making use of the provisions of Part IX of the EPC may give tasks to the EPO and set up a select committee of the Administrative Council of the European Patent Organisation (hereinafter 'Select Committee').

(17) The participating Member States should give certain administrative tasks relating to European patents with unitary effect to the EPO, in particular as regards the administration of requests for unitary effect, the registration of unitary effect and of any limitation, licence, transfer, revocation or lapse of European patents with unitary effect, the collection and distribution of renewal fees, the publication of translations for information purposes during a transitional period and the administration of a compensation scheme for the reimbursement of translation costs incurred by applicants filing European patent applications in a language other than one of the official languages of the EPO.

(18) In the framework of the Select Committee, the participating Member States should ensure the governance and supervision of the activities related to the tasks entrusted to the EPO by the participating Member States, ensure that requests for unitary effect are filed with the EPO within one month of the date of publication of the mention of the grant in the European Patent Bulletin and ensure that such requests are submitted in the language of the proceedings before the EPO together with the translation prescribed, during a transitional period, by Regulation (EU) No 1260/2012. The participating Member States should also ensure the setting, in accordance with the voting rules laid down in Article 35(2) of the EPC, of the level of the renewal fees and the share of the distribution of the renewal fees in accordance with the criteria set out in this Regulation.

(19) Patent proprietors should pay a single annual renewal fee for a European patent with unitary effect. Renewal fees should be progressive throughout the term of the patent protection and, together with the fees to be paid to the European Patent Organisation during the pre-grant stage, should cover all costs associated with the grant of the European patent and the administration of the unitary patent protection. The level of the renewal fees should be set with the aim of facilitating innovation and fostering the competitiveness of European businesses, taking into account the

3 OJ L 157, 30.4.2004, p. 45.

situation of specific entities such as small and medium-sized enterprises, for example in the form of lower fees. It should also reflect the size of the market covered by the patent and be similar to the level of the national renewal fees for an average European patent taking effect in the participating Member States at the time when the level of the renewal fees is first set.

(20) The appropriate level and distribution of renewal fees should be determined in order to ensure that, in relation to the unitary patent protection, all costs of the tasks entrusted to the EPO are fully covered by the resources generated by the European patents with unitary effect and that, together with the fees to be paid to the European Patent Organisation during the pre-grant stage, the revenues from the renewal fees ensure a balanced budget of the European Patent Organisation.

(21) Renewal fees should be paid to the European Patent Organisation. The EPO should retain an amount to cover the expenses generated at the EPO in carrying out tasks in relation to the unitary patent protection in accordance with Article 146 of the EPC. The remaining amount should be distributed among the participating Member States and should be used for patent-related purposes. The share of distribution should be set on the basis of fair, equitable and relevant criteria, namely the level of patent activity and the size of the market, and should guarantee a minimum amount to be distributed to each participating Member State in order to maintain a balanced and sustainable functioning of the system. The distribution should provide compensation for having an official language other than one of the official languages of the EPO, having a disproportionately low level of patenting activity established on the basis of the European Innovation Scoreboard, and/or having acquired membership of the European Patent Organisation relatively recently.

(22) An enhanced partnership between the EPO and central industrial property offices of the Member States should enable the EPO to make regular use, where appropriate, of the result of any search carried out by central industrial property offices on a national patent application the priority of which is claimed in a subsequent European patent application. All central industrial property offices, including those which do not perform searches in the course of a national patent-granting procedure, can play an essential role under the enhanced partnership, inter alia, by giving advice and support to potential patent applicants, in particular small and medium-sized enterprises, by receiving applications, by forwarding applications to the EPO and by disseminating patent information.

(23) This Regulation is complemented by Regulation (EU) No 1260/2012, adopted by the Council in accordance with the second paragraph of Article 118 of the TFEU.

(24) Jurisdiction in respect of European patents with unitary effect should be established and governed by an instrument setting up a unified patent litigation system for European patents and European patents with unitary effect.

(25) Establishing a Unified Patent Court to hear cases concerning the European patent with unitary effect is essential in order to ensure the proper functioning of that patent, consistency of case-law and hence legal certainty, and cost-effectiveness for patent proprietors. It is therefore of paramount importance that the participating Member States ratify the Agreement on a Unified Patent Court in accordance with their national constitutional and parliamentary procedures and take the necessary steps for that Court to become operational as soon as possible.

(26) This Regulation should be without prejudice to the right of the participating Member States to grant national patents and should not replace the participating Member States' laws on patents. Patent applicants should remain free to obtain either a national patent, a European patent with unitary effect, a European patent taking effect in one or more of the Contracting States to the EPC or a European patent with unitary effect validated in addition in one or more other Contracting States to the EPC which are not among the participating Member States.

(27) Since the objective of this Regulation, namely the creation of unitary patent protection, cannot be sufficiently achieved by the Member States and can therefore, by reason of the scale and effects of this Regulation, be better achieved at Union level, the Union may adopt measures, where appropriate by means of enhanced cooperation, in accordance with the principle of subsidiarity as set out in Article 5 of the Treaty on European Union. In accordance with the principle of proportionality, as set out in that Article, this Regulation does not go beyond what is necessary in order to achieve that objective,

HAVE ADOPTED THIS REGULATION:

CHAPTER I GENERAL PROVISIONS

Article 1 Subject matter

1. This Regulation implements enhanced cooperation in the area of the creation of unitary patent protection, authorised by Decision 2011/167/EU.
2. This Regulation constitutes a special agreement within the meaning of Article 142 of the Convention on the Grant of European Patents of 5 October 1973, as revised on 17 December 1991 and on 29 November 2000 (hereinafter 'EPC').

Article 2 Definitions

For the purposes of this Regulation, the following definitions shall apply:
(a) 'Participating Member State' means a Member State which participates in enhanced cooperation in the area of the creation of unitary patent protection by virtue of Decision 2011/167/EU, or by virtue of a decision adopted in accordance with the second or third subparagraph of Article 331(1) of the TFEU, at the time the request for unitary effect as referred to in Article 9 is made;
(b) 'European patent' means a patent granted by the European Patent Office (hereinafter 'EPO') under the rules and procedures laid down in the EPC;
(c) 'European patent with unitary effect' means a European patent which benefits from unitary effect in the participating Member States by virtue of this Regulation;
(d) 'European Patent Register' means the register kept by the EPO under Article 127 of the EPC;
(e) 'Register for unitary patent protection' means the register constituting part of the European Patent Register in which the unitary effect and any limitation, licence, transfer, revocation or lapse of a European patent with unitary effect are registered;
(f) 'European Patent Bulletin' means the periodical publication provided for in Article 129 of the EPC.

Article 3 European patent with unitary effect

1. A European patent granted with the same set of claims in respect of all the participating Member States shall benefit from unitary effect in the participating Member States provided that its unitary effect has been registered in the Register for unitary patent protection.
A European patent granted with different sets of claims for different participating Member States shall not benefit from unitary effect.
2. A European patent with unitary effect shall have a unitary character. It shall provide uniform protection and shall have equal effect in all the participating Member States.
It may only be limited, transferred or revoked, or lapse, in respect of all the participating Member States.
It may be licensed in respect of the whole or part of the territories of the participating Member States.
3. The unitary effect of a European patent shall be deemed not to have arisen to the extent that the European patent has been revoked or limited.

Article 4 Date of effect
1. A European patent with unitary effect shall take effect in the participating Member States on the date of publication by the EPO of the mention of the grant of the European patent in the European Patent Bulletin.
2. The participating Member States shall take the necessary measures to ensure that, where the unitary effect of a European patent has been registered and extends to their territory, that European patent is deemed not to have taken effect as a national patent in their territory on the date of publication of the mention of the grant in the European Patent Bulletin.

CHAPTER II EFFECTS OF A EUROPEAN PATENT WITH UNITARY EFFECT

Article 5 Uniform protection
1. The European patent with unitary effect shall confer on its proprietor the right to prevent any third party from committing acts against which that patent provides protection throughout the territories of the participating Member States in which it has unitary effect, subject to applicable limitations.
2. The scope of that right and its limitations shall be uniform in all participating Member States in which the patent has unitary effect.
3. The acts against which the patent provides protection referred to in paragraph 1 and the applicable limitations shall be those defined by the law applied to European patents with unitary effect in the participating Member State whose national law is applicable to the European patent with unitary effect as an object of property in accordance with Article 7.
4. In its report referred to in Article 16(1), the Commission shall evaluate the functioning of the applicable limitations and shall, where necessary, make appropriate proposals.

Article 6 Exhaustion of the rights conferred by a European patent with unitary effect
The rights conferred by a European patent with unitary effect shall not extend to acts concerning a product covered by that patent which are carried out within the participating Member States in which that patent has unitary effect after that product has been placed on the market in the Union by, or with the consent of, the patent proprietor, unless there are legitimate grounds for the patent proprietor to oppose further commercialisation of the product.

CHAPTER III A EUROPEAN PATENT WITH UNITARY EFFECT AS AN OBJECT OF PROPERTY

Article 7 Treating a European patent with unitary effect as a national patent
1. A European patent with unitary effect as an object of property shall be treated in its entirety and in all the participating Member States as a national patent of the participating Member State in which that patent has unitary effect and in which, according to the European Patent Register:

(a) the applicant had his residence or principal place of business on the date of filing of the application for the European patent; or

(b) where point (a) does not apply, the applicant had a place of business on the date of filing of the application for the European patent.

2. Where two or more persons are entered in the European Patent Register as joint applicants, point (a) of paragraph 1 shall apply to the joint applicant indicated first. Where this is not possible, point (a) of paragraph 1 shall apply to the next joint applicant indicated in the order of entry. Where point (a) of paragraph 1 does not apply to any of the joint applicants, point (b) of paragraph 1 shall apply accordingly.

3. Where no applicant had his residence, principal place of business or place of business in a participating Member State in which that patent has unitary effect for the purposes of paragraphs 1 or 2, the European patent with unitary effect as an object of property shall be treated in its entirety and in all the participating Member States as a national patent of the State where the European Patent Organisation has its headquarters in accordance with Article 6(1) of the EPC.
4. The acquisition of a right may not be dependent on any entry in a national patent register.

Article 8 Licences of right
1. The proprietor of a European patent with unitary effect may file a statement with the EPO to the effect that the proprietor is prepared to allow any person to use the invention as a licensee in return for appropriate consideration.
2. A licence obtained under this Regulation shall be treated as a contractual licence.

CHAPTER IV INSTITUTIONAL PROVISIONS

Article 9 Administrative tasks in the framework of the European Patent Organisation
1. The participating Member States shall, within the meaning of Article 143 of the EPC, give the EPO the following tasks, to be carried out in accordance with the internal rules of the EPO:
- (a) to administer requests for unitary effect by proprietors of European patents;
- (b) to include the Register for unitary patent protection within the European Patent Register and to administer the Register for unitary patent protection;
- (c) to receive and register statements on licensing referred to in Article 8, their withdrawal and licensing commitments undertaken by the proprietor of the European patent with unitary effect in international standardisation bodies;
- (d) to publish the translations referred to in Article 6 of Regulation (EU) No 1260/2012 during the transitional period referred to in that Article;
- (e) to collect and administer renewal fees for European patents with unitary effect, in respect of the years following the year in which the mention of the grant is published in the European Patent Bulletin; to collect and administer additional fees for late payment of renewal fees where such late payment is made within six months of the due date, as well as to distribute part of the collected renewal fees to the participating Member States;
- (f) to administer the compensation scheme for the reimbursement of translation costs referred to in Article 5 of Regulation (EU) No 1260/2012;
- (g) to ensure that a request for unitary effect by a proprietor of a European patent is submitted in the language of the proceedings as defined in Article 14(3) of the EPC no later than one month after the mention of the grant is published in the European Patent Bulletin; and
- (h) to ensure that the unitary effect is indicated in the Register for unitary patent protection, where a request for unitary effect has been filed and, during the transitional period provided for in Article 6 of Regulation (EU) No 1260/2012, has been submitted together with the translations referred to in that Article, and that the EPO is informed of any limitations, licences, transfers or revocations of European patents with unitary effect.

2. The participating Member States shall ensure compliance with this Regulation in fulfilling their international obligations undertaken in the EPC and shall cooperate to that end. In their capacity as Contracting States to the EPC, the participating Member States shall ensure the governance and supervision of the activities related to the tasks referred to in paragraph 1 of this Article and shall ensure the setting of the level of renewal fees in accordance with Article 12 of this Regulation and the setting of the share of distribution of the renewal fees in accordance with Article 13 of this Regulation. To that end they shall set up a select committee of the Administrative Council of the European Patent Organisation (hereinafter 'Select Committee') within the meaning of Article 145 of the EPC.

The Select Committee shall consist of the representatives of the participating Member States and a representative of the Commission as an observer, as well as alternates who will represent them in their absence. The members of the Select Committee may be assisted by advisers or experts.
Decisions of the Select Committee shall be taken with due regard for the position of the Commission and in accordance with the rules laid down in Article 35(2) of the EPC.
3. The participating Member States shall ensure effective legal protection before a competent court of one or several participating Member States against the decisions of the EPO in carrying out the tasks referred to in paragraph 1.

CHAPTER V FINANCIAL PROVISIONS

Article 10 Principle on expenses

The expenses incurred by the EPO in carrying out the additional tasks given to it, within the meaning of Article 143 of the EPC, by the participating Member States shall be covered by the fees generated by the European patents with unitary effect.

Article 11 Renewal fees

1. Renewal fees for European patents with unitary effect and additional fees for their late payment shall be paid to the European Patent Organisation by the patent proprietor. Those fees shall be due in respect of the years following the year in which the mention of the grant of the European patent which benefits from unitary effect is published in the European Patent Bulletin.
2. A European patent with unitary effect shall lapse if a renewal fee and, where applicable, any additional fee have not been paid in due time.
3. Renewal fees which fall due after receipt of the statement referred to in Article 8(1) shall be reduced.

Article 12 Level of renewal fees

1. Renewal fees for European patents with unitary effect shall be:
   (a) progressive throughout the term of the unitary patent protection;
   (b) sufficient to cover all costs associated with the grant of the European patent and the administration of the unitary patent protection; and
   (c) sufficient, together with the fees to be paid to the European Patent Organisation during the pre-grant stage, to ensure a balanced budget of the European Patent Organisation.
2. The level of the renewal fees shall be set, taking into account, among others, the situation of specific entities such as small and medium-sized enterprises, with the aim of:
   (a) facilitating innovation and fostering the competitiveness of European businesses;
   (b) reflecting the size of the market covered by the patent; and
   (c) being similar to the level of the national renewal fees for an average European patent taking effect in the participating Member States at the time the level of the renewal fees is first set.
3. In order to attain the objectives set out in this Chapter, the level of renewal fees shall be set at a level that:
   (a) is equivalent to the level of the renewal fee to be paid for the average geographical coverage of current European patents;
   (b) reflects the renewal rate of current European patents; and
   (c) reflects the number of requests for unitary effect.

Article 13 Distribution

1. The EPO shall retain 50 per cent of the renewal fees referred to in Article 11 paid for European patents with unitary effect. The remaining amount shall be distributed to the participating Member States in accordance with the share of distribution of the renewal fees set pursuant to Article 9(2).

2. In order to attain the objectives set out in this Chapter, the share of distribution of renewal fees among the participating Member States shall be based on the following fair, equitable and relevant criteria:
- (a) the number of patent applications;
- (b) the size of the market, while ensuring a minimum amount to be distributed to each participating Member State;
- (c) compensation to the participating Member States which have:
  - (i) an official language other than one of the official languages of the EPO;
  - (ii) a disproportionately low level of patenting activity; and/or
  - (iii) acquired membership of the European Patent Organisation relatively recently.

CHAPTER VI FINAL PROVISIONS

Article 14 Cooperation between the Commission and the EPO
The Commission shall establish a close cooperation through a working agreement with the EPO in the fields covered by this Regulation. This cooperation shall include regular exchanges of views on the functioning of the working agreement and, in particular, on the issue of renewal fees and their impact on the budget of the European Patent Organisation.

Article 15 Application of competition law and the law relating to unfair competition
This Regulation shall be without prejudice to the application of competition law and the law relating to unfair competition.

Article 16 Report on the operation of this Regulation
1. Not later than three years from the date on which the first European patent with unitary effect takes effect, and every five years thereafter, the Commission shall present to the European Parliament and the Council a report on the operation of this Regulation and, where necessary, make appropriate proposals for amending it.
2. The Commission shall regularly submit to the European Parliament and the Council reports on the functioning of the renewal fees referred to in Article 11, with particular emphasis on compliance with Article 12.

Article 17 Notification by the participating Member States
1. The participating Member States shall notify the Commission of the measures adopted in accordance with Article 9 by the date of application of this Regulation.
2. Each participating Member State shall notify the Commission of the measures adopted in accordance with Article 4(2) by the date of application of this Regulation or, in the case of a participating Member State in which the Unified Patent Court does not have exclusive jurisdiction with regard to European patents with unitary effect on the date of application of this Regulation, by the date from which the Unified Patent Court has such exclusive jurisdiction in that participating Member State.

Article 18 Entry into force and application
1. This Regulation shall enter into force on the twentieth day following that of its publication in the *Official Journal of the European Union.*
2. It shall apply from 1 January 2014 or the date of entry into force of the Agreement on a Unified Patent Court (the 'Agreement'), whichever is the later.
By way of derogation from Articles 3(1), 3(2) and 4(1), a European patent for which unitary effect is registered in the Register for unitary patent protection shall have unitary effect only in those participating

Member States in which the Unified Patent Court has exclusive jurisdiction with regard to European patents with unitary effect at the date of registration.
3. Each participating Member State shall notify the Commission of its ratification of the Agreement at the time of deposit of its ratification instrument. The Commission shall publish in the *Official Journal of the European Union* the date of entry into force of the Agreement and a list of the Member States who have ratified the Agreement at the date of entry into force. The Commission shall thereafter regularly update the list of the participating Member States which have ratified the Agreement and shall publish such updated list in the *Official Journal of the European Union.*
4. The participating Member States shall ensure that the measures referred to in Article 9 are in place by the date of application of this Regulation.
5. Each participating Member State shall ensure that the measures referred to in Article 4(2) are in place by the date of application of this Regulation or, in the case of a participating Member State in which the Unified Patent Court does not have exclusive jurisdiction with regard to European patents with unitary effect on the date of application of this Regulation, by the date from which the Unified Patent Court has such exclusive jurisdiction in that participating Member State.
6. Unitary patent protection may be requested for any European patent granted on or after the date of application of this Regulation.
This Regulation shall be binding in its entirety and directly applicable in the participating Member States in accordance with the Treaties.

Done at Brussels, 17 December 2012.

For the European Parliament
The President
M. SCHULZ

For the Council
The President
A. D. MAVROYIANNIS

8. EU Regulation No 1260/2012

Council Regulation (EU) No 1260/2012 of 17 December 2012 implementing enhanced cooperation in the area of the creation of unitary patent protection with regard to the applicable translation arrangements

THE COUNCIL OF THE EUROPEAN UNION,

Having regard to the Treaty on the Functioning of the European Union, and in particular the second paragraph of Article 118 thereof,

Having regard to Council Decision 2011/167/EU of 10 March 2011 authorising enhanced cooperation in the area of the creation of unitary patent protection,[1]

Having regard to the proposal from the European Commission,

After transmission of the draft legislative act to the national parliaments,

Having regard to the opinion of the European Parliament,

Acting in accordance with a special legislative procedure,

Whereas:

(1) Pursuant to Decision 2011/167/EU, Belgium, Bulgaria, the Czech Republic, Denmark, Germany, Estonia, Ireland, Greece, France, Cyprus, Latvia, Lithuania, Luxembourg, Hungary, Malta, the Netherlands, Austria, Poland, Portugal, Romania, Slovenia, Slovakia, Finland, Sweden and the United Kingdom (hereinafter 'participating Member States') were authorised to establish enhanced cooperation between themselves in the area of the creation of unitary patent protection.

(2) Under Regulation (EU) No 1257/2012 of the European Parliament and of the Council of 17 December 2012 implementing enhanced cooperation in the area of the creation of unitary patent protection, certain European patents granted by the European Patent Office (hereinafter 'EPO') under the rules and procedures of the Convention on the Grant of European Patents of 5 October 1973, as revised on 17 December 1991 and on 29 November 2000 (hereinafter 'EPC') should, at the request of the patent proprietor, benefit from unitary effect in the participating Member States.

(3) Translation arrangements for European patents benefiting from unitary effect in the participating Member States (hereinafter 'European patent with unitary effect') should be established by means of a separate Regulation, in accordance with the second paragraph of Article 118 of the Treaty on the Functioning of the European Union (TFEU).

(4) In accordance with Decision 2011/167/EU the translation arrangements for European patents with unitary effect should be simple and cost-effective. They should correspond to those provided for in the proposal for a Council Regulation on the translation arrangements for the European Union patent, presented by the Commission on 30 June 2010, combined with the elements of compromise proposed by the Presidency in November 2010 that had wide support in the Council.

1 OJ L 76, 22.3.2011, p. 53.

(5) Such translation arrangements should ensure legal certainty and stimulate innovation and should, in particular, benefit small and medium-sized enterprises (SMEs). They should make access to the European patent with unitary effect and to the patent system as a whole easier, less costly and legally secure.
(6) Since the EPO is responsible for the grant of European patents, the translation arrangements for the European patent with unitary effect should be built on the current procedure in the EPO. Those arrangements should aim to achieve the necessary balance between the interests of economic operators and the public interest, in terms of the cost of proceedings and the availability of technical information.
(7) Without prejudice to the transitional arrangements, where the specification of a European patent with unitary effect has been published in accordance with Article 14(6) of the EPC, no further translations should be required. Article 14(6) of the EPC provides that the specification of a European patent is published in the language of the proceedings before the EPO and includes a translation of the claims into the other two official languages of the EPO.
(8) In the event of a dispute concerning a European patent with unitary effect, it is a legitimate requirement that the patent proprietor at the request of the alleged infringer should provide a full translation of the patent into an official language of either the participating Member State in which the alleged infringement took place or the Member State in which the alleged infringer is domiciled. The patent proprietor should also be required to provide, at the request of a court competent in the participating Member States for disputes concerning the European patent with unitary effect, a full translation of the patent into the language used in the proceedings of that court. Such translations should not be carried out by automated means and should be provided at the expense of the patent proprietor.
(9) In the event of a dispute concerning a claim for damages, the court hearing the dispute should take into consideration the fact that, before having been provided with a translation in his own language, the alleged infringer may have acted in good faith and may have not known or had reasonable grounds to know that he was infringing the patent. The competent court should assess the circumstances of the individual case and, inter alia, should take into account whether the alleged infringer is a SME operating only at local level, the language of the proceedings before the EPO and, during the transitional period, the translation submitted together with the request for unitary effect.
(10) In order to facilitate access to European patents with unitary effect, in particular for SMEs, applicants should be able to file their patent applications at the EPO in any official language of the Union. As a complementary measure, certain applicants obtaining European patents with unitary effect, having filed a European patent application in one of the official languages of the Union, which is not an official language of the EPO, and having their residence or principal place of business within a Member State, should receive additional reimbursements of the costs of translating from the language of the patent application into the language of the proceedings of the EPO, beyond what is currently in place at the EPO. Such reimbursements should be administered by the EPO in accordance with Article 9 of Regulation (EU) No 1257/2012.
(11) In order to promote the availability of patent information and the dissemination of technological knowledge, machine translations of patent applications and specifications into all official languages of the Union should be available as soon as possible. Machine translations are being developed by the EPO and are a very important tool in seeking to improve access to patent information and to widely disseminate technological knowledge. The timely availability of high quality machine translations of European patent applications and specifications into all official languages of the Union would benefit all users of the European patent system. Machine translations are a key feature of European Union policy. Such machine translations should serve for information purposes only and should not have any legal effect.

(12) During the transitional period, before a system of high quality machine translations into all official languages of the Union becomes available, a request for unitary effect as referred to in Article 9 of Regulation (EU) No 1257/2012 should be accompanied by a full translation of the specification of the patent into English where the language of the proceedings before the EPO is French or German, or into any official language of the Member States that is an official language of the Union where the language of the proceedings before the EPO is English. Those arrangements would ensure that during a transitional period all European patents with unitary effect are made available in English which is the language customarily used in the field of international technological research and publications. Furthermore, such arrangements would ensure that with respect to European patents with unitary effect, translations would be published in other official languages of the participating Member States. Such translations should not be carried out by automated means and their high quality should contribute to the training of translation engines by the EPO. They would also enhance the dissemination of patent information.

(13) The transitional period should terminate as soon as high quality machine translations into all official languages of the Union are available, subject to a regular and objective evaluation of the quality by an independent expert committee established by the participating Member States in the framework of the European Patent Organisation and composed of the representatives of the EPO and the users of the European patent system. Given the state of technological development, the maximum period for the development of high quality machine translations cannot be considered to exceed 12 years. Consequently, the transitional period should lapse 12 years from the date of application of this Regulation, unless it has been decided to terminate that period earlier.

(14) Since the substantive provisions applicable to a European patent with unitary effect are governed by Regulation (EU) No 1257/2012 and are completed by the translation arrangements provided for in this Regulation, this Regulation should apply from the same date as Regulation (EU) No 1257/2012.

(15) This Regulation is without prejudice to the rules governing the languages of the Institutions of the Union established in accordance with Article 342 of the TFEU and to Council Regulation No 1 of 15 April 1958 determining the languages to be used by the European Economic Community.[2] This Regulation is based on the linguistic regime of the EPO and should not be considered as creating a specific linguistic regime for the Union, or as creating a precedent for a limited language regime in any future legal instrument of the Union.

(16) Since the objective of this Regulation, namely the creation of a uniform and simple translation regime for European patents with unitary effect, cannot be sufficiently achieved by the Member States and can therefore, by reasons of the scale and effects of this Regulation, be better achieved at Union level, the Union may adopt measures, where appropriate by means of enhanced cooperation, in accordance with the principle of subsidiarity as set out in Article 5 of the Treaty on European Union. In accordance with the principle of proportionality, as set out in that Article, this Regulation does not go beyond what is necessary in order to achieve that objective,

HAS ADOPTED THIS REGULATION:

Article 1 Subject matter

This Regulation implements enhanced cooperation in the area of the creation of unitary patent protection authorised by Decision No 2011/167/EU with regard to the applicable translation arrangements.

2 OJ 17, 6.10.1958, p. 385/58.

Article 2 Definitions

For the purposes of this Regulation, the following definitions shall apply:

(a) 'European patent with unitary effect' means a European patent which benefits from unitary effect in the participating Member States by virtue of Regulation (EU) No 1257/2012;

(b) 'Language of the proceedings' means the language used in the proceedings before the EPO as defined in Article 14(3) of the Convention on the Grant of European Patents of 5 October 1973, as revised on 17 December 1991 and on 29 November 2000 (hereinafter 'EPC').

Article 3 Translation arrangements for the European patent with unitary effect

1. Without prejudice to Articles 4 and 6 of this Regulation, where the specification of a European patent, which benefits from unitary effect has been published in accordance with Article 14(6) of the EPC, no further translations shall be required.

2. A request for unitary effect as referred to in Article 9 of Regulation (EU) No 1257/2012 shall be submitted in the language of the proceedings.

Article 4 Translation in the event of a dispute

1. In the event of a dispute relating to an alleged infringement of a European patent with unitary effect, the patent proprietor shall provide at the request and the choice of an alleged infringer, a full translation of the European patent with unitary effect into an official language of either the participating Member State in which the alleged infringement took place or the Member State in which the alleged infringer is domiciled.

2. In the event of a dispute relating to a European patent with unitary effect, the patent proprietor shall provide in the course of legal proceedings, at the request of a court competent in the participating Member States for disputes concerning European patents with unitary effect, a full translation of the patent into the language used in the proceedings of that court.

3. The cost of the translations referred to in paragraphs 1 and 2 shall be borne by the patent proprietor.

4. In the event of a dispute concerning a claim for damages, the court hearing the dispute shall assess and take into consideration, in particular where the alleged infringer is a SME, a natural person or a non-profit organisation, a university or a public research organisation, whether the alleged infringer acted without knowing or without reasonable grounds for knowing, that he was infringing the European patent with unitary effect before having been provided with the translation referred to in paragraph 1.

Article 5 Administration of a compensation scheme

1. Given the fact that European patent applications may be filed in any language under Article 14(2) of the EPC, the participating Member States shall in accordance with Article 9 of Regulation (EU) No 1257/2012, give, within the meaning of Article 143 of the EPC, the EPO the task of administering a compensation scheme for the reimbursement of all translation costs up to a ceiling, for applicants filing patent applications at the EPO in one of the official languages of the Union that is not an official language of the EPO.

2. The compensation scheme referred to in paragraph 1 shall be funded through the fees referred to in Article 11 of Regulation (EU) No 1257/2012 and shall be available only for SMEs, natural persons, non-profit organisations, universities and public research organisations having their residence or principal place of business within a Member State.

Article 6 Transitional measures

1. During a transitional period starting on the date of application of this Regulation a request for unitary effect as referred to in Article 9 of Regulation (EU) No 1257/2012 shall be submitted together with the following:

(a) where the language of the proceedings is French or German, a full translation of the specification of the European patent into English; or
(b) where the language of the proceedings is English, a full translation of the specification of the European patent into any other official language of the Union.

2. In accordance with Article 9 of Regulation (EU) No 1257/2012, the participating Member States shall give, within the meaning of Article 143 of the EPC, the EPO the task of publishing the translations referred to in paragraph 1 of this Article as soon as possible after the date of the submission of a request for unitary effect as referred to in Article 9 of Regulation (EU) No 1257/2012. The text of such translations shall have no legal effect and shall be for information purposes only.

3. Six years after the date of application of this Regulation and every two years thereafter, an independent expert committee shall carry out an objective evaluation of the availability of high quality machine translations of patent applications and specifications into all the official languages of the Union as developed by the EPO. This expert committee shall be established by the participating Member States in the framework of the European Patent Organisation and shall be composed of representatives of the EPO and of the non-governmental organisations representing users of the European patent system invited by the Administrative Council of the European Patent Organisation as observers in accordance with Article 30(3) of the EPC.

4. On the basis of the first of the evaluations referred to in paragraph 3 of this Article and every two years thereafter on the basis of the subsequent evaluations, the Commission shall present a report to the Council and, if appropriate, make proposals for terminating the transitional period.

5. If the transitional period is not terminated on the basis of a proposal of the Commission, it shall lapse 12 years from the date of application of this Regulation.

Article 7 Entry into force

1. This Regulation shall enter into force on the twentieth day following that of its publication in the *Official Journal of the European Union*.

2. It shall apply from 1 January 2014 or the date of entry into force of the Agreement on a Unified Patent Court, whichever is the later.

This Regulation shall be binding in its entirety and directly applicable in the participating Member States in accordance with the Treaties.

Done at Brussels, 17 December 2012.

For the Council
The President
S. ALETRARI

www.ingramcontent.com/pod-product-compliance
Lightning Source LLC
Chambersburg PA
CBHW061355240926
51846CB00007B/1417
* 9 7 8 9 4 6 2 3 6 3 5 0 2 *